DANGEROUS NEW THREATS
TO AMERICA'S SECURITY

*To Travis and Margaret,
Rightfully proud parents of
a very impressive, young
Midshipman —
With great affection and
warmest best wishes —
Steve
17 APRIL 2023*

DANGEROUS NEW THREATS TO AMERICA'S SECURITY
*Failed Political Leadership
and
The Race to Deter or Win the "Big One."*

Stephen M. Duncan

ALSO BY
Stephen M. Duncan

The Sanctuary:
*Cherishing the Blessings of the Past and
Making New Memories on the Chesapeake Bay*
2020

First Duty:
Presidents, the Nation's Security and Self-Centered Politics
2019

A Chrysanthemum With Grit
2017

Master Craftsmen:
*Friends, Colleagues and Other Contemporaries
Who Have Made a Difference*
2016

Only the Most Able:
*Moving Beyond Politics in the
Selection of National Security Leaders*
2013

By His Grace:
A Professional Life of Adventure and Service
2007

A War of a Different Kind:
*Military Force and
America's Search for Homeland Security*
2004

A Woman of Noble Character
1999

Citizen Warriors:
*America's National Guard & Reserve Forces
& the Politics of National Security*
1997

ACCLAIM
for the works of **Stephen M. Duncan**

A War of a Different Kind
Military Force and America's Search for Homeland Security

> "New wars require new attitudes and an understanding of the new conditions we face. A War of a Different Kind gives us all this and more in a thoroughly researched and well-written history of our own times."
>
> **Hon. Caspar W. Weinberger**
> **15th Secretary of Defense**

> "Combining the research of a scholar and the knowledge of an insider, Steve Duncan has written with clear insight about the challenges our nation will face in the first half of the twenty-first century."
>
> **Gen. Charles C. Krulak USMC (Ret.),**
> **31st Commandant, U.S. Marine Corps**

Only the Most Able
Moving Beyond Politics in the Selection of National Security Leaders

> "A must-read...for all Americans who desire a government that works."
>
> **Hon. Pendleton James**
> **Former Special Assistant to the President**

> "Under present arrangement, no systemic scrutiny and evaluation of civilian leadership exists. Only until the magnitude of...failure is sufficiently great are ad hoc evaluation processes thrown into place. Duncan is correct. There must be a better way. How much worse can it get?"
>
> **Dr. James A. Stever**
> **Professor Emeritus, University of Cincinnati**

Citizen Warriors
America's National Guard & Reserve Forces & the Politics of National Security

> "Steve Duncan's Citizen Warriors is the best treatment I've ever seen on a vitally important subject—America's National Guard and Reserve Forces. He knows the history intimately...."
>
> **Hon. Dick Cheney**
> **17th Secretary of Defense**

Copyright © 2023 by Stephen M. Duncan

All rights reserved.
No part of this book may be reproduced or utilized in any form or by any means, electronic or mechanical, without permission in writing.
Inquiries should be sent to Stephen M. Duncan at: stephenmduncan@msn.com.

Published by Highland & Claymore Press
Mount Vernon, Virginia

Printed in the United States of America.

Cover and book design by Nancy Newland, Rare Bird Design.

FOR

The thousands of men and women who, for 247 years, have sacrificed much, and on many occasions everything, to create, to protect, and to preserve the freedoms of our Republic.

CONTENTS

	Prologue	xi
I.	The Beginning of a Tradition and the Necessary Departures From It	3
II.	The Big Stick Policy and a New Broad View of American Interests	11
III.	The Fury of an Aroused Democracy	19
IV.	Isolationism and the Start of The Cold War	29
V.	Stand Together or Fall Separately	37
VI.	Pragmatism, Political Will and Human Rights	49
VII.	The End of the Cold War and a New Hot War in Iraq	61
VIII.	The Dangerous Road to Ineffective Deterrence	73
IX.	Russia: The Early Warning Signs	85
X.	Russia: The Failure of Deterrence, a Hot War in Ukraine and Cold War II	99
XI.	The Will and Moral Courage of Free Men and Women	121
XII.	China: The Early Warning Signs	137
XIII.	China: Taiwan and Other Acts of Aggression	153
XIV.	Iran: Nuclear Armed Terrorist?	171
XV.	North Korea: International Outlaw	189
XVI.	Inexcusable and Unacceptable Failures of Leadership	203
XVII.	A Republic If You Can Keep It	223
	Postscript	249
	Acknowledgements	257
	Notes	258

PROLOGUE

It is very likely that in the future, the year 2022 will be considered historically very consequential. It is unlikely to be locked into our national consciousness as much as the years of the Pearl Harbor and 9/11 attacks or the end of the Cold War because thousands of Americans did not die in attacks by aggressors on the American homeland. Nevertheless, analysts and other respected American leaders are already referring to it as an important date in "The Era of Catastrophic Risk,[1] the first year of a "Dangerous Decade" in an "Age of Uncertainty,"[2] and even "a pivotal moment in history."[3] A respected, veteran American diplomat has briefly summarized the reasons for these characterizations: "…the danger …stems from a sharp decline in world order" which "threatens to become especially steep, owing to a confluence of old and new threats that have begun to intersect at a moment the United States is ill positioned to contend with them."[4]

    I was born in the year of the attack on Pearl Harbor. I was a small boy when the Cold War commenced. Only three years later, U.S. forces were sent to the front lines of a new hot war in Korea. While I was attending the U.S. Naval Academy, the world came dangerously close to a nuclear Armageddon during the Cuban Missile Crisis of October 1962. Two and a half years later, I began my service aboard an amphibious flagship in Vietnam. That experience was followed by additional service in Vietnam as the Weapons Officer of a small ship that provided close-in gunfire support of U.S. ground troops. After 18 years in the Naval Reserve, I was appointed as a senior civilian official in the Department of Defense where I served for more than five years and was privileged to be serving during the Persian Gulf War of 1990-91 (Operations *Desert Shield* and *Desert Storm*) and when the Cold War ended. I testified in more than 50 politically charged hearings in the U.S. Senate and U.S. House of Representatives on national security policy matters. I have spent much of the subsequent three decades writing and teaching about those matters.

    Thus, it was with considerable concern that I watched America relax its vigilance on developing new threats to our security during the decade of the 1990s. After the terrorist attacks of 9/11 2001, I shared the pride of all Americans as "patriotic ardor burned bright" and "righteous anger and resolve …joined in support of our leaders, our Armed Forces, our country."[5] But, as one former senior Government official observed, "moments of moral clarity are rare in life, and they are exceedingly precious. They usually follow upon hours— years—of moral confusion; they seldom arrive all at once or definitively; and they are never accompanied by a lifetime guarantee."[6]

For the last decade and a half, I have watched with the same kind of concern that I had in the 1990s as U.S. political leaders, anxious to focus their attention on more politically rewarding domestic matters and perhaps unreasonably comforted by the absence of any immediate, direct threat to America's security, permitted U.S. military strength to quickly decline while the strength of our most likely future adversaries was quickly growing. Despite many continuous warning signs, our Presidents and Congress have generally acted as if they have not noticed the dramatic changes in the relative military power of the U.S. and that of the authoritarian states of China, Russia, Iran and North Korea or the many aggressive and dangerous actions those countries have taken in recent years.

All post-Cold War illusions by American political leaders that the risks of the U.S. becoming involved in a war were nonexistent, or at least very low, should have been dispelled on February 24, 2022, when Russia began its brutal and massive invasion of Ukraine. But, for the most part, the leaders continued business as usual with respect to the need to rebuild our Armed Forces. They did not stop to consider the facts that wars are unpredictable; that future developments in the war in Ukraine and actions taken by other potential adversaries might have a major impact upon America's security; that known and long-standing deficiencies in the readiness of the U.S. Armed Forces have greatly decreased both our ability to deter our potential enemies from engaging in war, and our preparation for one should it be forced upon us; that those deficiencies cannot be corrected in the short term; and that we might not have time to take the necessary corrective actions. The leaders who had political power had no interest or real understanding of these important national security issues, and the people who did understand them, had no political power.

On October 18, 2022, the results of an important study of America's Military Strength were published. A critical finding was that the U.S. Armed Forces are "weak relative to the force needed to defend national interests on a global stage against actual challenges in the world as it is, rather than as we wish it were."[7] Sixteen days later, the Four-Star Commander of the U.S. Strategic Command addressed defense professionals at a conference. "This Ukraine crisis that we're in right now...is just the warm-up," he said. The big one is coming. And it isn't going to be very long before we're going to get tested in ways that we haven't been tested [for] a long time."[8] Addressing the probable result of a continuing reduction in U.S. military strength as that of our likely adversaries increases, he declared that "it isn't going to matter how good our [operating plan] is, or how good our commanders are, or how good our forces are—we're not going to have enough of them. And that is a very near-term problem."[9]

The underlying assumption and theme of this book is that most Americans do not understand either the seriousness or the immediacy of the threats to our security which we face today if they are aware of them at all; that because they are not grounded in important facts about the specific nature of the threats, they are not prepared to make sound judgments about what must be done about them; that our most senior political leaders in the White House and Congress have irresponsibly failed to make serious efforts to educate the public about the threats, the potential costs to the Nation if we fail to take prompt action to deal with them, and what courses of action are available.

The purpose of this book is to offer such facts and such judgments in the hope that at a time when clarity about the threats to America's security is essential, they will contribute to an arousal of the Nation to do what must be done—very soon! Because it is impossible to separate politics and the war policies of a government, i.e., the "higher conduct of a war," from the military operations that constitute an important, although not exclusive part of the means adopted to attain the ends of policies,[10] I have discussed the political, as well as the military aspects of U.S. national security policies during several presidential administrations. My focus on the policies and actions of various Presidents is not intended to be anything remotely approaching a full evaluation of their performance in the White House since I do not discuss their domestic policies except tangentially. Nor do I pretend that the book is perfectly impartial, but I have attempted to make it so. To that end, I have included extensive End Notes to document sources of information and to explain particular points. My conclusions are based not only upon research, but also upon personal experience.

I offer the book not as an exhaustive academic study of the subjects addressed, but rather as a primer for the general public, as well as for readers who are particularly interested in national security, foreign policy, and American military and political history. I have given historical context to it by surveying the views of several U.S. Presidents and the public at large about the continuing tension in the American political system between the Nation's pragmatic security interests and political passions; between political realists and idealists; and between Internationalists and Isolationists. An important element of U.S. history is "the gap between the way Americans think and talk about their national interests and the way they actually behave in times of perceived crisis." As one critic of American foreign policy has noted, for more than a century, the U.S. has oscillated… from periods of restraint, indifference, and disillusion to periods of almost panicked engagement and interventionism."[11]

In order to assist readers in evaluating the performance of recent U.S. political leaders on national security matters, I have provided a standard by which that performance may be measured, namely, Churchill's actions on several matters which were critical to Great Britain's survival in the early years of World War II before the Pearl Harbor attack and soon after that attack.

During this time of increasing danger, Americans and their national political leaders once again have vitally important choices to make about our security. The situation is made more complex by the fact that thankfully, for the moment at least, our passions have not been inflamed by a catastrophic attack on America itself, or upon our vital security interests beyond our borders. We must, however, take prompt and very energetic action to deter such attacks. We do not have the luxury of time.

Stephen M. Duncan

Mount Vernon, Virginia
March 2023

We are persuaded that one of the most effectual means of preserving Peace, is to be prepared for War; and our attention shall be directed to the objects of common defence, and to the adoption of such plans as shall appear the most likely to prevent our dependence on other Countries for essential supplies.

President George Washington
Annual Address to the United States Senate
and House of Representatives
8 January 1790

Our detached and distant attention invites and enables us to pursue a different course. If we remain one people, under an efficient government, the period is not far off when… we may choose peace or war, as our interest guided by justice shall counsel.

President George Washington
Farewell Address 1796

I.

THE BEGINNING OF A TRADITION AND THE NECESSARY DEPARTURES FROM IT

The year 1796 was a difficult one for President George Washington. He was bothered by rheumatism, his dentures, and an aching back. He appeared to be worn out from his two terms as the Nation's Chief Executive and the cares of his office. The capabilities of the members of his current cabinet were markedly inferior to those of the members of his first cabinet. He was very frustrated by the decisive partisanship being exercised by former colleagues and supporters like Thomas Jefferson and James Madison, now members of the new Republican Party, who were fighting for policies which strengthened the rights of states at the expense of a united and strong central or Federal Government in which he believed.

He was bruised by attacks on his policies. He strongly resented the meddling by France in American politics, particularly after France declared war on Great Britain and other nations soon after his second inauguration.[1] He was suspicious of everyone, including many of his former supporters, who had sympathized with the French Revolution without acknowledging its bloodthirsty spirit and the clear evidence of the anarchy and indiscriminate mob violence which had supplanted the rule of law. Only three years earlier, King Louis XVI, who had provided critical support to America's fight for independence, had been decapitated before a crowd of twenty thousand people screaming for revenge. His remains had been desecrated.

After the French declaration of war in January 1793, Washington had made clear his desire that America remain impartial toward the belligerents and free from any involvement in that conflict, so that his still developing new country could prosper with its own resources and growing population without the necessity of large military expenditures. He had a realistic understanding that America was then too weak and unstable to fight another war with a major European nation. The following year Congress passed its first Neutrality Act in

order to avoid any involvement in that continental war. But, by 1796, intervening events had given the President increased concern about the potential for a military clash with France.

Having decided with finality not to seek a third term, Washington turned to the question of who should help him draft the valedictory remarks he intended to present to the citizens of his young nation. Because of the considerable changes that had been "wrought by the intervening years," he discarded a draft that had been written by Vice President John Adams in the last year of Washington's first term. Instead, he assigned the task to Alexander Hamilton, his aide-de-camp during the Revolution, a leading member of the 1787 Constitutional Convention, the primary author of *The Federalist Papers*, and the head of the Federalist Party. No one was more familiar than Hamilton with the President's sentiments.

The magisterial document which became known as Washington's Farewell Address, was not delivered in a speech by the President, but rather by publication on September 16, 1796, in the *American Daily Advertiser*, a Philadelphia newspaper selected by Washington. Touching on "the importance of national unity, the value of the Constitution and the rule of law, the evils of political parties, and the proper virtue of a republican people,"[2] the Address is even now considered to be one of the ground-breaking statements of American political values in the 18th Century.

The President also expounded a foreign policy "based on practical *interests* instead of *political passions*."[3] Sympathy with a foreign nation for purely ideological reasons, he said, "could lead America into 'the quarrels and wars of the latter without adequate inducement or justification.'"[4] He warned that "There can be no greater error than to expect, or calculate upon real favors from Nation to Nation," and that America should "steer clear of *permanent* alliances with any portion of the foreign world" and should instead "safely trust to *temporary* alliances [based on 'policy, humanity, and *interest*] for extraordinary emergencies." Referring without name to Jefferson's and Madison's strong sympathy with France, he took issue with "ambitious, corrupted or deluded citizens (who devote themselves to the favorite nation)" and sacrifice the *interests* of their own country."[5]

It has been rightly observed that the Farewell Address "embodied the *political realism* of the 18th Century—cool, cerebral and cold-blooded." Recently, a leading geopolitical analyst has summarized the difference between political *realists* and *idealists* in this fashion: "Realists generally opt for *interests* over *values*, since our values cannot be imposed everywhere; they opt for order over freedom, since without order there is anarchy and therefore no freedom for anybody. Idealists frequently clash with realists when the debate focuses on the level of [military, diplomatic, economic] intervention in this particular country and that one."[6]

In expressing these views, Washington was aware of the fact that the policies he espoused were almost risk free, at least for the foreseeable future of the citizens who read them. Unlike many of the countries in Europe, which had real or potential enemies on at least one of their borders, and which were often embroiled in what a future European leader would refer to as wars "of chieftains or of princes, of dynasties or national ambition,"[7] the new United States of America only had oceans on its eastern and western borders and weak, peaceful countries on its northern and southern borders. In addition, it had the safety of time and space. Unlike the situation in today's age of hypersonic nuclear missiles, instantaneous worldwide communications, and other technologies which were unimaginable only a few decades ago, in which time is sometimes measured in nanoseconds, if not minutes, contacts with Europe at that time were limited to the 2–3-month transit of sailing ships over the Atlantic. As Washington put the matter in his Address, "Our detached and distant situation invites and enables us" to avoid involvement in European conflicts.

*   *   *

The political views of Thomas Jefferson, our third President and the first nominee of the Democratic-Republican Party, or the Jeffersonian Republican Party as it was also known, were considerably different from those of President Washington on a range of issues, including foreign affairs. Curiously, in his Inaugural Address, Jefferson spoke of "Peace, commerce and honest friendship with all nations, *entangling alliances* with none" but other words and his actions more accurately reflected his beliefs.

For Jefferson, ever the romantic *idealist* of the Revolution, "America was not only a great power in the making but an 'empire for liberty'—an ever-expanding force acting on behalf of all humanity to vindicate principles of good government."[8] In a letter to the noted chemist and theologian, Dr. Joseph Priestly, Jefferson wrote that "we feel that we are acting under obligations not confined to the limits of our own society. It is impossible not to be sensible that we are acting for all mankind; that circumstances denied to others, but indulged to us, have imposed on us the duty of proving what is the degree of freedom and self-government in which a society may venture to leave its individual members."[9] Circumstances never required Jefferson to preside over a major dispute with a foreign power or an armed conflict in which the intensity of his beliefs were tested.

This was not the case with James Madison, Jefferson's successor and political intimate. On June 18, 1812, Madison signed a congressional Declaration of War against Britain. The war was not, however, due so much to a breach by Britain of any formal agreement with the U.S., but rather the result of several factors, all of which directly affected American interests. They included Britain's efforts to restrict U.S. trade with France and its colonies, the Royal Navy's impressment of American merchant seaman[10] and its violation of other American maritime rights, and Britain's continuing encouragement of Native American hostility against America's westward expansion beyond the lands that were the subject of the Louisiana Purchase.

Over subsequent decades, America's size and power grew as the population of the country grew. Facing no serious threat to its security, the country was free to pursue a foreign policy of detached neutrality with respect to foreign conflicts and its Armed Forces remained small. There were two additional reasons why defense spending was limited. First, since the beginning of the Republic Americans had been concerned that a large standing army could be used by a tyrannical leader to curtail liberties won at such great cost in the Revolution. The second reason probably had practical roots. Since military campaigns in the 18th Century usually started with the spring and continued only until winter weather prevented operations, it is unlikely that many leaders of the new nation were interested in paying for a professional army on a year-round basis. Moreover, in the absence of a serious outside threat, it was believed that the militias of the individual states could effectively deal with domestic disturbances.

* * *

A biographer of William McKinley asserted that when he was campaigning in the Presidential Election Year of 1896, he looked upon the great industrialists "as leaders in the march of national progress, the source of high wages and full employment for all the people," and he thought of their financial backing of his candidacy "as a contribution to the patriotic cause of protection [i.e., tariffs]."[11] William Jennings Bryan, McKinley's Democrat opponent, campaigned on a platform of stricter federal control of trusts and railroads, the free and unlimited coinage of both silver and gold, and the abolition of tariffs, which he considered a breeder of trusts. The country was weary of hard times and many Americans responded to Bryan's eloquence and his call for renewed attention to the rights of the common man.

The foreign policy of the U.S. at the time was based upon the tradition of isolation from the powers of Europe, but it was not lacking in focused attention on developments closer to home in the Western Hemisphere and in the Far East. Americans were a peace-loving people, but there had never been a time when the country had not been ready to a call for war with any country that violated the Monroe Doctrine or presented threats to American security and commercial rights in the Pacific. McKinley's election as President did not foretell any particular change in policy. In his Inaugural Address, he declared that "Our diplomacy should seek nothing more and accept nothing less than is due us. We want no wars of conquest; we must avoid the temptation of territorial aggression. War should never be entered upon until every agency of peace has failed; peace is preferable to war in almost every contingency."

From the earliest stages of his Administration, however, foreign affairs was the primary subject of McKinley's Cabinet meetings. The strained American relations with Spain stood first on the agenda, but developments in the Pacific were receiving increasing attention. For decades, the U.S. had asserted an interest in Hawaii. It was a natural gateway to the potentially large commercial opportunities in the Far East. American traders there had been followed by large numbers of American missionaries. The strategic value of the islands had been recognized when the United States gained a Pacific coastline. The Government wanted to maintain a naval station in Pearl Harbor to deter any possible aggression from Asian countries. The quasi-protectorate of the United States "had so long been internationally recognized that Americans had come to regard any action on Hawaii as their own domestic concern."[12] It was thus no surprise that when Americans learned in the spring of 1897 that the now westernized Empire of Japan, which had "entered on a period of soaring imperial ambition,"[13] was taking an energetic interest in the islands, they were outraged. The American rage was made greater when Japan sent a cruiser to Honolulu to back up its demand for indemnity for American efforts to restrict Japanese immigration.

At the same time, many U.S. efforts were being undertaken to convince the political leaders of the decaying Empire of Spain to abandon that country's rich colony of Cuba. Congress had formally recognized the belligerency of insurrectionists there and both of America's political parties had expressed sympathy for Cuban independence. The American public had also demonstrated a strong sympathy with the struggle for independence and that attitude was made stronger by an old American hostility to the despotic misrule and cruelty of Spanish leaders in Madrid in the governance of the island. To choke off the insurgency, Spain sent more than 200,000 troops to Cuba. To starve the rebels operating in the countryside, the rural population was herded into garrisoned towns where starvation and a lack of sanitation resulted in the deaths of thousands of peasants. President McKinley characterized such concentrations as "extermination" and an "abuse of the rights of war." It was clearly in America's interest not to permit a foreign nation to continue to exercise brutal control over one of its colonies which was only ninety miles from the coast of Florida. McKinley was, of course, aware of the American public's desire for action to correct the situation in Cuba, but initially, he continued to resist the clamor for war.

Still hoping that the Spanish Government would proceed with its promises of political reform, McKinley pleaded for patience from the public while he attempted to dampen the militaristic enthusiasm of Theodore Roosevelt, his Assistant Secretary of the Navy. But, he also sent the American Battleship *Maine* on a friendly visit to Cuba as a show of force and for the protection of American interests there.

On the night of February 15, 1898, a massive explosion, then of unknown origin, sank the *Maine* as it sat anchored in Havana Harbor, taking more than 260 officers and enlisted men to their deaths.[14] In March, McKinley demanded that Spain end the brutality being inflicted upon Cubans and begin negotiations on the subject of independence for the island. Spain refused to give up its last major colony in the New World. On April 20, Congress authorized the President to use the Armed Forces to secure the independence of

Cuba. On April 25, it passed a formal Declaration of War.

Within three months, the United States decisively defeated Spanish forces on land and sea. On December 12, 1898, the U.S. and Spain entered into the Treaty of Paris, which officially ended the Spanish-American War and granted the U.S. its first overseas empire with the ceding of the former Spanish possessions of the Philippine Islands, Puerto Rico, and Guam. As the 19th Century was coming to a close, the U.S. was now recognized as a new and powerful nation on the world stage. But vulnerabilities remained. Subsequent to the sinking of the *Maine*, the strength of the Navy was insufficient to defeat a second-rate naval power. The fleet had only seven modern armor-clad ships, and one of them, the *Oregon*, was in the Pacific, separated by a journey of many weeks from the eastern seaboard, which would presumably bear the brunt of any conflict with a European power.

In 1900, President McKinley was a candidate for reelection. The theme of his campaign was that the war had not been one of conquest, or one fought for the purpose of acquiring territory for reasons relating to American ambitions or security, but rather that it had been fought "for humanity's sake."[15] He won the election handily and his margins of victory in both the popular and electoral votes were greater than they had been four years earlier.

Much has been given us, and much will rightfully be expected from us. We have duties to others and duties to ourselves; and we can shirk neither. We have become a great nation, forced by the fact of its greatness into relations with the other nations of the earth, and we must behave as beseems a people with such responsibilities.

President Theodore Roosevelt
Inaugural Address, 1905

We entered this war because violations of right had occurred which touched us to the quick and made the life of our own people impossible unless they were corrected and the world secured once for all against their recurrence. What we demand in this war, therefore, is nothing peculiar to ourselves. It is that the world be made fit and safe to live in.

President Woodrow Wilson
Speech to Congress
January 8, 1918

II.

THE BIG STICK POLICY AND A NEW BROAD VIEW OF AMERICAN INTERESTS

The ascent of Vice President Theodore Roosevelt to the presidency upon the death by assassination of President McKinley on September 14, 1901 brought together two irreversible factors: first, the de facto new status of America as one of the world's most consequential nations; second, an immensely energetic, intelligent, pugnacious and ambitious new President who believed that Americans had duties to others, as well as to themselves, that they could shirk neither, and that the country had become a great nation, forced by the fact of its greatness into relations with other nations of the earth. He believed that America should be sufficiently strong and ready to defend its interests around the and ideals "would have an enabling effect on the world."[1]

Roosevelt is considered by many today to be the first modern President because he significantly expanded the power and influence of the presidency, often through Executive Orders and Proclamations. It was his view that the President had the right to use all powers to accomplish his goals except those that were expressly denied to him. He made it clear in his Inaugural Address in 1905 that he did not feel bound by the old tradition of steering clear of security relationships with foreign nations. In describing his approach to diplomacy and his foreign policy generally, he referred to the favorite African proverb, "speak softly, and carry a big stick, and you will go far." He described this policy as "the exercise of intelligent forethought and of decisive action sufficiently far in advance of any likely crisis."[2] In practice, the policy had five components. First it was necessary to possess military capabilities sufficiently great to coerce adversaries to a particular course of action or to deter them. Since the county was still suspicious of a large standing army and because America is a maritime nation, that meant the maintenance of a powerful Navy. The second component required the U.S. to act justly toward other nations. The third component was a refusal to bluff. "The one thing I won't do," he wrote in an August 6,

1906, letter to Andrew Carnegie, "is to bluff when I cannot make good; to bluster and threaten and then fail to take the actions if my words need to be backed up."

The remaining components were to attack only when prepared to strike hard, and the willingness to allow an adversary to save face in defeat.[3] Generally speaking, Roosevelt much preferred to base national security policy decisions on hard, practical realities like a strong Navy, rather than on purely ideological grounds and he believed that even the resolution of moral questions, such as human rights, are usually linked to questions of power.

Roosevelt's assertive approach to Latin America and the Caribbean came to be known as the 1904 Roosevelt Corollary to the Monroe Doctrine of 1823. The original Doctrine was essentially passive since it merely asked that European nations not increase their influence or recolonize any part of the Western Hemisphere. When certain European creditors threatened Venezuela, Roosevelt became concerned that the crisis might spark an invasion of that country. He declared that he would use military force as a last resort to resolve such disputes and restore internal stability to nations in the region.

To demonstrate America's new power and his willingness to use it, he presided over a program of naval construction. He later ordered 16 battleships of the Navy's Atlantic Fleet, manned by 12,793 officers and men, to circumnavigate the globe from December 1907 to February 22, 1909.[4] The cruise was a diplomatic and national security triumph. Though he received the Nobel Peace Prize for hosting the conference of envoys from Russia and Japan who negotiated the terms of peace which ended the Russia-Japan War, Roosevelt later declared that the cruise of America's Great White Fleet was "The most important service that I rendered to peace."[5]

Even though he had been elected with McKinley in 1900, Roosevelt first ran for President in 1904 after serving for almost four years in the office. He won the election with 56.4 of the popular vote and 336 Electoral votes to his Democrat opponent's 140. Prior to his inauguration ceremony, he declared that he would not serve another term believing that a limited number of terms was a check against dictatorship.

He came to regret that decision in 1911 when he concluded that his friend, his former Secretary of War, his hand-picked successor, and then Republican President William Howard Taft, was not capable of strong leadership. Roosevelt was still very popular throughout the country, but after Taft received the Republican nomination in 1912, he accepted the nomination of the Progressive or "Bull Moose" Party. Between them, Roosevelt and Taft received 50 percent of the popular vote in the General Election, but Woodrow Wilson, the Democrat nominee, received 42 percent and a plurality of the total vote, thus assuring his election.

* * *

President Wilson could hardly have had a more different approach than Roosevelt to national security issues, but he too believed, if to a lesser extent than Roosevelt, that America could have security interests beyond the protection of its own borders. He was a lifelong academic who had essentially no experience in foreign relations and who placed much more importance on philosophical moral principles and values than on considerations of raw power. When he entered office, he was eager to spread democracy throughout the world.

In 1915, Wilson sent American Marines to Haiti to quell the chronic revolution there. The next year, he sent Marines to the Dominican Republic for the same purpose. In 1916, he also practiced what has been characterized as "an old-fashioned form of imperialism by buying the Virgin Islands from their colonial master, Denmark."[6]

When the fighting that became World War I erupted in Europe in August 1914, the English author and commentator H.G. Wells published a number of articles in London newspapers that subsequently appeared as a book which reflected British sentiment at the time. Wells argued that the Central Powers[7] had started the war and that the defeat of German militarism could bring about an end to it. The title of the book was initially *The War That Will End War*, but the alternative wording *The War to End All Wars* became more popular.

Wilson urged Americans to remain neutral. It was his simplified view that the underlying cause of the war was the militant nationalism of the major European powers and the ethnic hatreds that existed in much of Central and Eastern Europe. Later scholars concluded that the tragedy of the trench warfare that "produced deadlock on the Western Front" and sucked up lives "at the rate of 5,000 and sometimes 50,000 a day," was due to numerous misconceptions, miscalculations, and mistakes, such as the false assumption that the interconnectedness of the European nations through trade would stop a continent-wide war because the economic consequences would be too great; the unfounded belief that the war would be concluded in a matter of weeks, or at least by the end of the year; an over-reliance upon a French philosophy of warfare based almost exclusively on offensive operations and the maintenance of high morale; the failure of military planners to consider the likely political and treaty-based consequences of their offensive operations; and the unreasonable expectations of military leaders in occupied territories of a form of martial etiquette, including cooperation and obedience, from civilians whose country the military leaders had invaded, and whose home and property had been stolen or destroyed.[8]

On May 7, 1915, a German submarine torpedoed the British-owned luxury steamship *Lusitania* without warning, killing 1,195 people, including 128 Americans. Former President Roosevelt demanded swift retaliation, but Wilson decided to act with caution and keep the country in its neutral status. In August 1915, a German submarine sunk another British ocean liner. Despite being advised by members of his Cabinet to seek a Declaration of War against Germany, Wilson demurred again.

In 1916, President Wilson campaigned for re-election to the White House. He campaigned with the slogans "He kept us out of war" and "America First," a policy idea that generally emphasized nationalism and non-interventionism. It appeared that he was engaged in an effort to placate the country's isolationists, even though he was personally somewhat of an internationalist. On April 7, 1916, former President Roosevelt wrote to a friend and expressed the view that Wilson's failure to seek a Declaration of War after the sinking of the *Lusitania* was nothing short of cowardly. "What a dreadful creature Wilson is!" he exclaimed "I cannot believe our people have grown so yellow as to stand for him"[9] From the porch of Sagamore Hill, his home in Oyster Bay, New York, the former President urged the country to become more prepared for war. "I believe in the fullest liberty within our borders," he said, "and therefore I believe in efficiency in preparedness to prevent the restriction of this liberty by people outside our own borders.….Preparedness means discipline; and in a democracy it is of the highest importance for us to discipline ourselves; and in so doing we would prepare ourselves, not merely to defend our own rights against alien foes, but to ensure the habits of orderly liberty and disciplined efficiency, which will enable us to resolve our own social and industrial problems.[10] Four days prior to the Presidential Election, Roosevelt delivered a speech in which he attacked Wilson for his "tame submission to brutal [German] wrongdoing...and [his] failure to prepare" for war.[11] Nevertheless, Wilson narrowly defeated the Republican candidate, former Associate Justice of the Supreme Court Charles Evans Hughes.

Then, in January 1917, British intelligence intercepted and decoded a secret diplomatic communication from the German Foreign Office to the German Ambassador to Mexico in which Germany proposed a military alliance between Germany and Mexico if the U.S. entered the war against Germany. Under the terms of the proposed alliance, the states of Texas, Arizona, and New Mexico would be returned to Mexico. On February 1, Germany resumed its campaign of unrestricted submarine warfare. Several American ships were sunk. When the contents of what became known as the Zimmermann Telegram were released to the American public and the German Foreign Secretary admitted on March 3 that the telegram was genuine, Americans were outraged. Roosevelt railed again about Wilson's timid and vacillating course."[12]

Wilson finally had enough. On April 2, he appeared before Congress to request a Declaration of War against Germany. Curiously, he emphasized that the primary objective of the war should not be to ensure the safety and security of American shipping, or even of the American public. Rather, it was to make the world "safe for democracy" since the U.S. was "one of the champions of the rights of mankind." On April 6, Congress declared war.

Predictably, four days later, 58-year-old Theodore Roosevelt went to the White House to see Wilson. Nineteen years after his gallant leadership of the charge of the Rough Riders up San Juan Hill in Cuba, and eight years after he completed his second term as President, Roosevelt proposed to the cautious academic who had defeated him in 2012, to form a new volunteer division of the Rough Riders with him as its commander. He would later say that "I told Wilson that I would die on the field of battle; that I would never return if he would let me go." Also, predictably Wilson rejected the proposal, telling his personal secretary that Roosevelt was unscrupulous and that "the best way to treat Mr. Roosevelt is to take no notice of him. That breaks his heart and is the best punishment that can be administered."

Ten months before the end of the First World War, President Wilson addressed Congress to describe the fourteen points that he believed to be the "only possible" program for world peace. Once again, he argued the necessity of morality and ethics as the basis of the foreign policy of a democratic society. "We entered this war," he said, "because violations of right had occurred which touched us to the quick and made the life of our own people impossible unless they were corrected, and the world secured once for all against their recurrence. What we demand in this war, therefore, is nothing peculiar to ourselves. It is that the world be made fit and safe to live in."

In the present European situation I feel very much as if I were groping for a door in a blank wall.

President Franklin D. Roosevelt
Letter to a Friend
Early 1934

When you see a rattlesnake poised to strike, you do not wait until he has struck before you crush him.

President Franklin D. Roosevelt
Radio Address
September 11, 1941

III.

THE FURY OF AN AROUSED DEMOCRACY

In the decade following the end of the First World War, few issues arose which involved a clash between American isolationists and those referred to as internationalists. During the early 1930s, most Americans were struggling to deal with very difficult circumstances. Even though relative peace had reigned since the end of the Great War, the stock market crash and the Great Depression had created a general climate of despair. The old isolationist tradition that the only proper business of the United States was at home was widely embraced and few Americans heard, much less cared about the sounds of aggression that were coming from places like Ethiopia—where Italy's colonial governors in the Horn of Africa, under the increasingly radical fascist rule of Prime Minister Benito Mussolini, were acting with increased aggression to expand the borders of Italy's imperial foothold, and Spain—where a civil war between conservative monarchists (including a large military clique and the landed aristocracy) and socialists was in its early stages. Fewer still recognized the potential dangers associated with the rise of the new German Chancellor, Adolph Hitler. We were safe from the crises in Europe—so we thought—because we were separated from them by the Atlantic Ocean. That same year of 1936, Congress declared all loans to belligerent nations to be illegal.

Franklin D. Roosevelt, who had entered the White House after the election of 1932, had no principled belief by which he made foreign policy. He preferred to veer back and forth between isolationism and internationalism as political conditions required. He was less interested in fitting his foreign policy into a larger or long-term framework than in overcoming immediate problems and he tried to avoid foreign policy matters which might wreck his political popularity and the domestic programs he wanted.[1]

As Hitler set about rearming Germany openly, making increasingly aggressive demands and claims and taking actions in defiance of the terms of the Treaty of Versailles, which ended World War I, Roosevelt remarked to a friend that "In the present European situation

I feel very much as if I were groping for a door in a blank wall."

In March 1935, Hitler revealed that a German Air Force already existed, and he introduced a military draft that was designed to expand German's army from 100,000 to 500,000 troops. On March 7, 1936, Germany repudiated the Treaties of Locarno[2] and German troops marched into the demilitarized zone of the Rhineland.[3] German generals had advised against the move because they were certain that it would bring a reaction from France, which had the largest army in Europe, and it became known later that Hitler's troops would have turned back if France had resisted. But, neither France nor England even made an effective protest. Neither country had any fight. Hitler had judged well the mettle of his potential adversaries and the timidity of the democracies.

A lone voice of warning was, however, receiving increasing attention in Britain. On November 8, 1936, Winston Churchill, the former First Lord of the British Admiralty, rose in the House of Commons to declare that unless a united front against German rearmament and territorial expansion was soon established, Britain and all of the nations of Europe would "just be driven helter-skelter across the diplomatic chessboard until the limits of retreat [were] exhausted and then out of desperation, perhaps in some most unlikely quarter, the explosion of war [would] take place, probably under conditions not very favorable to those who [had] been engaged in [the] long retreat."

Three days later, a debate in the House of Commons opened on the speed and effectiveness of Britain's defense preparations. Replying to Churchill's charges of the Government's neglect of defense preparations between 1933 and 1935, Prime Minister Stanley Baldwin spoke of the political difficulties he would have faced if he had taken steps to build up Britain's armed forces at that time. He asserted that he had been unable to do so because public opinion was not in favor of such steps. In a remarkable admission of his vacuous leadership, which had placed partisan political considerations above the urgent needs of the country, he added: "Supposing I had gone to the country [i.e., called a General Election] and said that Germany was rearming and that we must rearm, does anybody think that this pacific democracy would have rallied to that cry at the moment?" He added that he could not think of anything "that would have made the loss of the Election from [his] point of view more certain."

Churchill had already driven home a rebuttal to Baldwin's argument with the force of a sledgehammer. "I have heard it said," he had declared, "that the Government had no mandate for rearmament until the general Election. Such a doctrine is wholly inadmissible. The responsibility of [the Government] for the public safety is absolute and requires no mandate. It is in fact the *prime object* for which Governments come into existence."

With war clouds becoming darker in Europe, isolationism remained strong in the U.S. and Roosevelt offered little leadership to those who were concerned about how a war in Europe might affect America. When Mussolini began making preparations for war against Ethiopia in 1934, Roosevelt believed that war would be a threat to peace everywhere and that the U.S. would necessarily be involved, but he did nothing more than to urge the Italian Dictator to settle issues with Ethiopia peacefully. In 1935, he signed the Neutrality Act of 1935 which required the President, in the event of war abroad, to embargo the export of arms to all belligerents, without consideration of which one had initiated aggression. Most importantly, he made no serious effort to educate the American people on the approaching dangers. He "hoped that they would be educated by events."[4] According to Roosevelt's biographer, "The record is clear. As a foreign policy maker, Roosevelt during his first term was more pussyfooting politician than political leader."[5]

In late 1937 and 1938, the President finally began to search for ways to awaken Americans to the rising dangers abroad, including the rising power of Japan, which had been occupying Manchuria, a Chinese territory, since 1931, and some avenue to a formula for peace. But, he remained keenly sensitive to the isolationists in Congress. In November 1937, the Rome-Berlin-Tokyo Axis was formally established. The leaders of Germany and Japan had surely noted the failure of the western democracies to respond to the aggression in Ethiopia and Manchuria.

On November 5, Hitler informed his generals of his plans for the conquest of eastern Europe. On March 12, 1938, German tanks and troops swept into Austria. Spain was now the venue of combat involving forces from several countries. Shortly after the Munich Agreement on September 29, in which the western democracies acceded to Hitler's demands for the partition of Czechoslovakia, German troops crossed into the Sudetenland, unopposed. British citizens now had mixed feelings about the appeasement policies of the Government of Prime Minister Neville Chamberlain, but one voice showed no mixed feelings at all. "We have," Winston Churchill said, "sustained a total and unmitigated defeat." In March 1939, the entire country of Czechoslovakia was annexed by Germany and eliminated as an independent nation. Roosevelt's reaction to the development "was little more than the old diplomacy of protest and pinprick."[6]

At three o'clock in the morning of September 1, 1939, President Roosevelt was informed that Germany had invaded Poland. After discussions with French and British officials, the American Embassies in Warsaw and London informed the White House that France and Britain would fight. "Well," Roosevelt observed, "it's come at last. God help us all." At least some reality had finally set in.

On the evening of September 3, the President spoke to what he called "the whole of America." Explaining that he had hoped that some miracle might prevent war, he declared to his radio audience that "You must master at the outset a simple but unalterable fact in modern foreign relations between nations. When peace has been broken anywhere, the peace of all countries everywhere is in danger. It is easy for you and me," he continued, "to shrug our shoulders and to say that conflicts taking place thousands of miles from the continental United States, and, indeed, thousands of miles from the whole American Hemisphere, do not seriously affect the Americas—and that all the United States has to do is to ignore them and go about its own business. Passionately though we may desire detachment, we are forced to realize that every word that comes through the air, every ship that sails the sea, every battle that is fought, does affect the American future...." But, he then added that "This nation will remain a neutral nation," and that "As long as it remains within my power to prevent, there will be no black-out of peace in the United States."

When France fell and the Nazis controlled all of western Europe, Roosevelt was faced with the bleak reality that only Britain stood between America and Hitler's European fortress. But, in 1940 he was also bucking the historical practice of American Presidents to serve only two terms by campaigning for a third term. He justified the action on the ground that there was a world crisis which demanded continuity of leadership. Because of the continuing political influence of the isolationists in Congress, however, it was not until his famous speech in Charlottesville, Virginia on June 10, 1940, that he warned that America could not afford to become "a lone island in a world dominated by the philosophy of force." During the presidential campaign, he was squeezed all possible political benefit from his role as Commander-in-Chief, but like President Wilson, he was running on a platform pledging that while the U.S. would assist those countries fighting against aggression, it would not participate in foreign conflicts or send military forces outside of America except in case of attack. Even that pledge of assistance was dangerously slow in coming.

On May 15, 1940, Churchill sent his first telegram to as Prime Minister to Roosevelt to plea for "the loan of forty or fifty of your older destroyers to bridge the gap between what we now have and the large new construction we put in hand at the beginning of the war." The ships were vitally necessary, he said, both to repel the expected and perhaps imminent seaborne invasion by Germany and to protect Britain's critically important supply routes from the already highly successful attacks by German submarines and the expected attacks by another hundred Italian submarines in what would become known as the Battle of the Atlantic. The embattled Prime Minister found it necessary to renew his plea for the destroyers on June 11 and again on July 31, saying "with great respect I must tell you that in the long history of the world, this is a thing to do *now*," and warning the President that "the voice and force of the United States may count for nothing if they are withheld too long." Roosevelt saw the request for destroyers as a colossal political risk only a few months before the election. His initial response was "vague and unsatisfying."[7]

The prospect of potentially having to prepare the country for war by drastically increasing the size of the Armed Forces and retooling its factories and workers was breathtaking. But, by August of 1940, the Battle of Britain had begun and it was not clear that the Royal Air Force could defeat the German Luftwaffe and prevent Germany's control of the air and its ground forces from landing on Britain's shores. This development finally shocked America out of its lassitude.

On September 8, Roosevelt declared a state of emergency. Eight days later, he signed into law the Selective Training and Service Act, which required all men between the ages of 21 and 45 to register for the nation's first peacetime draft. Despite the facts that the European democracies were already under Hitler's control and that Germany's war against Britain had been ongoing for more than a year, the vote on the legislation in the House of Representatives was only 203-202.

While the attention of the American people was suddenly being focused on the war in Europe, serious trouble was also brewing in another foreign quarter. In the summer of 1937, the so-called War Lords of Japan ordered the invasion of China. Believing that war with the West was inevitable, on July 26, 1940, a new Japanese Cabinet adopted a program of building a new order in Greater East Asia, a plan for massive expansion to secure for Japan the oil and mineral wealth of southern Asia. Friction between Japan and the U.S. increased rapidly. Believing that Japan was violating the letter and spirit of treaties signed by Japan as well as international law, destroying the independence of China, and transgressing American commercial and other rights in the Orient, Roosevelt froze all Japanese assets in the United States.[8] A commercial blockade of Japan was subsequently put into effect.

In November 1940, the President was given a decisive victory in the Presidential Election. He interpreted the result as a mandate for the United States to become the "arsenal of democracy." A step in that direction occurred in March 1941 when, after several months of negotiation, Congress finally passed legislation which authorized what became the Lend Lease Agreement, by which the U.S. would "lend" supplies to Britain, deferring payment. The primary motivation of the policy "was not altruism or disinterested generosity. Rather, it was designed to serve America's interest in defeating Germany without entering the war."[9]

Roosevelt still had to deal with the conflicting demands of the isolationists and the internationalists. As usual, he responded to the situation with a combination of improvisation and subterfuge. Some suggestion that he might act with more freedom of action to prepare the country for war now that the election was behind him was a remark that he made in a Radio Address on September 11, 1941. "When you see a rattlesnake poised to strike," he said, "you do not wait until he has struck before you crush him." Nevertheless, "the President," said Harry Hopkins, Roosevelt's closest foreign policy confidant, who also lived in the White House, "would rather follow public opinion than lead it." This comment was later confirmed by Roosevelt's biographer, who wrote that "as Roosevelt anxiously examined public opinion polls during 1941, he once again was failing to supply the crucial factor of his own leadership in the equation of public opinion."[10]

That approach to developments in an increasingly dangerous world was in sharp contrast to that of Churchill, who said in a speech on The War Situation to the House of Commons on September 30, 1941 that "Nothing is more dangerous in wartime than to live in the temperamental atmosphere of a Gallup poll, always feeling one's pulse and taking one's temperature....There's only one duty, only one safe course, and that is to try to be right and not to fear to do or say what you believe to be right."

The United States knew that rattlesnakes were poised to strike from both Europe and Asia, but still, no comprehensive or effective action was taken to crush them. Roosevelt did not know that at an Imperial Conference of senior Japanese civil and military officials on November 5, Emperor Hirohito had given his formal approval of his Government's proposal to continue negotiations with the U.S. for a brief period of time, and if the negotiations failed to lead to an agreement, to commence war against America by implementing Admiral Isoroku Yamamoto's plan to destroy the U.S. Pacific Fleet in its Pearl Harbor base.[11]

On the afternoon of Sunday, December 7, Roosevelt and Hopkins had just finished eating lunch in the White House when the telephone rang. It was Frank Knox, the Secretary of the Navy. "Mr. President," Knox said, "it looks as if the Japanese have attacked Pearl Harbor." Four days later, Hitler made a strategic mistake of gigantic proportions when he informed the Reichstag and the world that Germany was declaring War on the United States. Italy immediately followed suit.

A World War was now a fact. Any remaining meaningful domestic isolationist opposition to the U.S. joining the European war or fighting Japan soon disappeared. There was neither time nor room for anything other than national unity. Churchill would later write that at that moment he knew that Britain had been saved, that Hitler's and Mussolini's fates were sealed. He believed that the war would be long and that "Many disasters, immeasurable cost and tribulation lay ahead, but [that] there was no more doubt about the end." United, the democracies "could subdue everybody else in the world."[12] But, the outcome had not been inevitable. One can only speculate in hindsight about what the effect on America's security might have been if but a few developments had turned out differently, but it is important to consider them.

What if Hitler had defeated Britain and most or all of the other countries which constituted the British Empire in 1940 or early 1941, thereby giving Hitler freedom to run amok across all of the remaining democracies in Europe and to take control of the oil reserves of Middle Eastern countries?

What if Japan had waited a few months or a year before attacking Pearl Harbor in order to help Germany defeat Britain without the involvement of the United States in the war?

What if in addition to the eighteen American warships that were sunk or damaged in the attack on Pear Harbor, including eight battleships, the Japanese had the luck to find that America's aircraft carriers were also in the port at that time and to sink or badly damage all of them, thereby giving Japan time to complete its contemplated six-month campaign to seize the Dutch East Indies, the Philippines, [and] Malaya—the core of the new Japanese citadel,"[13] and to perhaps conquer other areas?

What if the Japanese had achieved a considerably more dramatic victory in the Pearl Harbor attack by remaining in the neighborhood of Hawaii for a couple of days "pummeling the submarine yard and setting ablaze the above ground tank farm containing 4.5 million barrels of precious oil?"[14]

What if Hitler had not made the colossal and obvious strategic error of declaring war on America shortly after the Pearl Harbor attack, thereby giving Germany a year or two of additional time to continue building the strength of the German armed forces and to expand and consolidate its geopolitical ambitions, without having to immediately confront the human and industrial resources of an enraged United States?

What if the February 1943 raid by six British-trained commandos on the German Norsk Hydro heavy-water plant in the village of Vemok in southern Norway had failed? The heavy water (deuterium oxide) being made by the plant was a vital ingredient of the Atomic Bomb that German scientists were working to produce. The several month delay in the production of heavy water which was the result of the raid disrupted Germany's nuclear program and perhaps sealed its fate. Kurt Diebner, a German atomic scientist, was quoted after Germany's surrender as saying that "It was the elimination of German heavy-water production in Norway that was the main factor in our failure to achieve a self-sustaining atomic reactor before the war ended."[15]

What if Hitler had not been misled by his own scientists into believing that an atomic bomb-building project "was impractical and that nuclear energy would be useful mainly to power submarines?" One German nuclear scientist would explain after the war that the scientists misled Hitler because "the führer would 'have [had] their heads' if he thought a bomb could be built and they failed to produce one in six months."[16]

* * *

At the outset of World War II, then Colonel Dwight David Eisenhower wrote a letter to his brother Milton in which he said that "Hitler should be aware of the fury of an aroused democracy."[17] Some people have attributed to Admiral Yamamoto, who planned the attack on Pearl Harbor, the comment "I fear we have awakened a sleeping giant and filled him with a terrible resolve." Scholars have challenged the authenticity of that quotation, but there is no doubt that from his two years of study at Harvard as a junior officer, his later service as the Naval Attaché at the Japanese Embassy in Washington, and his long study of the American oil industry, Yamamoto understood that if Americans were sufficiently outraged, Japan could not win a long war with them. The advanced technologies of today make it highly unlikely that any significant armed conflict in the future will be long. America will have no choice but to attempt to deter such conflicts and to be already fully prepared to instantly fight and win them.

Five years after World War II ended, the first volume of Churchill's War Memoirs was published. The theme of the volume was:

How the British people held the fort ALONE till those who hitherto had been half blind were half ready.

If the Communists were permitted to force their way into the Republic of Korea without opposition from the free world, no small nation would have the courage to resist threats and aggression by stronger Communists neighbors.

President Harry S. Truman
1950

IV.

ISOLATIONISM AND THE START OF THE COLD WAR

The occasion was the March 31, 1949, Mid-Century Convocation of the Massachusetts Institute of Technology in Boston. Winston Churchill, now out of political office for almost four years, had been invited to deliver the Keynote Address. Fresh off the heels of the most destructive war in history, the democracies of the world were desperate for peace, or at least a prolonged period of recuperation. Hitler and Mussolini were dead. President Harry S. Truman had occupied the White House since the death of Franklin D. Roosevelt on April 12, 1945. Japan lay prostrate before the world and its government was being directed by General Douglas MacArthur in his position as the Supreme Commander for the Allied Powers. Because of its economy and its then sole possession of the Atomic Bomb, America was the undisputed greatest power on earth. The isolationist strain of ideology in the U.S. had been made practically impossible and had almost disappeared.

It had been three years since Churchill had accepted Truman's invitation to make an earlier speech at the small Westminster College in Fulton, Missouri. Even then geopolitical developments were a dangerous or at least a troublesome future. The Soviet Union had already been engaged in an aggressive effort to bend the countries of Eastern Europe and the Middle East to its will and to extend its influence, if not its outright domination, to the Persian Gulf. At a time when the U.S. was demobilizing thousands of its soldiers each day, Russia had been demanding that it be allowed to establish army and navy bases in the Bosporis Strait and the Dardanelles and it was beginning to mass its troops on the borders of Turkey, thus placing control of the eastern end of the Mediterranean at risk.[1] In expressing his concern about these developments to Secretary of State James Byrnes, Truman had declared that "Unless Russia is faced with an iron fist and strong language, another war is in the making." He had added that "Only one language do they understand—'How many divisions have you?'"[2]

On February 9, 1946, Soviet Premier Joseph Stalin had declared in his first major public speech after the end of the World War that war between the East and West was inevitable because of the "capitalist development of the world economy" and that the USSR would concentrate on increasing its military strength in advance of that war. That speech would later be described as the beginning of the Cold War. As we shall see in Chapter IX, seventy-six years later, almost to the day, Russian President Vladimir Putin would deliver a speech that was eerily similar to Stalin's and which marked the beginning of Cold War II.

Thirteen days after Stalin's Address, George F. Kennan, the U.S. Ambassador to Moscow, had sent his famous "Long Telegram" to America's Secretary of State warning that the Soviet Government was committed to the belief that if Soviet power was to be secure, it was "necessary that the internal harmony of [American] society be disrupted, [the American] way of life be destroyed, [and] the international authority of [the American] state be broken." Kennan had concluded that the United States did not need to engage in a war with the Soviet Union in order to blunt and counter the USSR's aggressive moves. The main element of any U.S. policy, he believed, "must be that of a long-term patient but firm and vigilant containment of Russian expansive tendencies." This containment concept soon began to guide American foreign policy.

It was in this context that Churchill had declared in his March 5, 1946, speech at Fulton the famous words "From Stettin in the Baltic, to Trieste in the Adriatic, an Iron Curtain has descended across the Continent. Behind that line lie all the capitals of the ancient states of Central and Eastern Europe.... All these famous cities and the populations around them lie in what I must call the Soviet sphere... subject...not only to a Soviet influence, but to a very high and, in many cases increasing measure of control from Moscow." He continued. "From what I have seen of our Russian friends and allies during the war, I am convinced that there is nothing they admire so much as strength, and there is nothing for which they have less respect for than weakness, especially military weakness." His speech was the first clear articulation of the threat that the Soviet Union and Communism posed to the peace and stability in the post-World War II world. It was not a call for war, but a counsel of military preparedness. In a speech in New York on March 25, 1949, he elaborated on this theme about authoritarian Russian leaders. "You can only deal with them on the following basis...

by having superior force on your side on the matter in question—and they also must be convinced that you will use—you will not hesitate to use—these forces, if necessary, in the most ruthless manner...that you are not restrained by any moral consideration if the case arose from using that force with complete material ruthlessness. And that is the greatest chance of peace, the surest road to peace."

Churchill's "Iron Curtain" speech was not broadly welcomed. The immediate reaction in many quarters was hostility, not unlike that which he encountered in Britain after his early warnings about Hitler's and Nazi Germany's military buildup. World War II had only recently ended and like the British public in the early 1930s, no one wanted to hear about new threats.

In a speech to Congress on March 12, 1947, however, Truman had announced a new American foreign policy which was designed to corroborate Churchill's opinion of the need for military preparedness and to contain the geopolitical expansion of the Soviet Union and Communism as advocated by Kennan. He had asserted that because Communist regimes were threatening free peoples, they necessarily represented a threat to international peace and the national security of the United States. The policy had soon become known as the Truman Doctrine.

Three months later on June 5, the eve of the third anniversary of D-Day, Secretary of State George C. Marshall had delivered a speech at the Harvard University Commencement which had the same aim as The Truman Doctrine, but which proposed a different methodology. The Second World War had left a wake of destruction that had completely broken the business structure of European countries. Massive food shortages had created widespread hunger and misery. The U.S. Government feared that a starving, devasted Europe might turn to Communism (as China would do two years later).

Declaring that the "United States should do whatever it is able to do to assist in the return of normal economic health in the world, without which there can be no political stability and no assured peace," Marshal proposed a plan to provide European countries with $13 billion in economic aid. The purpose of the aid would be "the revival of a working economy in the world so as to permit the emergence of political and social conditions in which free institutions can exist." On December 10, 1953, the retired Five Star General of the Army George C. Marshall, who Churchill had hailed as "the organizer of victory" in the War, was awarded the Nobel Peace Prize for what had become known as the Marshall Plan.

By the time the Presidential Election year of 1948 opened, articles in newspapers were increasingly concerned about the possibility of war with the Soviet Union because of its continuing efforts to obtain political control of the City of Berlin. President Truman, who had entered the presidency with no foreign policy experience, but who had clearly demonstrated forceful, confident, and decisive leadership traits during the final months of the World War and since, had decided to take action other than just hopeful diplomacy. On March 17, he had asked Congress for immediate passage of new legislation regarding universal military training and a temporary reinstatement of the draft. The political will for peace, he had said, must be backed by the strength for peace. "We must be prepared to pay the price for peace, or assuredly we shall pay the price of war."[3] "Truman deserved great praise for his courage," one leading newspaper had declared, "as well as his disregard for political considerations, since calling for the draft in an election year seemed the poorest possible political strategy."[4]

On June 24, 1948, Soviet forces blockaded all barge, rail, road, and water access to West Berlin, which was under Allied control. The Soviets had decided that if they could force their former allies to evacuate Berlin, future Communist control of all of Germany might be possible. Deprived of electrical power and the steady supply of food and coal, the 2.1 million people living in the Western sectors of the City, who were still suffering from the hardships which were the result of the World War, now faced additional hardships.

Truman's freedom of action had appeared to be very limited. He had serious political problems. Only two months earlier, a Gallup Poll had reported his approval rating at only 36 percent. He also had a military problem. The Western garrison in Berlin amounted to only fifteen thousand troops and there were only sixteen Western divisions located outside of Berlin in the Western zone of occupation. It was estimated that the Russians had eighty-four divisions stationed in eastern Germany and in other satellite countries.

Despite these facts, the President had refused to acquiesce to the Russian actions. Ignoring the possible political consequences, he had ordered that an airlift of supplies be conducted through air corridors from West Germany which were still open. Huge logistical and organizational problems had been involved, but the airlift operations had soon begun.

The Berlin Airlift was still being conducted when Churchill rose to speak at MIT in March 1949.[5] It would be reported that his remarks "condensed fifty years of world history into a thorough and cautionary analysis of the fledgling Cold War." Noting that science and new technologies had placed "novel and dangerous facilities in the hands of the most powerful countries" and that the multiplication of ideas had proceeded at an incredible rate, he lamented that the vast expansion was "not accompanied by any noticeable advance in the stature of man, either in his mental faculties, or his moral character.... The scale of events around him [had] assumed gigantic proportions while he [had] remained about the same size. By comparison, therefore, he [had] actually became much smaller."

In discussing the First World War, he declared that "The United States, for reasons which were natural and traditional, but no longer so valid as in the past, stood aloof and expected to be able to watch as a spectator, the thrilling, fearful drama unfold from across what was then called 'the broad Atlantic'. These expectations were not borne out by what happened." In referring to he Second World War, he observed that "Once again, the English speaking world gloriously but narrowly emerged, bleeding and breathless, but united as we never were before." He concluded by saying "I cannot speak to you…without expressing… the thanks of Britain and of Europe for the splendid part America is playing in the world. Many nations have risen to the summit of human affairs, but there is a great example where new-won supremacy has not been used for self-aggrandisement, but only for further sacrifice."

*   *   *

On June 25, 1950, North Korea invaded South Korea. The details and consequences of that invasion for the U.S. are discussed in Chapter XV. For the purposes here, it is sufficient to say that the U.S. was caught totally unprepared. Moreover, the Truman Administration had not hidden its desire not to become involved in another armed conflict on the Asian continent. Indeed, on January 12, 1950, then U.S. Secretary of State Dean Acheson had announced publicly that the American "defensive perimeter" did not extend to South Korea. Since the U.S. had withdrawn its troops from South Korea the previous year, Kim Il Sung, the Communist leader of the North Korean puppet regime, had determined that South Korea could be quickly overrun. He informed Stalin that a war against South Korea would be won in three days.[6]

There was no doubt that after the devastation of World War II, the last thing that the American people wanted was another war. America had entered the Second World War only after Japan and Germany had declared war directly on it. Whatever might be said about the North Korean attack, it was not an attack directly on the U.S. Moreover, sustained public support, which is required in war, is emotionally exhausting. One scholar put the matter this way. "A nation's capacity for high-tension political commitment is limited. Nature insists on a respite. People can no longer gird themselves for heroic effort. They yearn to immerse themselves in the privacies of life. Worn out by the constant summons to battle, weary of ceaseless national activity…they seek a new dispensation, an interlude of rest and recuperation."[7]

In his Memoirs, Truman would later reflect upon his own thinking at the time. "[T]his was not the first occasion when the strong had attacked the weak. I recalled some earlier instances: Manchura, Ethiopia, Austria. *** Communism was acting in Korea just as Hitler, Mussolini, and the Japanese had acted….I felt certain that if South Korea was allowed to fall Communist leaders would be emboldened to override nations closer to our own shores. If the Communists were permitted to force their way into the Republic of Korea without opposition from the free world, no small nation would have the courage to resist threats and aggression by stronger Communist neighbors."[8] North Korea was supported by China and the Soviet Union. South Korea was supported by United Nations forces, principally those of the United States.

Pearl Harbor and the dangers of World War II had jolted the sleepy, isolationist American nation and dragged it to superpower status, but the horrible fact in June 1950, was that the country was totally and inexcusably unprepared for another war. The first American troops who were thrown into combat in South Korea were garrison troops stationed in Japan. The American units were "poorly armed, in terrible shape physically, and more often than not, poorly led. The mighty army that had stood victorious in two great theaters of war, Europe and Asia, just five years earlier, was a mere shell of itself."[9]

The problem then was the same one which has plagued the American Armed Forces many times over several decades. Militarily, the country was trying to get by on the cheap. The blame "belonged to everyone—the President, who wanted to keep taxes down..and keep the defense budget down to a bare-bones level; the Congress, which if anything wanted to cut the budget even more; and the theater commander," General MacArthur, who was responsible for the lack of adequate training. But, it was Truman who was most responsible. "[T]he President [had] to take full responsibility" for the matter.[10]

America provided half of the Allied ground troops and almost all the naval and air forces in Korea. The cost to the U.S. in blood and treasure was thirty-four thousand dead and some $15 billion. The cost to the North and South Koreans and the Communist Chinese, was much higher. But, by the time the Korean Armistice was signed on July 27, 1953, the objective of reversing North Korea's aggression had been realized.[11]

Today, South Korea is governed within a democratic system that features regular rotations of political power and robust political pluralism. Since the end of the Korean War, South Korea has been transformed from a poor agrarian society to one of the world's most highly industrialized nations and its economy continues to grow at a remarkable pace. North Korea continues to be ruled by one of the world's longest-running dynastic dictatorships. Three generations of the Kim family have ruled with absolute and brutal authority. Periodic purges of senior officials by Kim Jong-un, the current Supreme Leader and grandson of Kim Il Sung, are normal. It has no functioning judiciary. The nation is one of the world's poorest and the state controls all means of production and owns almost all property.

We live...not in an instant of peril, but in an age of peril. All of us have learned—first from the onslaught of Nazi aggression, then from Communist aggression—that all free nations must stand together, or they shall fall separately.

President Dwight D. Eisenhower
June 10, 1953

V.

STAND TOGETHER OR FALL SEPARATELY

Senator Robert A. Taft of Ohio was not the usual kind of politician. He was not a back slapper at all, but he had a remarkable pedigree. The elder son of William Howard Taft, our 27th President and 10th Chief Justice of the United States, the younger Taft graduated from Harvard Law School, he was highly principled and was famous for his appetite for hard work and political integrity. He was considered to be the most powerful Republican in the Senate. He was so respected that in 1957, a Senate committee named Taft as one of America's five greatest senators.

As a prominent non-interventionist, he opposed U.S. involvement in World War II prior to the Pearl Harbor attack. After the War, he spoke out against the Nuremberg War Trials. He conceded that the Defendants, including German Field Marshal Hermann Goering, were despicable, but he declared that "the trial of the vanquished by the visitors cannot be impartial no matter how it is hedged about with the forms of justice," because the trials violated the fundamental principle of law that "a man cannot be tried under an ex post facto statute."

After Taft was elected to the Senate in 1938, he sought the Republican presidential nomination in 1940 but lost. He tried again in 1948, but he had opposed the creation of NATO and he lost again. He sought the nomination a third time in 1952, but lost to General Dwight D. Eisenhower, who won the General Election. Long before the 1952 Presidential Election, Taft's views on foreign policy were well known.

In foreign affairs, he applied the same libertarian strain of isolationism philosophy that shaped his domestic policy views. He believed that war should never be undertaken by the U.S. for any purpose other than to save the liberty of the American people, and then only when it was directly threatened.[1] He objected to the United Nations and other international organizations. For much of his career, he advocated what he called "the policy of the free hand," whereby the United States would avoid entangling alliances and interference in foreign disputes.[2] He has been described as a "prudential optimist, an American conservative who rejected the Hobbesian view of human nature."[3]

By the time of the 1952 election year, Dwight Eisenhower had a worldwide reputation for leadership and was immensely popular at home. He had led the Allied forces to victory in Europe in the War as a Five Star General of the Army serving as the Supreme Commander, Allied Expeditionary Force in Europe. He had then served as the Army Chief of Staff from 1945 to 1948. After retiring from the Army for two years to serve as the President of Columbia University, Eisenhower agreed to President Truman's request to return to active duty in the Army and accept operational command of the new North Atlantic Treaty Organization.

No one really knew whether Eisenhower was a Democrat or a Republican or what his views were on domestic and even some foreign policy issues. He had never registered with a political party or voted in a Federal Election. He was actually very independent-minded, asserting that it would be impossible for him "to adopt a political philosophy so narrow as to merit the label 'liberal' or 'conservative,' or anything of the sort."[4] It was thus not entirely surprising that on December 18, 1951, President Truman, who imagined, or at least hoped that Eisenhower was a Democrat, inquired for the second time about his intentions with respect to the 1952 Presidential Election. Well aware that Eisenhower, who by then had retired again from the Army and returned to Columbia University, was committed to the concept of collective defense and a strong NATO, Truman said that it was his own immediate duty to keep isolationists out of the White House. Eisenhower demurred. When he attempted without success to persuade Senator Taft, the presumed future Republican nominee in the 1952 election, to support NATO, and after voters in several states voted for him in the early Primary Elections, his reluctance to become a candidate quickly dissipated and he announced his candidacy as a Republican. He defeated Taft for the nomination. With the possible exception of President Washington, no presidential candidate in U.S. history had the national security experience of Eisenhower. On November 4, he was elected President, receiving 55 percent of the popular vote and 442 Electoral Votes. The Democrat candidate, Governor Adlai Stevenson of Illinois, received 89 Electoral Votes.

Broadly speaking, President Eisenhower governed with the internationalist approach of Roosevelt and Truman, but he was not doctrinaire or partisan on foreign policy issues. Having promised during the campaign that if elected, he would make a personal trip to Korea to assess the situation on the ground there for the purpose of ending the War, he did just that before his inauguration. Believing that he had received a mandate by American voters to end the War, he seriously considered all options, including the use of tactical nuclear weapons on the Kaesong area and he made sure that the North Koreans and Chinese knew that option was being seriously considered. An Armistice Agreement soon was signed on July 27, 1953. In contrast, when Britain, France and Israel sought U.S. support in 1956 for their effort to drive Egyptian leader Gamal Abdel Nasser out of Egypt because of his nationalization of the Suez Canal, Eisenhower refused the request immediately.

On January 12, 1954, one year after Eisenhower assumed the presidency, the new Administration announced a new policy of "massive retaliation" against Communist aggressors. A strong fiscal conservative, Eisenhower believed that military and foreign assistance spending had to be reduced. The new policy was aimed at "getting maximum protection at a bearable cost." The idea was to deter Communist aggression by threatening to use "massive retaliatory power," i.e., nuclear weapons, in response to future Communist acts of war. That policy would not last beyond the end of Eisenhower's second term.

*   *   *

Five months after he entered the White house, President Eisenhower delivered a forceful speech in which he struck back at Taft and other critics of his Cold War foreign policy. In the weeks prior to the speech, Taft had argued that if efforts to reach a peace agreement on Korea failed, the United States should withdraw from the United Nations forces and establish its own policy for dealing with North Korea. Declaring that the Nation's security was the most important of all of the problems confronting the American people because it involved a struggle for freedom, Eisenhower noted that the fight was being waged "neither for land nor food nor for power – but for the soul of man himself." To win the struggle, he said, America had to remain militarily strong because "we cannot count upon any enemy striking us at a given, ascertainable moment. We live," he continued, "not in an instant of peril, but in an age of peril."[5] He attacked Taft's policy views as involving an "oversimplified concept, which I believe is equally misleading and dangerous. It is what we might call the "fortress" theory of defense. Advocates of this theory ask: 'Why cannot the strongest nation in the world—our country—stand by itself? Why does the United Nations matter? …[W]hy cannot we make our own decisions, fight and stand as only we ourselves may choose?"

He answered the rhetorical question by declaring that "All of us have learned—first from the onslaught of Nazi aggression, then from Communist aggression—that all free nations must stand together or they shall fall separately. ***This, essential, indispensable unity means working together—always within a clearly defined, clearly understood framework of principle." This principle clearly reflected the strategic war-fighting imperatives espoused by Major General Fox Connor (1874-1951), Eisenhower's former Army mentor.[6] He concluded the argument by asking "Who is there who thinks that the strength of America is so great, its burdens so easy, its future so secure, that it could [retreat from the necessary] unity?" This speech and Eisenhower's subsequent performance as President temporarily buried the isolationist wing of the Republican Party and enshrined an internationalist principle in American foreign policy.

In 2017, a poll of over 100 historians ranked Eisenhower among the five greatest Presidents in the Nation's history.[7]

*   *   *

When President John F. Kennedy assumed the presidency in January 1961, he declared in his Inaugural Address that "…the torch has been passed to a new generation of Americans…" The new Special Counsel to the President, who was also his alter ego, would later write that the young men who were the new senior officials in the new Administration were men "who had been concerned about the lack of ideas and idealism in the sterile clash between repressive Communism and narrowly negative anti-Communism, but who were also determined," as Kennedy declared in the Inaugural Address, to "pay any price, bear any burden, meet any hardship, support any friend [or] oppose any foe in order to assure the survival and the success of liberty."[8] The eloquent address suggested future policies that would be vigorously international in nature and which would include greater U.S. military intervention in third world countries in the periphery of the Cold War, particularly in newly independent states in

Asia and Africa which soon became battlegrounds in which the U.S. and the Soviet Union supported competing factions.

In the 1960 Presidential Election, Kennedy had campaigned against Richard Nixon, Eisenhower's Vice President, by challenging the Eisenhower Administration's policy of "massive retaliation" as unrealistic. While Eisenhower had been worried about excessive U.S. expenditures for defense Kennedy believed that the country could afford sufficient additional defense spending to catch up to and surpass the Soviet Union. More importantly, Kennedy believed that Eisenhower's policy was not effective. Several armed conflicts in The Third World had been neglected because the only response would have been nuclear retaliation. Moreover, with the development of nuclear-tipped International Ballistic Missiles and Submarine Launched Ballistic Missiles, the USSR could possibly survive a retaliatory nuclear attach from the U.S. and fire back with its second-strike capability.

Kennedy wanted more options. During his first year in office, a new policy of Flexible Response was adopted. It would permit the U.S. to respond to Communist aggression with a customized response which might include diplomatic, political, and military strategies, and which could be made proportional to the circumstances of the Communist aggression. Kennedy also increased the size of the Special Forces of the U.S., which were established by the Army in 1952 for the purpose of engaging in unconventional warfare, including intelligence, commando, and other operations. He soon became closely associated with the Green Berets.

The most significant extension of the containment policy to the third world took place in Vietnam. In April 1954, representatives of the world's powers met in Geneva in an effort to resolve problems in Asia, the most difficult of which was a long conflict between the French, who were intent on continuing colonial control of Vietnam, and Vietnamese nationalist forces whose leadership were Communist. While the representatives were meeting, a 57-day battle between the Vietnamese and the French Army came to a dramatic conclusion at Dien Bien Phu on May 7, 1954. The French defeat clearly signaled the end of France's aspirations in Vietnam. Concerned that a victory by the nationalist forces would trigger further Communist expansion throughout Southeast Asia (the "Domino Theory"), the U.S. had supported France, but it had refused France's request for more direct intervention in the war.

Agreement was reached in July at Geneva that Vietnam would be temporarily divided at the 17th parallel, that France would withdraw its troops from Northern Vietnam, and that within two years, elections would be held to select a president and to reunite the country. Within a year, the U.S. contributed to the establishment of a new anti-Communist government in South Vietnam and it began providing financial and military assistance to that government. When President Eisenhower left office, the U.S. had 1,000 military advisors in South Vietnam who were training the Army of the Republic of Vietnam and the paramilitary Civil Guard. Refusing to wait for the elections, North Vietnam and its Communist allies in South Vietnam (the Viet Cong) commenced a military campaign to forcibly unify all of Vietnam under the leaders of the Communist North.

Successive American Presidents believed that they were responsible for the containment of the Communist efforts to expand, especially after North Vietnam's breach of the Geneva Agreement. Communist expansion, however, was already a fact. In 1949, the Chinese civil war had come to an end with the victory of the Chinese Communist Party (CCP) over the Nationalist Party, or Kuomintang. The U.S. had promptly suspended diplomatic ties with the new People's Republic of China (PRC). A year later, Communist North Korea had invaded South Korea. During the 1940s and 1950s, Communist revolts had occurred in the Philippines and Malaya. And, the French defeat at Dien Bien Phu was fresh on the minds of Kennedy's senior advisors.

In August 1961, President Kennedy informed his advisors for the first time that he might have to send U.S. combat troops to Vietnam. He worried that an American withdrawal and a Communist triumph would destroy him and the Democrat Party in a replay of the "Who Lost China?" debate that had plagued President Truman in the early 1950s. "There are limits to the number of defeats I can defend in one twelve-month period," he said to one adviser. "I've had the Bay of Pigs, pulling out of Laos, and I can't accept a third."[9] According to one national security theorist, Kennedy "knew that he could not get out of Vietnam before the elections in November 1964 without inviting his own political eclipse."[10] By the end of 1962, there were 11,500 members of the U.S. Armed Forces in Vietnam, almost 9,000 more than had been there at the beginning of the year. Kennedy eventually authorized 15,000 advisors in addition to the 1,000 that Eisenhower had authorized. Many years later, the U.S. Department of State's Historian would conclude that "The execution of Kennedy's foreign policy did not quite live up to the stirring rhetoric of his Inaugural Speech."

*   *   *

When Lyndon Johnson entered the White House in November 1963 upon the death of President Kennedy, few people could predict with confidence what his approach to foreign policy would be. He had a sometimes-embarrassing lack of knowledge on the subject. A domestic program of Great Society legislation was clearly his grand ambition, his most important objective. Nevertheless, he asserted that the Vietnam conflict was a war against Communism that had to be won. As a Democrat, he too remembered the blame that had been attached to the Truman Administration in the late 1940s for the perceived "loss of China" to the Communists. "I am not going to lose Vietnam," he said. "I am not going to be the President who saw Southeast Asia go the way China went."[11]

On August 2, 1964, the American destroyer U.S.S. *Maddox* (DD-731), was steaming in international waters 10 miles off the coast of North Vietnam in the Gulf of Tonkin. The ship was attacked unsuccessfully by three Communist patrol boats. No American casualties were suffered. The next day, as the *Maddox* and another destroyer were approaching the coast, a violent thunderstorm erupted causing the sonar equipment on the two ships to act erratically. In the confusion, the ships reported that they were being attacked. Most national security authorities would later conclude that there was no clear evidence of a second attack, but Johnson immediately ordered retaliatory airstrikes against coastal targets in the North. He appeared on nationwide television to announce his 'positive reply' to North Vietnamese aggression.

It would be argued later that Johnson's action was no more than a cynical play in an election year, but on August 7, Congress passed a Joint Resolution that had been requested by Johnson that granted authority to the President "to take all necessary measures to repel any armed attack against the forces of the United States and to prevent any further aggression." He subsequently treated the Resolution as the functional equivalent of a congressional Declaration of War. Thus it was, that the U.S. had taken the first step down a path that led to unforeseeable consequences and a badly divided nation.

As Johnson presided over the increasing American involvement in the Vietnam conflict after his election in 1964, his conduct was not based upon any internationalist, isolationist, or other principles, but upon the principle of political expediency and self-interest. Despite his inexperience in national security matters, he began to make key decisions on his evolving policies on the advice of only a small group of advisors. He preferred making small, incremental decisions and authorizing only small escalations and sharply limited military actions which were reversible, and therefore could be carried out at minimal risk and cost.[12] Slowly at first, but surely, American responsibility for the war became inevitable because of his deceit with the American people and his lack of the *political will* necessary to make a big decision on the question of either withdrawing from Vietnam, or committing whatever resources were required to achieve a clearly defined American strategic objective there. His practice of only making small decisions precluded the kind of critical thinking and rigorous re-examination of existing policies that are necessary for success. By the end of 1964, some 23,000 U.S. military personnel were in Vietnam.

In July 1965, Defense officials concluded that the war in Vietnam was very likely to be a long-term commitment with increasing military manpower requirements, primarily from the Army. Increased draft calls and extensions of the tours of duty of Active U.S. Army forces were projected to be insufficient to meet the requirements for Vietnam and the Army's other worldwide commitments, so the Joint Chiefs of Staff recommended a mobilization, or at least a partial mobilization of the Army's Reserve Components, the National Guard and Army Reserve. Johnson would not even consider the issue. A mobilization of large numbers of part-time Reservists would awaken the country to the true costs of the war. He wanted to both declare his intent to "win" the war, and to declare that the Nation would scarcely have to inconvenience itself while fighting a war ten thousand miles away.[13] He wanted Vietnam to be "a war without a price, a silent, politically invisible war."[14] By the end of 1966, the total U.S. military strength in South Vietnam was 385,000 personnel.

By 1967, Johnson had lost the full trust of his most senior military officers. More importantly, public support of the war was diminishing rapidly. There were several causes. A major cause was his ineffective performance in war leadership. Members of the media were beginning to find cracks in his credibility. People who he referred to as

"Eastern Intellectuals" were also quick to report instances of his crude and sometimes coarse personality. They seemed to resent the fact that he lacked the polish and eloquence of Jack Kennedy.

Another major cause was, to a considerable extent, beyond Johnson's control and had nothing to do with the exhaustion of the public or what has been called the "changing cycles of American politics,"[15] e.g, between internationalism and isolationism. It did involve an unprecedented new factor: cultural politics. By 1967, radicalism among young people in the Baby Boomer generation was engulfing several college campuses. A spirit of ugly belligerence had developed, producing a growing rebellion against authority generally and the rules of personal conduct on campus with which generations of previous students had had no difficulty. The new, aggressive student militancy soon resulted in the destruction of property and in other violations of law. Riots in American cities had become commonplace. Antiwar protests, especially against the presence of ROTC units on campus, was increasing, which was not entirely surprising since the media and academia were already two of the most staunchly anti-war communities in the country and they were in daily contact with the students.

That conduct, which would later be described as also involving "protest music that thrilled…many hearts, exhilarating antiwar rallies, …[and] love-soaked, dope-hazed evenings in places like Woodstock,"[16] might have been more understandable if it was clear that the protestors had critically analyzed and were fully informed on the complex issues relating to the war. In fact, most of the privileged students who were protesting had, by virtue of their attendance at a college, received a student's deferment from fighting their country's battles in Vietnam. Nevertheless, many remained fearful of that possibility and were easily enticed into what the President of one distinguished college called the "blatant sophomoric nihilism…of American undergraduate life."[17] They were also easily led into believing the conventional portrayal of the U.S. Armed Forces as a group of unwilling draftees which was overrepresented by minorities. The truth was that two-thirds of those who served in Vietnam—and 73 percent of those who died—were volunteers.[18]

Thus, it was that when North Vietnamese and Viet Cong forces commenced the Tet Offensive[19] on January 3, 1968, the response of the American public was not a celebration of the fact that the Offensive had resulted in a crushing military and political defeat for the North,[20] but rather one of shock. The politicized and vivid reporting of the

Offensive by the U.S. media convinced the American public that an overall successful outcome in Vietnam was not as imminent as they had been led to believe by Johnson.[21] Fifty-nine days later, with his approval rating lingering at 36 percent and only seven months remaining in the presidential campaign, President Johnson announced that he would no longer seek re-election.

Johnson simply had not had the *political will* to tell the American people all of the unvarnished truths about U.S. objectives in Vietnam, including the probable risks and costs of achieving them. A distinguished and friendly presidential historian who later helped Johnson write his memoirs, has written about the absence of this kind of communication: "While accepting recommendations for a major war expansion, Johnson simultaneously rejected counsel to inform Congress and country of the likelihood of a protracted and costly struggle." She continued. "In war, more than at any other time, the people must be sufficiently informed to understand the choices that are being made. In the end, no statesman can successfully pursue a war policy unless he has instilled a sense of shared direction and purpose, unless people know what to expect and what is expected of them. By all these standards of candor and collaboration between a leader and the people in the critical time of war, Lyndon Johnson…failed."[22]

*Richard Nixon's foreign policy goals were long-range. and he pursued them without regard to domestic political consequences.
When he considered our nation's interests at stake, he dared confrontations, despite the imminence of elections and also in
the midst of the worst crisis of his life.*
Former Secretary of State Henry Kissinger
April 27, 1994

*Rhetoric alone would not persuade anyone that America would stand firm.
They would have to see proof of our resolve.*
President Gerald Ford
May, 1975

Our moral sense dictates a clear-cut preference for those societies which share with us an abiding respect for individual human rights.
President Jimmy Carter
Inaugural Address, January 20, 1977

VI.

PRAGMATISM, POLITICAL WILL AND HUMAN RIGHTS

During the period 1969 to 1981, three Presidents occupies the Oval Office. Foreign and national security policy was the primary interest of one. One inherited a foreign policy agenda and his attention to it was often diverted because of serious domestic problems. The third had no experience and little or no interest in national security and related policy matters, as his performance in office clearly demonstrated.

When Richard Nixon entered the White House in January 1969, he brought a reputation as perhaps the foremost anti-Communist politician of the Cold War, a reputation honed by his service on the House Un-American Activities Committee. His political base was within the conservative wing of the Republican Party. At the same time, he was a highly intelligent pragmatist and this characteristic was apparent in his foreign policy, where he looked for geopolitical opportunities that did not fall neatly along partisan, internationalist/isolationist, or other ideological lines.

Only five days after his inauguration, the new President presided over the first meeting of his National Security Council. The principal subject was Vietnam. Having already considered a series of options prepared by Dr. Henry Kissinger, his National Security Adviser, on the question of how to deal with the war in Vietnam, Nixon made a difficult but very important strategic decision. The U.S. would withdraw, but gradually. He would reverse the long build-up of U.S. forces in Vietnam over the previous decade, a decade in which U.S. military strength had increased from a small number of advisers to 543,000 troops.

Nixon and Kissinger both perceived the world in balance-of-power terms. They were unwilling to cede American influence in any part of the world where it existed.[1] But, by January 1969, the U.S. no longer had the nuclear superiority that had influenced and supported the national security policies of Truman, Eisenhower and Kennedy. It was now necessary to develop policies for the implementation of the new strategy for Vietnam that took that fact into account, along with the political reality of decreasing domestic support for American involvement in the war.

Initially, President Nixon placed his hopes on a negotiated settlement at the peace talks then underway in Paris which would smooth the way for the American withdrawal. He knew, however, that if those talks failed, he would have the problem of explaining to other countries, especially to those situated near Communist China, that despite its withdrawal from Vietnam, the U.S. still shared the common objective of resisting Communist aggression. To that end, he established a policy of "Vietnamization," a program designed to strengthen the armed forces of South Vietnam in number, equipment, leadership, and combat skills to enable them to assume responsibility for their own defense. The policy was not an isolationist policy, but rather one that recognized that the U.S. could no longer rely solely on its military strength to achieve its geopolitical objectives; that it was now necessary to rely upon the cooperation of other countries.[2]

By the summer of 1970, Nixon's national security and foreign policies involved a clearly identifiable theme, a well-defined global strategy. In an era of nuclear parity, the hardline anti-Communist warrior wanted to enter into negotiations with the Communist world while withdrawing from Vietnam under the best conditions that could be obtained. He and Kissinger believed that there were limits on American power and on the U.S. responsibility to become engaged in the small wars of the future. He wanted to be an activist, to pursue policies that might be perceived as unpredictable, but which would always be calculated "to get the United States off the defensive in relations with the Communist world."[3]

He also sensed an opportunity to obtain some kind of détente with the Soviet Union and China. The goal of détente was a period of limited cooperation to reduce tensions. No formal treaty or alliance was involved and the policy did not imply trust of either the Soviet Union or China. It was obvious to Nixon that Communism was not going to disappear anytime soon and that international stability would not be possible without U.S. accommodations with both of the Communist countries. The forces of history were "moving America from the position of [post-World War II] dominance to one of leadership"[4] and that leadership had to be earned. Because of the decades of American hostility toward both China and the USSR a considerable amount of political will was required, but Nixon soon launched a diplomatic opening to China. Because the relationship between the two other countries was strained, the announcement of a U.S.-China summit meeting in Beijing, which took place in February 1972, resulted in an immediate improvement in relations between the U.S. and the USSR. That eventually produced two important agreements to control the growth of nuclear weapons. The agreements, the Strategic Arms Limitation Treaty and the Anti-Ballistic Missile Treaty laid the groundwork for future arms reduction treaties.

When the Paris Peace Talks had produced no results by December 1972, and despite the pervading public opinion in the U.S., which was by then more strongly against American involvement than ever before, Nixon once again demonstrated the *political will* which characterized his presidency by ordering a full-scale resumption of the U.S. aerial bombing campaign in North Vietnam. The North could not withstand the resulting widespread devastation and its leaders quickly agreed to come to terms. In January 1973, an agreement was signed ending the war.[5] A respected military historian later wrote that the renewed bombing campaign provided "a classic example of the overwhelming use of military might to achieve a political end quickly."[6] Regrettably, in August 1973, and despite a pledge to the President of South Vietnam by Nixon to "take swift and severe retaliatory action" if North Vietnam should violate the terms of the Paris Agreement, Congress passed legislation prohibiting any further American military involvement in Vietnam.

President Nixon also left his mark on several other national security policies and he certainly continued to believe in American leadership, but he always remained a pragmatist. A good example was his approach to reform of the military draft in the middle of the conflict in Vietnam. In the 1950s and 1960s, each incumbent administration, Democrat and Republican, had favored retention of the draft. By 1968, however, Nixon had changed his own mind. His conviction that the draft could and should be ended apparently rested on three foundations, one demographic, one social and economic, and one political.[7] A practical demographic fact was that the baby-boom generation would mature during the 1970s. A large pool of young people would be available from which a volunteer force could be recruited. The social-economic factor related to the inequities in the way the draft system was working. A random lottery had replaced draft-board decisions, but draft exemptions for college students and others and a perceived economic burden on those drafted made it appear unfair after the fact. Finally, there were obvious political benefits to a clean break with the draft as soon as possible after the end of an unpopular war.

There was also a national security strategy factor. Prior to Vietnam, a "two-and-a-half war" concept had—at least in theory—guided military force planners. Nixon adopted a "one-and-a-half war" strategy that required only such peacetime general-purpose forces as were necessary for simultaneously fighting an all-out conventional war with a major power in either Asia or Europe (one war) and a limited war, e.g., providing assistance against non-Chinese threats in Asia (half of a war).[8]

By 1973, the new policy of an All-Volunteer Force was quickly becoming a reality. The last general draft call was issued in December 1972. The last induction took place in June 1973. On August 23, 1973, the Secretary of Defense established a new Total Force Policy, the purpose of which was to integrate "the Active, National Guard, and Reserve forces into a homogenous whole."[9] The implementation of the new policies would encounter many obstacles, but when the Persian Gulf War of 1990-91 commenced, the remarkable performance of the U.S. Armed Forces[10] presented a vivid reminder of the wisdom of these and other national security policies of President Nixon, many of which were initiated while the Nation was dealing with the Watergate Scandal, a period which Kissinger would later characterize as "the worst crisis of his life."

* * *

After graduating from Yale and then its Law School in 1938, Gerald Ford returned to his home state of Michigan to open a new law practice in Grand Rapids. Shortly after the Pearl Harbor attack, he enlisted in the Navy and was immediately commissioned as an Ensign. He served in combat actions in the Pacific and on October 13, 1945, after receiving several campaign decorations, he was promoted to Lieutenant Commander.

When he was released from active duty in February 1946, he returned to Grand Rapids and the practice of law. He also became active in local Republican politics. In 1948, the novice politician challenged an incumbent Republican Congressman who was a fervent isolationist. As a result of his wartime experiences, Ford's worldview was now that of an ardent internationalist who believed that "Our military unpreparedness before World War II had only encouraged the Germans and the Japanese."[11] The major issue in the campaign was foreign policy. Few people thought he had any chance in the election, but he won with 61 percent of the vote. He served in the U.S. House of Representatives for 25 years, ultimately becoming Minority Leader, where he became known as a moderate conservative, or an "Eisenhower Republican."

On October 10, 1973, Vice President Spiro Agnew resigned. He had been under investigation by the Justice Department for possible charges of conspiracy, bribery, extortion, and tax fraud. Ford was immediately nominated by President Nixon to fill the vacancy and on December 6, after confirmation votes in the Senate and House of Representatives and in the middle of the developing Watergate scandal, he took the oath of office in the House Chamber. It was the first time that the vacancy provision of the 25th Amendment to the U.S. Constitution had been implemented. Eight months later, a strong consensus had developed in Congress that Nixon had committed at least one impeachable offense and Senate leaders informed the President that if an impeachment trial took place in the Senate, he would be convicted. On August 9, Nixon resigned, and Ford assumed the presidency.

To no one's surprise, especially in view of the fact that Ford asked Nixon's senior policy advisers to remain in his Administration, the new President continued the same internationalist foreign policies established by Nixon and Kissinger, including détente. But he faced staggering problems. The Nation's economy was in terrible shape. The Watergate scandal was dominating the attention of the public. He had to manage the domestic policies of the Cold War, including the end of the Vietnam War. Tensions with the Soviet Union remained. And, as with most other Presidents, there was the danger of unexpected crises.

During the first few months of 1975, Communist forces in Vietnam brought that country to the edge of defeat. Congress refused Ford's request for additional military aid for our former ally and offered nothing more than humanitarian assistance. In late April, the Communist forces overran Saigon and the President had no choice but to order the evacuation of all remaining American personnel and as many of the South Vietnamese who had strongly supported the U.S. effort there as was possible.

The emotional impact of the tens of thousands of Americans killed or seriously wounded in Vietnam and the devastating injury to American credibility and prestige caused by what Ford called "a humiliating withdrawal" from that country, was almost beyond measure. There was great concern among the Administration's national security professionals that America's loss of *political will* in Vietnam would encourage the country's adversaries around the world to challenge American interests with impunity and that the U.S. would lose whatever remaining influence it had in Asia.

Ford's first test of political will on a national security matter occurred nine months after he assumed office. On May 12, 1975, only days after the fall of Saigon and less than a month after the brutal, Communist Khmer Rouge regime took power in Cambodia, gunboats of the Cambodian Navy seized the American merchant ship S.S. *Mayaguez* and its 39 American crew members in international waters off the Cambodian coast. The U.S. had no diplomatic relations with the Khmer Rouge, no warships in the area, and insufficient ground forces in neighboring Thailand to take any action. Congressional leaders were unenthusiastic about any rescue operation and pursuant to the War Powers Act, a statute of doubtful constitutionality, they demanded involvement in any action that might be taken to resolve the matter.

Ford would have none of it. "The President has the authority to act," he said. And, like most President's before that time and since, he felt a strong obligation to act to save Americans who were in foreign hands just as Theodore Roosevelt did in the famous "Perdicaris Alive or Raisuli Dead" incident.[12] He ordered an immediate response. He was sensitive to the fact that U.S. allies would scrutinize U.S. conduct "to determine whether the fall of Saigon marked an aberration or America's permanent retreat from international responsibility."[13] He was determined, he would later say, to end the crisis swiftly and decisively, and not to permit the recent U.S. setbacks in the area "to become a license for others to fish in troubled waters. Rhetoric alone, …would not persuade anyone that America would stand firm. They would have to see proof of our resolve."[14]

The difficulties of mounting a military operation to recover the ship and crew were, however, formidable. The U.S. had very little intelligence on the location of the imprisoned crew members and the strength of the Cambodian forces. American forces would have to be brought to the area of the incident from long distances. The risks to the crew members during a rescue operation would be significant. Because of the recent developments in Vietnam, the morale of U.S. military leaders was low. They offered no ideas of their own about such an operation and "left it to the civilians to prod it into action."[15] Doubts about a rescue operation by the Secretary of Defense compounded the problems.

Despite the obstacles, a successful operation was conducted and the political will displayed by the President and his muscular response to the seizure of the ship and crew were broadly approved by the public. *Newsweek* called the operation "a daring show of nerve and steel…swift and tough—and it worked."

*   *   *

To most observers, President Jimmy Carter's four years in the White House remain a symbol of failed leadership.[16] Before he assumed the presidency, he had been a one-term governor of Georgia and he had no national security or other international policy-making experience. Consequently, he brought no overarching ideological plan or worldview to his responsibilities other than a general goal of making human rights a key part of American foreign policy. He had ignored calls for greater specificity during the 1976 Presidential Election campaign and had only called for "a new moral authority" to govern America's foreign relations and a foreign policy "designed to serve mankind."[17] In practice, Carter criticized important American allies, including those who had loyally stood by the U.S. in its containment of the Soviet Union, for their human rights shortcomings, as well as U.S. adversaries. This approach strained relations with allied countries on a range of matters and did nothing to narrow existing disputes with the adversaries.

Carter soon encountered serious national security problems, many of his own making. Rather than attempting to negotiate arms reductions with the Soviet Union, he initiated a form of unilateral disarmament by urging Congress to approve significant reductions in strategic missile programs and to reduce the overall defense budget. His own Secretary of Defense believed that the goal of U.S. defense spending should be as much as 7 percent of the GNP, but during Carter's term of office, and despite the dramatic recent improvements in the capabilities of the Soviet Armed Forces, defense spending was "just over 5 percent."[18]

A second unilateral and ill-advised action was his order to withdraw all 32,000 American ground troops from South Korea. The troops had been placed there after the Korean War to deter any renewed aggression by North Korea. When the press asked for an explanation,

Carter had none and only replied through his Press Secretary that it was his "basic inclination to question the stationing of American troops overseas."[19] After a fierce, bipartisan backlash, Carter announced that he would greatly reduce the number of troops being withdrawn. Although the number fluctuates, as of early 2022, forty-five years and six Presidents after Carter's aborted attempt to remove them, more than 28,000 American troops remained in South Korea.

Carter soon leaped into another internal national security battle. Since the U.S. entered into a treaty with Panama in 1903 for the construction and operation of a 51-mile Canal, it had proven its strategic importance. In the event of war, the Canal had made it possible for U.S. Navy ships to promptly transit from the Atlantic to the Pacific, or vice versa, instead of taking the much longer and more difficult route around Cape Horn at the southern tip of Chile and up the east or west coast of the continent. U.S. control of the Canal had prevented potential and real enemies from having the same advantage.

Carter believed that a new treaty turning control of the Canal over to Panama was necessary, not for any reason relating to American security, but "to correct an injustice to Panama."[20] Public opinion polls showed that a large majority of the American public strongly opposed any effort to relinquish control of the Canal, and that view was shared by the Senate Armed Services Committee. Nevertheless, in September 1977 Carter signed a new treaty doing just that. In March 1978, the Democrat controlled Senate ratified the treaty by a margin of one vote.

President Carter did enjoy one foreign policy success when he mediated a dispute between Egypt and Israel in September 1978, but the Camp David Accords did little to revive his struggling presidency. On January 1, 1979, he made more Americans unhappy when he granted formal diplomatic recognition to Communist China and then unilaterally revoked the 1955 Mutual Defense Treaty between the U.S. and the Republic of China (Taiwan).

By 1979, concern was increasing about Carter's defense and foreign policies. He had entered the White House in 1977 vowing to cut the defense budget by $5-7 billion, dollars, a promise that was politically popular in the aftermath of the war in Vietnam, but short sighted. The budget cuts were now having serious operational consequences and, along with high inflation, rising fuel costs and other factors, they had made his first years in office "some of the leanest in modern times in terms of defense buying power."[21]

In a meeting with the Joint Chiefs of Staff on November 24, 1979, he was informed by the Army Chief of Staff that the Nation had a "hollow Army," one which could not perform its primary mission of reinforcing its forces in Europe because inadequate funding had caused the Army to have had neither the necessary number of divisions ready to deploy nor adequate air and sea lift to get them to Europe. A series of incidents had even raised questions about whether the Armed Forces could perform essential functions.[22] These developments had not escaped the attention of the American public. Opinion polls indicated that half of all Americans believed that the Soviet Union was militarily stronger than the U.S. and 53 percent believed that the U.S. needed to be more aggressive in its relations with the Soviet Union.[23]

Matters were rapidly becoming worse. The Chief of Naval Operations (CNO) informed Carter that the Navy was short 20,000 Petty Officers, the most senior and most skilled members of its enlisted force. The Navy's shortage of equipment and spare parts was so great that the service had resorted to "cross-decking."[24] Sailors were leaving the service in increasing numbers and as a result of that manpower shortage, the length of ship deployments had increased to eight to ten months, placing a greater strain on those who remained in the service. The message the CNO wanted to leave with the President was that the Armed Forces weren't just hollow, they were becoming "so inept and demoralized as to be downright dangerous."[25]

As his political problems mounted, Carter seemed to doubt his ability to lead the Nation through them. In early July, he convened a meeting of experts and politicians at Camp David, the presidential retreat. Purportedly, the President sat on the floor and having asked the participants in words to the effect of "Tell me what I am doing wrong," he scribbled notes as people offered advice.[26] Democrat Harry Truman and Republican Dwight Eisenhower would have been appalled by the scene, the question, and the obvious absence of presidential leadership.

Four months later, Islamic student militants loyal to Iran's new supreme religious leaders, seized the U.S. Embassy in Teheran and the Embassy staff, most of which were held hostage for 444 days. As time passed, Americans grew increasingly impatient with a seemingly impotent President who could not win the hostages' release. Foreign leaders were telling Carter that America's international standing was being damaged by his excessive passivity.[27]

President Carter was widely believed to be indecisive. In a highly publicized article in May 1979, one of his former speech writers depicted his former boss as a politician who lacked defined positions, who couldn't see the forest for the trees, and who was not particularly talented in dealing with Congress or the art of governing. "He thinks he 'leads' by choosing the correct policy, but he fails to project a vision larger than the problem he is tackling at the moment."[28] In the complex work of protecting the Nation's security, hard realities demand much more.

[W]hile [the leaders of the Soviet Union] preach the supremacy of the state, declare its omnipotence over individual man, and predict its eventual domination of all peoples on the Earth, they are the focus of evil in the modern world....I urge you to beware the temptation of pride—the temptation of blithely declaring yourselves above it all..., to ignore the facts of history and the aggressive impulses of an evil empire, to simply call the arms race a giant misunderstanding and thereby remove yourself from the struggle between right and wrong and good and evil....
President Ronald Reagan
March 8, 1983

This will not stand, this aggression against Kuwait.
President George Bush
August 5, 1980

VII.

THE END OF THE COLD WAR AND A NEW HOT WAR IN IRAQ

During the 1980 Presidential Election Campaign, Ronald Reagan spoke repeatedly of the need to rebuild the U.S. Armed Forces, to counter Soviet ambition and expansionism with a new policy of "peace through strength," and to otherwise aggressively protect American and free world interests all over the world. After he assumed office, the military buildup became the most important part of his national security and foreign policies, which had four major goals: protection of the Nation's security and its interests abroad; protection of U.S. allies; encouragement and support to countries attempting to escape from the yoke of Soviet Communism; and to bring the Soviets to the bargaining table in order to "achieve real nuclear arms reductions."[1] To those ends, he terminated the existing policy of détente.

In June 1982, the Soviet Union sat at "the apex of its military might, with a nuclear arsenal that out matched that of the United States and an overwhelming advantage in ships, tanks, and troops."[2] On June 2, President Reagan left on his first trip outside of North America. A highlight of the trip was to be the first speech to both houses of the British Parliament ever made by an American President. British expectations were low. In a cable to Prime Minister Margaret Thatcher prior to the visit, the British Ambassador to the U.S. said that "Reagan stands lower in the opinion polls than [President] Carter did at this period in his presidency," that he risks "being written off as a lame-duck President two years before the end of his term," and that in the speech, the President would be "walking another tightrope" as he attempted to deal with his unpopularity in both the U.S. and Europe. He added that Reagan would probably "project himself as...a peacemaker and not a warmonger."[3]

The speech, most of which Reagan wrote himself, would later be described, however, as the greatest of his presidency.[4] It was both blunt and hopeful. After referring to the Berlin Wall as "that dreadful gray gash across the city," a gash that was then almost 21 years old, he declared that "We are witnessing today a great revolutionary crisis.... It is the Soviet Union that [is running] against the tide of history by

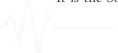

denying human freedom and human dignity to its citizens.... Today on the NATO line, our military forces face east to prevent a possible invasion. On the other side of the line, the Soviet forces also face east to prevent their people from leaving." He expressed "a hope for the long term—the march of freedom and democracy which will leave Marxism-Leninism on the ash-heap of history."

To reach that end, he believed that a major improvement in the capabilities of the U.S. Armed Forces was essential for two reasons. First, to deter a war with the USSR. Second, in order to permit the integration of overwhelming military power with diplomacy to "pressure the Soviet system on multiple fronts and drive the Communists to appoint a leader willing to make [negotiated] concessions."[5] He recognized, however, that it would take several years for the U.S. to overcome the USSR's numerical advantage in almost all weapons categories. Under the leadership of Cap Weinberger, who served as Secretary of Defense during the first seven years of Reagan's two terms, the Department of Defense focused on developing major improvements in the quality of U.S. weapons systems to offset the USSR's quantitative edge.

Many scholars believe that in foreign policy terms, "Reagan's presidency was probably the most sweeping anti-establishment triumph of the twentieth century."[6] He truly believed in the superiority of America's society, i.e., that America was both good and great. He projected optimism and confidence, refused to accept limits on American power and responsibility, and made no effort to avoid ideological conflict with the Soviet Union. The policies which he adopted to prevent the expansion of Soviet influence became known as the "Reagan Doctrine." He also equipped military forces and insurgent groups to fight communism in Afghanistan, Nicaragua, Angola, Grenada, and Poland and that support made it unnecessary to use American troops for the fighting.

These changes in policy required both conviction and strong political will since they were clearly contrary to the prevailing political wisdom. It would later be observed that he was criticized on the Left as a dangerous warmonger, by the Right as being too soft, and by most of the foreign policy establishment as naïve, unrealistic, and ill-informed. His political will was again on display in a speech on March 8, 1983. The speech was crafted to dissuade Christian Evangelicals from joining the Conference of Catholic Bishops in supporting a freeze on the deployment of NATO nuclear-armed missiles in Western Europe in response to the Soviet installation of such missiles in Eastern Europe. "In your discussions of the nuclear freeze proposals," he said, "I urge you to beware the temptation of pride—the temptation of blithely declaring yourselves above it all and label both sides equally at fault, to ignore the facts of history and the aggressive impulses of an *evil empire*, to simply call the arms race a giant misunderstanding and thereby remove yourself from the struggle between right and wrong and good and evil."

When Reagan became President, the national budgetary deficit was around $50 billion. By the mid-1980s, the deficits had surged above $200 billion. The Administration could claim in 1984 that the U.S. could fight an intensive war for up to thirty days, but it was estimated that several more years of the buildup of the Armed Forces would be necessary before a major war effort could be sustained for as long as ninety days.[7] The President's insistence on continuing increases in budgets for the Armed Forces was resisted by critics on both the Left and the Right. But, he believed—and had the *political will* to deal with the severe criticism of that belief—that the amount of money spent on defense should be dictated by national security needs and that it "could not be determined simply by looking at how much money the domestic budget had to spare."[8] Weinberger would later say that Reagan continually pressed the buildup of the Armed Forces "regardless of political consequences."[9]

Most Americans perceived Reagan to be exclusively or primarily, a hardline anti-Communist leader. His loathing of "godless Communism" was, in fact, a cornerstone of his political identity.[10] Nevertheless, he was not as doctrinaire or as rigidly tied to conservative dogma as were many of his supporters. A biographer would later write that he "wasn't really an ideologue in the sense that he wasn't poring over the writings of conservative people." Rather, his beliefs were "instinctual—he believed in America, traditional values.... Traditional, rather than Conservative."[11] He had a firm and unshakable sense of right and wrong. His combination of ebullient confidence in the superiority of American society and determination to triumph over the evil of Communism, became known as Reaganism.[12]

Three decades after he left the White House, it was easier to come to a consensus about Reagan's foreign and national security policies. A recent, comprehensive, and highly regarded study of those policies has concluded that Reagan "was a dreamer and visionary but not a utopian. He knew the earth was fallen, as were the men and women who walked it and ruled it. What he did believe is that American leadership could make that flawed world a better place."[13] To that end, "he strengthened America's national security institutions." Under Reagan "and his lieutenants, [the Pentagon, CIA and State Department] became rebuilt, modernized, and expanded."[14] America's alliances "also underwent a renewal. Arguably no President before or since has been more devoted to allies than Reagan."[15] He also restored America's self-confidence. He "did not just restore the country's faith in itself, he also restored the world's belief in America – not as a perfect nation, but as a strong and good nation."[16] In considering where Reagan fell on the continuum between political realists and idealists, one astute observer declared that "Ronald Reagan spoke the soaring rhetoric of Wilsonian moral rearmament, even as he surrounded himself with realists at the Pentagon, at the State Department, and inside the White House itself, whose advice he slyly accepted. This inherent compromise was a key element in his greatness."[17]

Reagan was willing to negotiate with adversaries. He was an Internationalist who understood that America was safer "when it engaged the world, acted with allies and shaped the security environment." But, while some of his advisers tended to see the goal of foreign policy as the stable management of unavoidable rivalry, e.g., through a balance of competing powers, Reagan saw the objective as the eventual victory of a superior system, and he worked to foster constructive instability on the margins of the Soviet empire as a means of "clarifying a moral choice—not just between two political systems, but also between good and evil."[18]

A biographer has written that "Reagan's anti-nuclearism [was] one of the best kept secrets of his political career, for it [failed] to conform to conventional wisdom."[19] In fact, it was no secret at all. On more than 150 occasions during his eight years in office he said that he favored elimination of nuclear weapons.[20] George Schultz, who served as Reagan's second Secretary of State, put the matter another way: "Reagan made no secret of his view that we should abolish nuclear weapons. But most people did not take this idea seriously...."[21] There is no doubt that his views on the subject were sincerely and deeply felt. At a summit meeting in Washington, D.C. on December 8, 1987, President Reagan and Mikhail Gorbachev, the leader of the Soviet Union, signed the Intermediate Nuclear Forces (INF) Treaty.[22] It was the first treaty between the superpowers of any kind to provide for the destruction of nuclear weapons.

The results of Reagan's negotiations with Gorbachev were on full display on December 7, 1988, the day of their last meeting before Reagan left office. Earlier that day, Gorbachev had given a remarkable speech to the General Assembly of the United Nations. He had declared that the use or threat of force no longer can…be an instrument of foreign policy." He had noted that "Little by little, mutual understanding [had] started to develop and elements of trust" had emerged causing "changes for the better in the substance and the atmosphere of the relationship between Moscow and Washington." He had then informed the UN that he had decided to unilaterally reduce the Soviet Armed Forces by half a million troops, to withdraw and disband six tank divisions from Eastern Europe, including 10,000 tanks, 8,500 artillery systems, and 800combat aircraft. He also pledged to change the military doctrine of the Soviet Union from one that was offensive in nature to one that was defensive.

It is indisputable that Ronald Reagan set in motion many of the things that led to the end of the Cold War. He was also one of the most consequential Presidents in U.S. history. Henry Kissinger, Reagan's old political nemesis, has written that while it was President George H. W. Bush who presided over the final disintegration of the Soviet empire, "it was Ronald Regan's presidency which marked the turning point."[23] Cardinal Casaroli, the Vatican Secretary of State, declared publicly that the Reagan military buildup, which he had opposed at the time, had placed unsustainable demands on the Soviet economy and thus precipitated the events that led to the disintegration of communism.[24]

Perhaps the best analysis of Reagan's contributions to the end of the Cold War was that of former British Prime Minister Margaret Thatcher. Writing in her memoirs, she said that "The credit for these historic achievements must go principally to the United States and in particular to President Reagan, whose policies of military and economic competition with the Soviet Union forced the Soviet leaders…to abandon their ambitions of hegemony and to embark on the process of reform which in the end brought the entire communist system crashing down."[25]

*   *   *

When Ronald Reagan left the White House in January 1989, he had a higher approval rating than any other President since Franklin D. Roosevelt.[26] It was not particularly surprising, therefore, that in the 1988 Presidential Election, America's voters took the unusual step of electing Reagan's Vice President and continuing Republican control of the Executive Branch.

It soon became apparent that George H. W. Bush had his own ideas about governance. He brought to his Administration the best, or in any event, the broadest national security experience of any President. He was a decorated combat veteran of World War II. He had almost two decades of executive experience in private industry. He had been elected to Congress and had subsequently served as the U.S. Ambassador to the United Nations, Chief of the U.S. Liaison Office in China,[27] Director of the Central Intelligence Agency, and as Vice President for eight years.

Unlike Reagan, he did not have a unique, overarching ideology that governed his approach to decision-making on national security and foreign policy matters. When the Reagan Administration assumed office Bush was "firmly in the camp of the 'pragmatists' or 'realists'" within the Administration on certain national security issues. Reagan's biographer has written that "on issues of superpower diplomacy and arms control [the] pragmatists did constant battle with the 'conservatives' or 'Reaganauts,' whom they called 'hard-liners' or 'crazies.' The conservatives were equally unflattering to their opponents, often describing them as 'accommodationists' and occasionally as 'one-worlders.'"[28] The biographer described this as simply "an odd scrap of opprobrium left over from the struggles between internationalists and isolationists before World War II," and concluded that the labels "lacked relevance beyond the byzantine confines of the Reagan court."[29]

Bush believed that the skills, experience and policy positions which are necessary to successfully govern a diverse nation of 247 million people (1989), are not a perfect reflection of those which are required to win an election; that a President must be concerned with the needs of the Nation as a whole, not just the needs of that part of the electorate which voted for him; that sound judgment is the coin of the realm for a good President; that as facts and circumstances change, a President must have the courage, the *political will*, to risk offending his opponents, the media, and even his political base if he believes that it is in the best interest of the Nation to do so; and that doing the right things on a particular problem many well be more important than his own re-election.[30]

Bush thus had a sound understanding of the differences between electioneering and governance. His governing methods were those of "a pre-internet age, with decisions forged in private meetings and messages sent by personal letter through back channels," and he surrounded himself with experienced policy hands who knew how to make government work."[31] His expertise was "the art and the ability to frame the results of negotiations in such a way that there were no losers, only winners."[32] The long-run framework of his foreign policy "was very deliberate: encouraging, guiding, and managing change without provoking backlash and crackdown."[33] The Soviet Union's repressive domination of Eastern Europe was his highest priority.

As I have previously observed,[34] if senior American policy makers had resorted in early 1989 to all known mathematical models, futurists, fortune tellers, astrologers, and other predictors of the future, it is unlikely that anyone of them could have foretold the number of historically important geopolitical developments that would take place over the four years of the Bush Administration. They included the liberation of Eastern Europe from the grip of Communism; U.S. engagement in an armed conflict in Panama, America's back yard; the commencement of a complex new U.S. and international fight against illegal drug trafficking; the disbanding of the Warsaw Pact;[35] the dissolution of the Soviet Union; the end of the Cold War; and a major hot war in the Middle East. These and related events brought about the greatest change in the strategic balance since the end of World War I.

Bush's efforts to provide encouragement to countries which were under the yoke of the Soviet Union were soon bearing tangible fruit. Early in 1989, the Administration had demanded the repeal of the Brezhnev Doctrine, by which the Soviet Union had asserted since its 1968 invasion of Czechoslovakia, that it had the right to provide "assistance, including assistance with armed forces," i.e., to intervene, in any Communist nation in which "the people's socialist gains" were in jeopardy. On October 25, Soviet leader Mikhail Gorbachev repudiated that doctrine and declared publicly that the Soviet Union had "no right, moral or political," to interfere in political developments in Eastern Europe. On November 9, the Berlin Wall was torn down.

Bush's response to that remarkable development was surprisingly low key. Instead of taking credit for it, or at least attempting to capitalize on it politically, he said to his Press Secretary "The last thing I want to do is brag about winning the Cold War or bringing the Wall down."[36] For this reaction, he was criticized by the Democrat leadership of the Senate and House of Representatives. But, a future Democrat Deputy

Secretary of State would write that "Bush's restraint had a larger purpose: he was determined not to rub Gorbachev's nose in the defeat of world Communism. He was…worried that a Western celebration of the Wall's collapse might encourage a backlash by hardliners in East Berlin and Moscow."[37] Bush thus led by "understanding that a world in convulsion was inherently unstable, and everything in him was about bringing stability, or a semblance of stability, to the unruliness of reality."[38]

Over the next two years, many additional historical developments occurred. On Christmas morning 1991, Mikhail Gorbachev telephoned President Bush to inform him that the Soviet Union had ceased to exist. In his public announcement two days later, the former Soviet leader declared that "An end has been put to the 'Cold War,' the arms race, and the insane militarization of our country, which crippled our economy, distorted our thinking and undermined our morals. The threat of a world war is no more."[39] All this, and not a single shot had been fired.

A presidential historian would later describe these developments this way: "Bush…guided the world through dangerous moments, whose peaceful outcome in hindsight continues to obscure their difficulty. The Cold War need not have ended so well. ***We cannot know for certain what a triumphalist, a more hawkish, or a more virulently nationalist President would have meant for global security in 1989 and immediately after. But the world, fortunately, had a prudent practitioner of Hippocratic diplomacy in office instead. He was… neither a radical nor a revolutionary; but was instead content to follow 'what worked.' This is what made him a success."[40] Few people who were alive on Christmas Day 1991 could have predicted the brutal, dangerous invasion of Ukraine which would start on February 24, 2022, at the order of another Russian leader.

*   *   *

In the early morning hours of August 1, 1990, two Iraqi Republican Guard Forces Command armored divisions and a mechanized infantry division attacked Kuwait with nearly a thousand tanks. Thirty minutes later, Iraqi Special Forces commando units landed by helicopter in the Kuwaiti capital and began seizing key government facilities. Within 96 hours, 120,000 Iraqi troops had poured into Kuwait, portions of eleven Iraqi divisions occupied inland oil fields, Kuwaiti ports had been captured and Iraqi President Saddam Hussein had proclaimed the annexation of Kuwait as "an eternal part of Iraq."

With the potential end of the 44-year-old Cold War in sight, a new hot war 8,000 miles away was the last thing America wanted. But, the Iraqi invasion was much more than a violation of Kuwait's sovereignty, a blatant violation of international law, and a threat to world stability. It was also a threat to vitally important U.S. national security interests. Iraq now controlled 20 percent of the world's known oil reserves, and if it took over neighboring Saudi Arabia, it would control more than 45 percent. That was an untenable prospect for the global economy, which was so dependent upon oil. Such a development would place the U.S. and its allies at Saddam's mercy because by manipulating world oil prices, he could fuel inflation and create worldwide economic instability.

The Iraqi invasion was but the latest development in the Persian Gulf that threatened important U.S. interests. Between 1984 and 1988, during the Iran-Iraq War, Iran began attacking oil tankers and other commercial ships with frigates, rockets, anti-ship cruise missiles, and other weapons. The Tanker War soon became the longest sustained attack on merchant shipping since World War II. A total of 451 ships were hit in the Gulf. By 1987, the amount of oil shipped through the Strait of Hormuz had fallen to less than 4 million barrels per day, down from more than 7 million in 1984. That same year, Iran began laying mines in the Gulf.[41] To help protect the world's oil supplies, the U.S. launched Operation *Ernest Will*, which involved the escort of tankers carrying oil and the use of minesweepers to clear the mines. Until the Iranian attacks ceased in September 1988, the U.S. and six European allied countries escorted 259 ships in 127 convoys.

An ironic side note to *Ernest Will*, involved a full-page "open letter" which appeared in the September 2, 1987, editions of *The New York Times*, *The Washington Post* and *The Boston Globe* from a future American President. The author of the letter, then a "flamboyant New York City real estate developer named Donald J. Trump," displayed his ignorance of national security matters by making a broadside attack against President Reagan's policy in the Persian Gulf. Accusing Reagan of a lack of backbone, he declared that "we defend the Persian Gulf, an area of only marginal significance to the United States for its oil supplies, but one upon which Japan and others are almost totally dependent.... The world is laughing at America's politicians as we protect ships we don't own, carrying oil we don't need, destined for allies who won't help."[42]

Two days after the August 1 invasion, the CIA Director informed President Bush that unless Iraq was forced out of Kuwait, the Persian Gulf region would be fundamentally altered and Saddam would "control the second and third largest proven oil reserves in the world with the fourth largest army in the world."[43] At a press conference on August 5, the President declared that "This will not stand, this invasion of Kuwait." In a televised address to the Nation on the morning of August 8, he declared that "a line had been drawn in the sand." He then announced a major deployment of U.S. forces to Saudi Arabia to take up "defensive positions." The operation would be called *Desert Shield*. He and Secretary of State James Baker immediately began an intense period of telephone and personal diplomacy to build an international coalition of 38 countries, including several Arab nations, that would oppose the invasion. Bush made 62 calls to various foreign leaders.[44] This is not the place to tell the full story of what would become known as the Persian Gulf War, or Operations *Desert Shield/Desert Storm*, but a quick summary is useful to illustrate how the U.S. Armed Forces had been rebuilt from the ashes of the humiliating withdrawal from Vietnam and how America's credibility and its capability to deter other armed conflicts was restored.

A lingering concern of many senior U.S. military leaders at the time was what was called the Vietnam Syndrome, a condition which might be defined as "skepticism, either prudent or debilitating according to your political taste, about both the legitimacy and the efficiency of America using military power overseas."[45] The Vietnam War had ended in 1975, but since then, battalions of journalists had routinely likened every American military operation to the unsuccessful ending of the war in Vietnam. The idea had proliferated in media and some policy circles that since American withdrew from Vietnam, the Nation had been in rapid decline. In his 1989 Inaugural Address, Bush had noted that Vietnam "cleaves us still" and he had warned that "no great nation can afford to be sundered by a memory." Nevertheless, many national security leaders continued to worry about the "blame America first" attitudes.

Bush did not hesitate. At his request, the UN Security Council immediately voted 14-0 to order Iraq out of Kuwait under the threat of sanctions. On August 4, he asked the Saudi King to permit U.S. forces to enter the Kingdom to protect its government and its oil fields. Permission was promptly given and Operation *Desert Shield* began. On

November 29, the UN Security Council gave Iraq until January 15, 1991, to withdraw its forces from Kuwait. The UN further authorized its member nations to use "all necessary means" to force Iraq out of Kuwait after that deadline. On January 12, the U.S. Senate and House of Representatives authorized the use of force. Five days later, after Iraq had failed to meet the January 15 deadline, offensive operations were commenced in Operation *Desert Storm*. On February 24, a massive ground assault was commenced by the UN forces against Iraq. It required only 100 hours to end the conflict and fulfill the UN mandate.

When a Cease Fire was ordered on February 28, after forty-three days of sustained combat, the Iraqi forces had been expelled from Kuwait and were almost totally destroyed. The war had been swift and limited. It would later be described as a "defining moment in military history; a campaign as momentous in operational terms as Cannae, Agincourt, Waterloo, the Somme, or Normandy."[46] A Pulitzer Prize-winning journalist wrote that "In terms of military objectives conquered, allied casualties minimized and popular support on the home front sustained the war was that rarest of prizes in the age of relativity—an absolute victory!"[47] On the evening of March 6, President Bush addressed a joint session of Congress and the American people. He concluded the Address with these words: "*This victory belongs...to the Regulars, to the Reserves, to the National Guard. This victory belongs to the finest fighting force this nation has ever known in its history.*"

In a private letter of congratulations after the conflict ended, Richard Nixon told Bush that he had "finally exorcized the Vietnam Syndrome from the American people." More importantly, Bush had protected the world's economy, maintained stability in the volatile Middle East, and devastated the army of a dangerous despot. America's national security interests had been well served.

...there are regimes...whose ends are irrational. It is a mistake to think that because a state [or a terrorist] has lunatic ends, it must be clumsy, erratic or incompetent in carrying them out. The fanatic can be both wise and wily. Indeed, the fanatic has a distinct advantage in choosing means. So utterly convinced is he of the rightness of his ends that he lacks ordinary inhibiting scruples in his choice of means. He need consider only their instrumental value, not their moral valence.

Charles Krauthammer
Pulitzer Prize Winning Commentator and Author
September 21, 1987

It does no good to be prepared to use force, or other instruments of power, if others do not believe you have the political will to actually use it in a sufficiently coercive manner.

Anthony Lake
National Security Adviser to
President Clinton 2000

VIII.

THE DANGEROUS ROAD TO INEFFECTIVE DETERRENCE

On Saturday, 8 June 1991, a unique and important national celebration took place in Washington, D.C. In contrast to the shabby, if not insulting treatment that had been accorded to the combat veterans of the war in Vietnam, this celebration was expressly intended to honor the gallant 550,000 U.S. troops who had achieved the magnificent victory in the 1990-1991 Persian Gulf War. Some 800,000 people were in Washington to attend the one and one-half mile Victory Parade down Constitution Avenue, past the Vietnam Veterans Memorial and across Memorial Bridge, which was bedecked with the National Flag. That morning, President George H. W. Bush had stood near the Tomb of the Unknowns at Arlington National Cemetery with the families of the 390 Americans who had died in the Gulf War. Many of those in attendance were crying. In a somber tone, the President declared that he hoped that "this time was the last time."[1]

It is likely that few people who attended the victory celebration were aware of Plato's admonition that only the dead have seen the end of war, or of the conclusion of Will and Ariel Durant in their 1968 book *The Lesson of History*. The Durant's asserted that in the 3,421 years of recorded history, only 268 had been free of war. The issue of whether war is inevitable has certainly been discussed for time immemorial. It was also the subject of a discussion between Albert Einstein and Sigmund Freud in 1932, shortly before Adolph Hitler became Chancellor of Germany. In a despairing letter to Freud, Einstein asked "Is there any way of delivering mankind from the menace of war? It is common knowledge that, with the advance of modern science, this issue has come to mean a matter of life and death for civilization as we know it." Perhaps, he wondered, "man has within him a lust for hatred and destruction." In his response, Freud wrote that men, like all male animals, are programmed to settle conflicts by fighting. "Violent compulsions," he said, may sometimes be counterbalanced by "ties of sentiment," but only within narrow bounds.[2]

It is generally recognized that Autocrats are much more likely than democratically elected leaders to indulge their personal ambitions for vengeance or glory, to attempt to distract their publics from failures or immediate concerns, or to pursue some religious crusade. "[I]t's the places ruled by strongmen with few checks [on their power]," particularly if they run resource-rich economies, that appear to be the most warlike with their neighbors."[3]

At the end of the year 1991, the prospects for an extended period of peace appeared to be great. The Cold War was over. The Soviet Union no longer existed. Communism was dying all over the world. As I noted in an earlier book,[4] even by the time of the June 1991 Gulf War Victory Parade, "the United States was the world's only remaining superpower. No armed forces in the world could match our war-fighting capabilities. In his 6 March 1991 address to Congress shortly after the cease-fire, President Bush had declared that the victory in the Gulf War belonged 'to the finest fighting force this nation has ever known in its history.' No nation could [then] match our economic power. For 215 years, the U.S. experiment in democracy had demonstrated its vitality and durability."[5] It was not long, however, before complacency, indifference and amateurish new national leadership began to characterize important matters relating to the Nation's security, just as they had in other periods of America's history.

*   *   *

In January 1993, President Bush, a combat veteran and highly skilled and experienced Commander-in-Chief, the leader for whom "foreign policy had been his raison d'être,"[6] was replaced by Bill Clinton, the first Baby Boomer President. At age 18, the same age at which Bush had volunteered for combat duty in World War II, Clinton had commenced both a multi-year effort to use political and family influence to help him dodge the military draft, and a campaign of lies and deliberate obfuscation which was intended to hide that effort. Later, while traveling and protesting the war in Vietnam, he had informed an Army Colonel who was leading a ROTC program that he "loathed the military."[7]

When Clinton entered the Oval Office, he had no foreign policy or national security experience and was uninterested in those matters. They were a distraction, an inconvenience, something that was likely to interfere with his central interests, the ones that got him elected—

the economy and social and related issues. Despite the fact that the geopolitical world was changing rapidly, he had no serious worldview, no long-range conceptual view of America's role in the world. He believed it to be sufficient to handle national security developments in a tactical, or ad hoc manner. His decisions were driven by the circumstances and the political mood of the moment, rather than by strategic principles and America's long-term interests. According to respected students of Civil-Military Relations, Clinton and many in his Administration were cowed by miliary leaders "because the men in uniform were a constant reproach to their own strategic amateurism and privileged absence from service in their generation's war."[8]

Matters were made worse by the fact that the process used by Clinton to select the national security members of his Cabinet and other senior national security officials was the most casual and undisciplined process used by any President in decades.[9] The pool of qualified Democrats who were willing to serve in a senior Defense Department position was admittedly small, but very few of his senior political appointees in the Defense Department had ever worn a military uniform, had any significant executive experience, or otherwise been personally responsible for the kinds of subject matter and operational challenges that would justify their appointments. At the time of their appointments, many of them were merely serving as one of many staffers on a congressional committee or as one of many aides to a Member of Congress. They were generally perceived as militarily ignorant, culturally distant, and inadvertently condescending. Clinton's first Secretary of Defense was even forced to resign after the disastrous failure of the U.S. mission in Somalia in September and October 1993.[10]

By 1987, concern was growing within the U.S. Government about the increasing number of incidents of terrorism and the demonstrated "fanatical hatred" of the U.S. by several nations, including Iran, North Korea, Cuba and Nicaragua. In an article published in September of that year, Charles Krauthammer, a Pulitzer Prize winning commentator, physician and best-selling author, reflected upon such fanaticism and zealotry by terrorists and the leaders of nations.

"The fanatic," he wrote, can be both wise and wily. Indeed, the fanatic has a distinct advantage in choosing means. So utterly convinced is he of the rightness of his ends that he lacks ordinary inhibiting scruples in his choice of means. He need consider only their instrumental value, not their moral valence. Not for him messy moral conflicts when matching means and ends. Everything matches. Zealotry," he continued, "produces a kind of hyperrationality of technique. The trains carrying innocents to the Holocaust ran ramosely on time. That is fanaticism's special gift, its special horror: its ability to routinize, to rationalize, to bureaucratize murderous irrationality."[11]

On February 26, 1993, a truck bomb planted by Islamic terrorists in the underground parking garage of the North Tower of New York's World Trade Center was detonated. The huge blast killed six people, injured more than one thousand others, and caused massive destruction. Some 100,000 people worked in or visited the Trade Center Towers every day. The bomb had obviously been designed and planted with the purpose of killing innocent Americans in far greater numbers. Despite the fact that it was the largest incident ever handled to that time in the 128-year history of New York City's Fire Department, Clinton did not even visit the site of the attack, he did not energize the intelligence agencies and the Department of Defense, and he treated the bombing incident as a mere domestic criminal matter.

In addressing the UN's General Assembly a few months later, Clinton described his foreign policy as one of "enlargement." "Our overriding purpose," he announced, "must be to expand and strengthen the world's community of market-based democracies." He still did not understand that the attack on the World Trade Center was the work of a new, militant Jihadist movement; that the long-established principles of state sovereignty and democracy were an abomination to the new movement. Consequently, he had no informed plan for dealing with the new threat to America's security.

In 1994, the Clinton Administration took action which was very badly managed, the consequences of which are being visibly played out on the world stage even today. In pressuring Ukraine hard to relinquish its nuclear weapons by signing the Budapest Memorandum, which is discussed in Chapter X, Clinton refused to wait for either "the full-scale review of disarmament policy that the General Accounting Office had recommended in 1993, or for [his Deputy Secretary of State's] comprehensive appraisal of existing policies toward post-Soviet states,"[12] thus depriving Ukraine—at least prematurely—of its most powerful deterrent to future aggression by Russia.

During the 1992 Presidential Election Campaign, Clinton had promised to intervene in some way in the civil war between the ethnically divergent members of the former Yugoslav Federation. By the spring of

1994, he still could not decide what, if anything, to do. His habit of talking tough but doing nothing would later lead one informed observer to conclude that "our rhetoric was mightier, if not than our sword, than certainly our deeds and [political] will."[13] By mid-1995, Clinton's foreign policy was being severely criticized. A respected author, journalist, and columnist wrote that the Administration was "still unable to grasp the fact that you build for peace on military victory and military victory alone," and not with hapless 'peace programs.'" Clinton's policy in the Balkans, he said, was "characterized by a utopian, pseudo-therapeutic and essentially reactive view of the uses of American power."[14] Writing in retrospect later about the Administration's foreign policy failures, Clinton's National Security Adviser declared that "We seemed unable or unwilling to bring American power to bear in effective ways. It does no good," he said, "to be prepared to use force, or other instruments of power, if others do not believe you have the *political will* to actually use it in a sufficiently coercive manner."[15]

In an article that was published the month of the 1996 Presidential Election, Clinton's Deputy Secretary of State announced the promotion of human rights as a principal objective of the Administration's foreign policy, declaring that in accordance with a new doctrine of liberal internationalism, Americans had "a growing stake in how other countries govern, or misgovern, themselves," and that this proposition was "the essence of the national security rationale for vigorously supporting, promoting, and when necessary, defending democracy in other countries."[16] Aside from the fact that the doctrine would be highly resented and opposed by authoritarian foreign leaders as an intrusion into their country's internal affairs, it said nothing about maintaining sufficient American power to deter potential aggressive conduct by those leaders.

*   *   *

In geopolitical terms, *deterrence* is the practice of discouraging or restraining a nation-state, or terrorists, if possible, from taking unwanted actions, such as an armed attack on another nation. It involves a threat of force, i.e., a threat of direct military action—not the actual use of force —communicated effectively to a potential aggressor for the purpose of preventing some action, e.g., maintaining the status quo.

Successful "deterrence" (from the Latin for "to frighten from") is by its nature, a barely believable bluff. It does not depend on 100 percent certainty that one adversary will go to war if the other adversary crosses a defined red line. It has always relied on "the credible threat of retributive violence, i.e., of unbearable retaliation." It relies upon the presence of three factors: "First, it requires the *means*," i.e., the military capability "to inflict unacceptable pain on the aggressor. Second, it demands the firm and undoubted *resolve*," i.e., the *political will* "to employ these means. Third, deterrence requires a rational interlocutor who can objectively weigh the consequences of his intended actions."[17] While countries like Russia and China are arguably governed by rational interlocutors, many believe that religious fanatics—like the Taliban of Afghanistan—can never be deterred, only killed because their actions are governed more by passion than by rationality.

There is, of course, risk in pursuing deterrence. The country seeking to deter cannot afford to bluff. If its threat to use force is not believed by the aggressor and an attack is made, the only two outcomes are an armed conflict that might have been prevented, or the total loss of future credibility by the country that bluffed. There is nothing but risk in the absence of deterrence. Weakness, actual or perceived, is an invitation to aggression and terrorism. One critic of the Carter Administration's national security policies has framed his complaint this way: "We primly warn bullies that we might not share our candy with them tomorrow—so they take all the candy they can grab today."[18]

With the end of the Cold War, the Clinton Administration proposed or adopted policies which initiated a decline of American's power to deter war. It slashed military spending in the hope of reaping a "peace dividend." Clinton's first proposed defense budget for FY 1994 would have reduced troop strength to a level not seen since the war in Korea. By January 1998, defense spending was projected to be only 3 percent of the Gross Domestic Product (GDP), half of what it had been a decade earlier. In the previous eight years, the number of Army Divisions had already dropped from 18 to 10; in the period 1993 to 2000, the Navy's combat fleet had shrunk from 454 to 341 ships; the number of Active Air Force Tactical Fighter Wings (72 planes each) had gone from 24 to 13.[19]

The Administration also began using the Armed Forces not to deter or win the Nation's wars, but to address domestic social problems which were too challenging for political leaders. An entire chapter of an

Army doctrinal statement was devoted to "operations other than war,"[20] such as disaster relief, humanitarian assistance, support to domestic civil authorities, treaty verification, evacuation operations, arms control, counterdrug operations and national assistance. Members of the Administration proudly announced plans to have military Reservists repair housing, restore the environment, build a pier for fishing vessels in an economically depressed fishing community, dig wells, and survey the safety of dams, airport runways, and other parts of the domestic infrastructure.[21] One competence-challenged Administration official called for military forces to be actively involved in "defending America at home" by attacking "low literacy levels, high unemployment rates, increasing numbers of high school dropouts, unavailability of health care, rising crime, and drug abuse."[22]

* * *

Bill Clinton's eight years in the White House were years of almost unmitigated disaster for U.S. national security and foreign policies. Since then, America's national security policies have continued to involve a contentious debate over America's role in the post-Cold War world. The hard lines between isolationism and internationalism which existed in 1940 have been gone for decades, but, isolationism in the United States has never really been about a total avoidance of all other countries. Rather, it involves a strong reluctance to enter into the famous "entangling alliances" or to use American influence and economic power to encourage freedom and democracy in other nations, and to avoid warfare at all costs.

Perhaps a more accurate description of the contending forces would divide the two camps into political realists and political idealists. The realists tend to be conservative and to prefer national security and foreign policies which are designed primarily, if not exclusively, to protect America's own security needs and interests. They are highly suspicious of quasi-abstract crusades against evils that do not affect our security directly. They reject security policies that are driven primarily by moral impulses and those which lack strong popular support. They seek mature, unsentimental, lucid realism and clearly defined organizing principles and strategies about the use of military force.

Political idealists, who tend to be liberal internationalists, argue that American security interests can't be easily separated from its values;

that the use of U.S. military force to intervene in foreign countries for humanitarian purposes, i.e., to promote democracy, political reconciliation or economic development in the many chaotic and unstable nations of the Third World, is not only desirable, but necessary; that a multilateral approach to resolving foreign problems is always better than one where America places its security interests first.

*   *   *

The deep shock to Americans of the September 11, 2001, terrorist attacks resulted in intense national solidarity as badly shaken Americans came together in an atmosphere of fear, sadness, and patriotism. For awhile, the public rallied behind the wars in Afghanistan and Iraq. Political differences were set aside. The approval rating of George W. Bush, who had entered the Oval Office nine months earlier after a hotly contested election, rose 35 percentage points in the space of three weeks. The public's support for foreign military intervention was strong. In 2006, several years after the U.S. commenced combat operations in Afghanistan, 69 percent of adults expressed the view that the U.S. made the right decision in using military force there.[23] Moreover, throughout the contentious, long debate before the U.S. invaded Iraq, Americans also widely supported the use of military force to end Saddam Hussein rule in Iraq.[24] As the "war on terror" in Afghanistan and Iraq continued through the eight years of George W. Bush's presidency and into the Obama Administration, the 9/11 national consensus began to break. Polling conducted in 2013 found that "Getting the American public's attention, let alone commitment to deal with international issues [was] as challenging as it [had] ever been I the modern era. Feeling burned by Iraq and Afghanistan and burdened by domestic concerns, the public [was feeling] little responsibility and inclination to deal with international problems that [were] not seen as direct threats to the national interest." The depth and duration of the public's disengagement was "well beyond" the periodic spikes in isolationist sentiment that had been observed over the previous 50 years.[25]

Over the next few years, President Obama, then President Trump, then President Biden made clear their determination to withdraw all of America's military forces from Afghanistan, regardless of the consequences and contrary to the unanimous advice of their most senior military advisers and field commanders. Their decisions and actions were marked by confusion, lack of understanding of the realities, expediency, and self-serving political considerations which did not relate to the long-term security interests of the Nation.[26] All three Presidents parroted media claims of "Endless Wars" or "Forever Wars" and of a "war-weary" public and made no serious effort to speak hard truths with informed candor to the public as Churchill did throughout World War II. It was probably asking too much to hope that at least one of those Presidents would have Churchill's breadth of view and grasp of essentials, or that at least one would have pre-White House experience as a senior Executive Branch national security policymaker, or experience in military uniform, if not experience in combat, but all three refused to be guided by Churchill's concept of statecraft in war. It must be remembered that he had personally participated in four wars on three continents and had commanded at the highest levels during the two world wars.[27] Nevertheless, as Prime Minister in World War II, he never overruled his most senior military advisors when they unanimously disagreed with one of his proposed actions.[28]

No serious person believes that senior civilian or military officials were actually seeking Endless War. One analyst debunked the claims by stating the obvious: "The trope about ending endless wars is really a way of arguing that the U.S. foreign policy establishment has failed, that the supposed doctrine of interventionism is ineffective and counterproductive, and that the United States should retrench, withdraw, and do less in the world. ***Advocates of restraint believe that we can end wars by simply leaving them."[29] They assume incorrectly that wars have expiration dates; that their duration is evidence that they are a lost cause; that leaving without success in an acceptable way is anything other than losing; and that other potential enemies will not take notice.

There is strong reason to believe that the public was, in fact, open to a consideration of all alternatives. A National Opinion Research Center survey conducted in September and October 2020, found that after 19 years of fighting, forty-one percent of the respondents said that they had no opinion on whether the U.S. had accomplished its goals in Afghanistan.[30] A National Defense Survey conducted in February 2021 by a bipartisan survey team at Beacon Research and Shaw & Company Research is even more illustrative. It found that Americans were not trending toward isolationism and did not want the United States to retreat from global leadership. Half of the respondents expressed the view that the U.S. should be more engaged and take the lead regarding international developments, while only 27 percent expressed the view that the U.S. should be less engaged and merely react to events. Three-quarters of Americans, including substantial majorities of both political parties, were in favor of increasing defense spending. Nearly two-thirds of the respondents indicated their support for maintaining U.S. military bases around the world to deter attacks and respond quickly if needed.[31]

It is essential that our political leaders stop pandering to their partisan political bases and never forget that the Nation's security is, and must always be, their highest priority. To that end, they must recognize and deal with the threats to that security with realistic methods which are based on the world as it is today, not as they wish it was. When military force must be employed to protect a core American interest and unforeseen difficulties arise, the answer it not to place the difficulties in the "too hard" box and leave. Rather, it is to remain in the fight, change strategy as necessary to one that is best suited to end the conflict on the best possible terms and achieve a specific and reasonably possible objective, and to continuously explain to the public why the change is being made and what the risks and benefits of alternative options are.

War is inherently unpredictable. It must be remembered that the Cold War, which lasted for more than four decades, and which seemed endless, suddenly came to an end with the destruction of the Berlin Wall and the demise of the Soviet Union. It is very unlikely that future conflicts will end with the kinds of Ticker Tape and Victory Parades that followed the end of World War II and the 1990-91 Persian Gulf War. It may be a trite phrase, but it is nevertheless true that "the enemy has a vote" in determining the nature and ending of an armed conflict. Moreover, many military scholars are of the view that because the structured characteristics of the current international order are beyond the choice of any single political agent, even one as powerful as the United States, Forever Wars are highly likely for the foreseeable future.[32] We have no choice but to accept this reality and to be prepared for it.

In doing so, it is critical that the U.S. maintains its credibility. We can never again abruptly abandon our allies for political self-interest as Presidents Obama and Trump attempted to do, and President Biden did. Such actions are both strategically dangerous and dishonorable. In this context, the events of 1938 in England come to mind. Nineteen days before Prime Minister Neville Chamberlain returned from the

Munich Conference brandishing an agreement with Hitler that appeared to remove the imminent threat of war while allowing Hitler to annex the Sudetenland region of Czechoslovakia, Churchill wrote a letter to his close personal friend Lord Moyne. "We seem to be very near the bleak choice between War and Shame," he said. "My feeling is that [Chamberlain] shall choose Shame, and then have War thrown in…later on even more adverse terms than at present."

To remain steady in an armed conflict until specific objectives are achieved does not mean making open-ended commitments, or throwing unrestrained resources at a security problem, or inevitably relying primarily upon large numbers of U.S. ground combat forces ("Boots on the ground"). Rather, it means closely managing the problem, in the way that Israel deals with terrorist attacks and the broader problems of the Middle East. That country recognizes that it cannot prevent all possible terrorist attacks or quickly solve complex diplomatic and political problems that have existed for many decades. It focuses on maintaining powerful deterrents to new attacks, minimizing the damage from attacks that may occur, searching for political means to resolve problems peacefully, and closely managing the risks associated with individual threats.

The shrill voices opposing even these concepts appear to be limited to a small fraction of Republicans and to "Progressive, Left Wing" isolationists who represent what has been called "a newer, less-noticed strain of America-first ideology." Progressive isolationism is thought to be antiseptic. "It wants no entanglements or acknowledgment of threats that would let the conservative opposition argue for increases in spending on national security or defense. It wants that spending reprogrammed into uncapped domestic spending like Build Back Better."[33]

Those views must be rejected. People who hold them need a large dose of reality, an informed understanding of the world as it actually is today. Recent events in Ukraine, around Taiwan and those described in the chapters which follow, demonstrate in unequivocal terms that Americans live in an increasingly complex and increasingly dangerous world; that we need "a coherent, proactive foreign policy to build a credible multifront deterrent"[34] and sufficiently powerful Armed Forces that will deter Vladimir Putin and all of the world's other autocratic tyrants from engaging in activities that risk creating conditions that make war more, rather than less likely.

From what I have seen of our Russian friends and allies during the war, I am convinced that there is nothing for which they have less respect than weakness, especially military weakness.

Winston S. Churchill
Fulton, Missouri
March 5, 1946

The collapse of the Soviet Union was the greatest geopolitical catastrophe of the century.

Russian President Vladimir Putin
April 25, 2005

The United States does not view Europe as a battleground between East and West, nor do we see the situation in Ukraine as a zero-sum game. That's the kind of thinking that should have ended with the Cold War.

President Barack Obama
March 24, 2014

…we can no longer tolerate the current state of affairs in the world.

Russian President Vladimir Putin
Speech to the UN General Assembly
September 28, 2015

IX.

RUSSIA: THE EARLY WARNING SIGNS

When Churchill delivered his famous "Iron Curtain" speech in Fulton, Missouri and made the comment about Russia's respect only for an adversary's military strength, many people no doubt remembered his earlier speech on the eve of World War II. On August 21-22, 1939, the Soviet news agency announced that Hitler's Foreign Minister was flying to Moscow to sign a Non-Aggression Pact with the Soviet Union. Churchill would later write that "The sinister news broke upon the world like an explosion. ***[O]nly totalitarian despotism in both countries could have faced the odium of such an unnatural act.*** The [Fascist-Communist] antagonisms between the two empires and systems were mortal."[1]

In a broadcast on October 1, 1939, a month after the start of the war, he attempted to explain the Soviet Union's motive. "I cannot forecast to you," he said, "the action of Russia. It is a riddle wrapped in a mystery inside an enigma. But perhaps there is a key. The key is Russian national interest." That was no doubt true. Stalin was desperately trying to give his armies more time to prepare for the inevitable war with Germany.

Regrettably, throughout its history, the Russian "national" interest has been determined almost exclusively not by a voting public, but by strong authoritarian rulers. This has certainly been the case since the assumption of power by Vladimir Putin in 2000, who has consistently launched into tirades about the decadence and values of democracies and his disdain for politicians who pay attention to public opinion and who permit themselves to be pressured by an aggressive media.

When the Berlin Wall came down in 1989, Putin was a 37-year-old KGB Foreign Intelligence Officer serving in East Germany.[2] He had been born and raised in Leningrad, now St. Petersburg, and it was his hometown. He entered Leningrad (St. Petersburg) University in 1970 where the KGB targeted him for recruitment even before he graduated in 1975. He spent 17 years as a mid-level agent in the KGB's foreign intelligence wing, rising only to the rank of Lieutenant Colonel.

Fiercely patriotic, in May 1990, he was appointed as an advisor on international affairs to the Mayor of St. Petersburg. In June 1991, he was appointed head of the Mayor's Committee for External Relations. From 1994 to 1997, Putin was also appointed to other administrative and political positions in St. Petersburg. By the time he was 44 years of age, he had spent almost all of his life in the beautiful City of St. Petersburg, which became the capital of Russia in 1712.

On a daily basis, Putin was reminded of Russia's imperial history by the presence of majestic Neo-Classicism buildings constructed during the reign of Empress Catherine II; the Empire-style state buildings which had been built during the reign of Czar Alexander I; the Peter and Paul Fortress; magnificent cathedrals with unusually high spires or huge domes; the gold, double-headed eagle which was the symbol of the Russian Empire; the sumptuous Hermitage Museum at the Winter Palace, which served as the imperial residence of several Czars (The Museum is one of the world's finest and was created by Czarina Catherine the Great in 1764); other landmarks such as the Catherine Palace; the Peterhof, a collection of palaces, fountains and parks built by Peter the Great to rival Versailles; the 25 meters high, granite Alexander Column dedicated to the vanquisher of Napoleon; and other Victory Monuments which memorialize wars fought from the early 18th Century to the defense of Leningrad in World War II; and much more. Why is all of this relevant? Because, as Napoleon is said to have observed, "To understand a man, look at the world when he was twenty."

As Putin watched the Cold War coming to an end and independence movements springing up in eastern European countries that had been under the Soviet thumb since at least the end of World War II, he and most of today's ruling class in Russia were clearly shocked and humiliated. They believe that Russia has some kind of an existential need, and the natural right, for territorial expansion. They are keenly sensitive to the fact that the dissolution of the Soviet Union in 1991 deprived Russia of nearly half of the population and lands that had been amassed by the czars over the centuries. At the same time, the former Soviet global superpower was turned into "a rump, bankrupt nation beset by poverty, corruption and internal revolts."[3]

Over subsequent years, Putin worked in national administrative positions, rising rapidly as a result of inside influence, hard work, and luck. In July 1998, the then President of Russia, Boris Yeltsin, appointed the former KGB agent Director of the Federal Security Service, the KGB's domestic successor. The following year Putin was appointed Prime Minister. When Yeltsin unexpectedly announced his own resignation on December 31, 1999, he named Putin as Acting President. After a short campaign in which he promised to rebuild a weakened Russia, he was elected President in March 2000.

Upon taking office, Putin "started dismantling the nascent Russian democracy: taking control of media outlets, consolidating state industries and undermining opposition to his United Russia party, including the assassination of political opponents" as I will discuss below. "He was," two analysts have written, "creating something resembling a Soviet system of Communist Party control, just without the Soviet ideology and a personal structure of rule in place of the old Party nomenklatura."[4]

He installed Security Service veterans as his closest advisers. They immediately complained bitterly about what they believed to be "the West's encroachment on Moscow's traditional sphere of influence in Central and Eastern Europe," a concern that was consistent with what has been described as "Russia's deep ambivalence about its place in the world after the end of the Soviet Union" and its refusal to reconcile itself to the loss of control over neighbors in Europe's east.[5] It was not coincidental that a few days before he succeeded Yeltsin as President, Putin authorized an article in the Russian newspaper *Nezavismaya Gazeta* in which he warned that "For the first time in the past 200 to 300 years, Russia faces the real danger that it could be relegated to the second, or even the third tier of global powers." He asserted that his country was entitled to exert a privileged influence over the post-Soviet states, and it was clear that he was prepared to start the process of reclaiming "his nation's stature as an imperial power and [asserting] Russia's prestige, authority and will on the world stage."[6]

This is not the place to discuss the history of Russian imperialism, but certain points must be considered in order to understand Russia today. By the start of the 16th Century, Russian Czars conceived of their expanding land as a great empire. By 1648, it was a full-fledged colonial enterprise. By the 19th Century, it was a global power.[7] When the empire collapsed in the 1917 Revolution, the Bolsheviks at first expressed antipathy toward imperialism, but when the end of World War I did not bring the worldwide socialist revolution that was expected, "the Russian empire was resurrected by Vladimir Lenin and the Bolsheviks within the federal structure of the Soviet Union. For the next 70 years, Russia's traditional imperial mission became entangled with the expansionist aims of Communism. To meet the surging economic and military power of the United States, the Soviet Union in the 1940s established satellite states throughout eastern Europe, with Communist governments overseen by Moscow."[8]

In the first years following his assumption of power in the Kremlin, Putin apparently decided that he had to change his image if he was to be respected by those he intended to control. One student of Putin's increased power over more than two decades has described him as one of the world's most secretive leaders, but he has also noted that the veil was pulled back a little in a famous photo of Yeltsin leaving the Kremlin in December 1999. "Putin stands beside him, [a "nervous apprentice"] so pale he looks as though he has food poisoning."[9] Over the succeeding years, Putin cultivated the image of a tough guy by appearing in absurd photos showing him in such postures as at the controls of a fighter aircraft, riding a horse bare-chested, driving a race car, and even flying a microlight with a flock of rare cranes.[10] He underwent plastic surgery and played up the fact that he had been a Black-Belt martial artist when he was a KGB Colonel. He also worked to make himself synonymous with the Russian state, not unlike Hitler's reference to himself as the First Soldier of the German Reich.[11] He increasingly characterized personal disloyalty [to him] as a threat to the Russian state.[12]

Putin has been described as "a walking, talking cauldron of resentments, which he deploys for maximum manipulation."[13] His rule has been characterized by both corruption on a vast scale and a deep-seated ruthlessness, and "he has not hidden his willingness to engage in…murders, kidnapping or sabotage."[14] His intelligence and security organs have used a variety of lethal means over the past few decades to dispatch those who were perceived to oppose him or the Russian state. On February 27, 2015, opposition leader Boris Nemtsov was gunned down within sight of the Kremlin, just days after he had spoken out against Russian interventions in Ukraine. The murders and attempted murders have often been laced with morbid messaging in order to evoke fear "that you are never safe, never out of reach."[15]

Another example was the attempted poisoning of former Russian military intelligence officer and British spy Sergei Skripal and his daughter in Salisbury, England in 2018 through the use of an exotic nerve agent which can be administered by exposure to everyday items such as doorknobs or tea. As a result of that incident, British Prime Minister Theresa May expelled 23 Russian diplomats, that country's largest removal of foreign officials in more than 30 years. A similar incident had taken place in a London hotel bar in 2006 when Alexander Litvineko, a former Russian official who had criticized the Russian Government's ties to organized crime was killed by a poison in his tea. In January 2016, a British public inquiry officially implicated Putin in the murder. More recently, Alexi Navalny, a popular Russian opposition leader, lawyer, anti-corruption activist, and political opponent of Putin was poisoned with a nerve agent. An investigation implicated agents from Putin's Federal Security Service. Navalny recovered after receiving medical treatment for five months in Berlin, but when he returned to Russia, he was imprisoned for purported violations of his probation for a sentence in an earlier case which the European Court of Human Rights has determined to be politically motivated. He remains in prison.

*   *   *

In an address on April 25, 2005, Putin declared to the Russian public that "The collapse of the Soviet Union was the greatest catastrophe of the century." At the time, the United States was still recovering from the devastation of the 9/11 2001 terrorist attacks and attempting to determine the nature and scope of the existing and potential worldwide terrorist threats. Putin was focused on rebuilding Russia's armed forces, modernizing and expanding its nuclear arsenal, reviving and expanding its intelligence services and its activities, and planning for a new world order in which he was moving from an aspiring autocrat to an aggressive dictator, and Russia was once again becoming a powerful authoritarian rogue state which could use military force to do as it pleased without the restraints of international law and the pressures of democracies. His first victim was the former Soviet Republic of Georgia, which had declared its independence in early 1991. After a pro-Western change of power in Georgia in 2003, tensions had risen and relations between Georgia and Russia began to deteriorate. In September-October 2006, the Georgian Parliament voted unanimously to seek the integration of Georgia into NATO.

Putin's antagonism to the West, his hatred of America, and his irredentist grievances became obvious in what was described as "a long and icy speech" which caused shock and a chill to fall on an audience of Western diplomats and politicians attending the annual Munich

Security Conference in February 2007. Putin railed against what he called the monopolistic dominance of the U.S. in global relations. He accused the U.S. of arrogance, hypocrisy, of creating a "unipolar world" with "one center of authority, one center of force, one center of decision making" headed by "one master, one sovereign." He "accused NATO of breaking promises by expanding into Europe's east, and called the West hypocritical for lecturing Russia about democracy."[16] It would subsequently be recognized that the speech "amounted to a declaration of war on the West," and that "what happened in Georgia in 2008, Ukraine in 2014, Syria in 2015 and Ukraine again in 2022 has been a series of kinetic campaigns in that war."[17]

In July 2007, Russia announced that it would no longer adhere to the Conventional Armed Forces in Europe Treaty. By April 2008, a full diplomatic crisis between Georgia and Russia was reached as the Kremlin provided support to separatist movements in Georgia in the self-proclaimed Republics of South Ossetia and Abkhazia, all for the purpose of disqualifying Georgia from entry into NATO and stymieing its Western ambitions.

In August, an armed conflict began between Georgia, Russia and the Russian-backed areas of South Ossetia and Abkhazia. Claiming that Russian troops had unlawfully crossed the Russo-Georgia border, the Georgian Army entered the rebellious province of South Ossetia conflict zone on August 7. Russia then accused Georgia of "aggression against South Ossetia" and it began a full-scale invasion of Georgia involving tanks and air strikes on August 8. Russia called the invasion a "peace enforcement" operation. A cease fire agreement was finally reached on August 12, but on August 26, Russia formally recognized the independence of South Ossetia and Abkhazia from Georgia. Georgia promptly severed diplomatic relations. The reaction of Western nations to Russia's invasion was to sit on their collective hands on the theory that it was better to maintain economic and political ties with Russia in the hope that Putin would move closer to the Free World, rather than to punish him. The response was limited to a temporary suspension of dialog, before returning to business as usual.

Another early warning sign of Russia's hostility to the U.S. and a much more significant development, was a joint military exercise involving Russia and China which took place in 2003. Since then, and especially during the last decade, the two countries have conducted more than 30 additional joint exercises and war games to hone tactical and operational capabilities. As many as 10,000 troops have been involved. The frequency, complexity, and geographical scope of the joint exercises have increased in recent years as the military ties between the countries have deepened.

In a Joint Sea Exercise in 2016, the navies of the two countries conducted drills "to seize and control islands and reefs for the first time, plus other amphibious, air defense [anti-submarine warfare], and search and rescue operations."[18] The two navies also used a unique command information system for the first time in 2016. During a 2019 Joint Exercise, they conducted a live-fire air defense exercise which involved launching surface-to-air missiles against cruise missile targets.[19] It has been observed that the Joint Sea Exercises were "most successful… in signaling China and Russia's growing geopolitical partnership and increasingly aligned security interests."[20]

*   *   *

Having ignored or not treated seriously the many warning signs of Russia's aggressive intentions during the first thirteen years of Putin's absolute control of the Russian Federation, it is incredulous that the leaders of the Free World, especially the leaders of Western Europe, failed to pull their collective heads out of the sand during the next nine years when Putin's primary victim was Ukraine, the second largest country in Europe.

On August 24, 1991, Ukraine had officially declared itself to be an independent country. The Communist Parliament of Ukraine had proclaimed that the country would no longer obey the laws of the Soviet Union. On December 1, 1991, voters had approved a referendum which formalized independence from the USSR. Over 90 percent of Ukrainian citizens had voted for independence, with majorities in every region, including 56 percent of the voters in Crimea. At the end of December, the Soviet Union formally ceased to exist By 2021, approximately 183 nations had recognized the sovereign independence of Ukraine and established formal diplomatic relations with it.

In the years after Russia emerged from the ruins of the Soviet Union, the U.S. and Europe worked for several years on an effort to integrate Ukraine into a new post-Cold War order. As I noted earlier, President George H. W. Bush, who was very well versed in diplomacy, was particularly careful not to engage in triumphalism about the end of the Cold War that might have provoked violence from Communist bitter-enders and jeopardized his relationship with Mikhail Gorbachev, and his Russian successors, with whom Bush would have to work in reducing U.S.-Soviet/Russian tensions.[21]

In the post-Cold War period of the 1990s, the West also provided Russia with substantial financial and technical assistance. All of the European countries, including Russia, signed "multiple agreements pledging to uphold key principles, including refraining from the threat or use of force; renouncing any change of borders by force; and affirming the right of all states to choose their own political and economic systems and security alliances."[22]

In 1994, and after lengthy negotiations involving the heads of the three governments, Russia, the U.S. and Great Britain signed the Budapest Memorandum on Security Assurances. Under the terms of the Memorandum, the three nations committed to "respect the independence and sovereignty and the *existing borders* of Ukraine." In exchange, for those "assurances" and Western pledges of aid, Ukraine agreed to relinquish its nuclear arsenal, the third largest in the world, which it had inherited from the collapsed Soviet Union. The Clinton Administration ignored what has been described as "flashing warning signs" as it pressured Ukraine to accept unilateral disarmament— "depriving Kyiv of a deterrent against Russia while providing nothing real to replace it."[23] In 1997, NATO and Russia signed the Founding Act on Mutual Relations, Cooperation and Security between NATO and the Russian Federation (the "Founding Act"), a political agreement in which the parties identified several areas where they could work together to strengthen security. Three years later, Vladimir Putin came to power and major changes began.

It is believed that Putin always viewed Ukraine as critical to the successful pursuit of his nationalist and imperial ambitions, i.e., to the restoration of Russia to its position as a great power.[24] He has publicly blamed Vladimir Lenin, the founder of the Soviet Union, for giving what he views as historically Russian land to Ukraine a century ago— and for acknowledging the idea of a separate Ukrainian nationality in the first place.[25] More broadly, he desires a belt of countries around Russia to be exclusively a sphere of Russian influence, places for Russian economic and political domination. He covets Ukraine's strategic resources, including its huge agricultural capacities and its untapped energy supplies. He claims that he hates NATO because it's member countries pose a military threat to Russia—which is preposterous since no NATO member has reason to initiate hostilities against that huge country—but his primary reason lies elsewhere. Putin knows that once a neighboring country joins NATO, "he loses the military leverage over that neighbor because now if he wants to pressure Latvia, or Estonia, he's actually going to find himself at war with the United States."[26]

In November 2013, large scale protests erupted in response to then Ukrainian President Viktor Yanukovych's refusal to enter into a political and free trade agreement with the European Union. He preferred to seek loans from Russia and to cement closer ties with Putin. The protests continued for months. In February 2014, clashes between the protestors and police became violent, but on February 21, an agreement was reached between Yanukovych and the leaders of the parliamentary opposition to conduct early elections and to form a unity government. The following day, however, Yanukovych fled from the capital fearing the results of an impeachment vote. The same day, in a vote of 328-0, the Ukrainian Parliament removed him from office.

Events had unfolded rapidly thereafter. On February 23, Putin informed the chiefs of his Security Service that "we must start working on returning Crimea to Russia." The former Soviet Union had officially transferred the Black Sea peninsula of Crimea from the Russian Government to the Ukrainian Government in 1954, but by 2008, there had been hints that Russia had irredentist plans for Crimea and was only waiting for the right opportunity. The Ukrainian Foreign Minister had been very concerned, especially in light of Russia's declared policy of military intervention abroad to "protect" Russian citizens. There had also been reports of Russian supporters pressuring Ukrainians living in Crimea to leave it. Regrettably, the Obama Administration was either unaware of Churchill's approach to peace-making, or they rejected it. In an address to the House of Commons on October 5, 1938 about the Munich Agreement and British policy toward Germany, Churchill had declared that "I have always held the view that the maintenance of peace depends upon the accumulation of deterrents against the aggressor, coupled with a sincere effort to redress grievances."

On February 27, 2014, masked Russian Special Forces troops without insignia of any kind forcibly took control of the Crimean Parliament, raised a Russian Flag over the building, and captured strategic sites across Crimea. Russia soon installed a pro-Russian government. The new government then hastily scheduled a referendum on March 16 to determine the political status of Crimea.

A national poll taken in Ukraine in 2013 had found that 69 percent of the public had little or no confidence in Yanukovych, 79 percent were dissatisfied with the political state of affairs, and 87 percent were displeased with the economy. A second poll had found that support for joining Russia was only 23 percent. But, after the February 2014 takeover, Russia used its control of television stations to initiate a misinformation campaign which attacked Ukraine's interim Government as an illegitimate "fascist junta" and to make the predicted false claims that Russians living in Crimea were in grave danger and that they required the "protection" of the Russian armed forces. At a March 4 press conference. Putin assured the world that his country had no plans to annex Crimea.[27] This was precisely the tactic used by Hitler when he declared upon annexing the Sudetenland that Germany would hold no further territorial demands in Europe. In reality, it was only the beginning of his demands. Similarly, Putin's promise not to annex Crimea was only one of the many of his future lies. It would not be the last time that the gullible leaders and people of the NATO and other European countries believed him.

On March 14, 2014, the scheduled Crimean status referendum was declared to be unconstitutional by the Constitutional Court of Ukraine, but the ruling was ignored. The interim Ukrainian Government was not capable of dealing with the Russian assault there, and its military forces were overwhelmed by Russian forces. The results of the fraudulent March 16 referendum were also predictable and on March 18, Russia formally—and unlawfully—annexed Crimea. Shortly thereafter, Putin triggered a bloody armed conflict in Ukraine's eastern Donbas region, by covertly sending troops and heavy weapons into that area.

Six days after the annexation, President Obama demonstrated his ignorance of the real world and of the kind of power politics practiced by Putin when he declared that "The United States does not view Europe as a battleground between East and West, nor do we see the situation in Ukraine as a zero-sum-game. That's the kind of thinking that should have ended with the Cold War." He resisted calls to send military assistance to Ukraine because he was seeking Putin's cooperation on his presidency's main foreign policy objective, namely, the heavily criticized deal with Iran regarding that country's efforts to produce nuclear weapons.[28] Obama compounded the complex problems by disdainfully dismissing Russia as a mere regional power" acting "out of weakness." Perhaps he should have taken more history courses before entering politics. He might have learned that Hitler's Germany and Tojo's Japan were also regional powers, yet they managed to leave behind 50 million dead in World War II.[29] Two years later, in an interview with *The Atlantic*, Obama expressed his "military" opinion that Ukraine "is going to be vulnerable to military domination by Russia no matter what we do."[30]

Obama's 2012 "Pivot to East Asia" policy suggested that he was shifting his attention and interest away from Europe to Asia and was not concerned about Putin's intentions or Russia's growing military capability. Such a conclusion was corroborated by his comment in a 2012 debate in which he ridiculed Mitt Romney, his Republican opponent, for stating accurately at that time, that Russia was the greatest threat to America's security.

After the Russian annexation of Crimea, Obama the lawyer, who had no national security credentials or experience when he entered the White House, emphasized the centrality of international institutions such as the United Nations in the U.S. response to the Russian actions, places where legal and diplomatic arguments involving fine points of international law and custom could be made. One analyst of Obama's position wrote that "Such fanciful thinking will leave our allies with two choices: Bend a knew—or arm to the teeth. Either acquiesce to the regional bully or gird your loins, i.e., go nuclear."[31] In the end, sanctions were subsequently imposed halfheartedly by the West, but they had no significant impact.

The American General Officer who was then serving as the NATO Supreme Allied Commander in Europe would later express great regret at Obama's decision and the U.S. response. The "U.S. Europe command staff [had] developed a wonderful set of options for how to reply to the Russian invasion of Crimea and of the Donbas," he said. "I wish I had more success and had done better advocating for those options to our senior-most civilian leaders. There is more we should have done…." He went on to say that "In war, or preparation for war, you want to *deter* your enemy, not be deterred yourself. You want to seize the initiative rather than ceding the initiative to the enemy and being reactive to him.[32]

* * *

While Russia was taking over Crimea, it was also conducting operations in early 2014 in the eastern Ukrainian regions of Donetsk and Luhansk, but those operations involved a different approach. Rather than conducting a conventional invasion, Moscow "launched a political-warfare campaign to subvert the authority of the interim government of Ukraine. The objective was to first destabilize the situation and, if possible, convince the new Ukrainian authorities to accept a federalization scheme that would reduce their power nationwide and allow Russia to have substantial influence over individual regions.[33] When that plan failed, Russia supported a separatist insurgency.

On April 23, 2014, Mikhail Kasyanov, who had served as Putin's Prime Minister from 2000 to 2004, addressed a conference hosted by the Atlantic Council which was televised on C-SPAN. He said that the Russian people were generally supportive of Putin because of the intense propaganda which appears on the Russian state-owned television network and the absence of opposing viewpoints. He also said that when sanctions are imposed on Russia by the West because of some aggression by Putin, he simply uses the sanctions as an excuse for further aggression and the Russian public believes his explanation that the new aggression is necessary for Russia's security. Kasyanov continued by declaring that Putin is full of bluff, but that because of the weak responses by the West to his previous aggressions, he feels free to engage in more aggressive actions, believing both that the Western nations will eventually tire of the situation and that "everything is for sale" in the negotiations that will follow, including Western values like freedom.

On September 28, 2015. Putin addressed the UN General Assembly and presented his vision of Russia as a world power, capable of projecting its influence abroad. In the same address, he again described the United States and NATO as threats to global security. Over the following years, Russia steadily introduced new conventional military capabilities into the eastern regions of Ukraine as part of a vertical escalation of the conflict there. By 2021, the fighting between the Russian-backed separatists and Ukraine's armed forces in Donetsk and Luhansk had already resulted in more than 14,000 deaths. Developments in Ukraine that were much worse were yet to come.

Ukraine has never had its own authentic statehood.*** [The Western countries] have once again vocalized the all-too familiar formulas that each state is entitled to freely choose ways to ensure its security....Their one and only goal is to hold back the development of Russia. And they will keep doing so...just because we exist.*** I consider it necessary...to immediately recognize the independence and sovereignty of the Donetsk People's Republic and the Hugansk People's Republic.

Russian President Vladimir Putin
February 21, 2022

"...today's Russia remains one of the most powerful nuclear states...it has a certain advantage in several cutting age weapons...whoever tries to impede us, ...must know that the Russian response will be immediate and lead to consequences you have never seen in history."

Vladimir Putin
Speech at the start of the Invasion of Ukraine
February 24, 2022

X.

RUSSIA:
THE FAILURE OF DETERRENCE, A HOT WAR IN UKRAINE AND COLD WAR II

In ominous news reports commencing in late March and early April 2021, an indulgent and self-deceiving world was informed that Russia had begun to move military forces near its western border with Ukraine, Europe's second largest country, from as far away as central Russia and Siberia. As the weeks passed, the number of troops and the pieces of their supporting equipment rapidly increased. By mid-November, it was estimated that 100,000 Russian troops were in the border area. There was no obvious reason for such a large deployment of forces other than an invasion of Ukraine. But that country had not attacked Russia or otherwise presented any kind of a threat to it, and Kremlin spokesmen and Russian diplomats had declared several times that Russia was not considering or planning for an invasion. By February 14, 2022, the massive buildup had grown to 105 Battalion Tactical Groups,[1] 500 combat aircraft, and 40 combat ships in the Black Sea. Western intelligence officials were of the opinion that 60 percent of Russia's ground power and more than half of its air power was now very close to Ukraine.

Any doubt about the severity of the Russian threat to Ukraine disappeared on February 21. In a long-televised speech, Vladimir Putin denied the statehood of Ukraine, claimed that the entire country belonged to Russia, and signed a declaration which annexed to Russia the Moscow-backed separatist regions of Donetsk and Hugansk in Eastern Ukraine. The immediate effect of the annexations was to give Putin a pretext for sending Russian troops into those areas as soon as the new Russian-installed officials in those regions made a request.

America's political leaders and the American public should not have been shocked, either by Putin's February 21 speech or by his next speech on February 24 which announced Russia's brutal and blatantly unlawful, full-scale invasion of the independent and sovereign nation of Ukraine. After all, on several occasions over more than two decades, he had publicly declared his opinion of what the relationship between Russia and Ukraine should be and there was considerable precedent for his aggressive behavior. Power abhors a vacuum, and such developments almost always occur where the surprised parties have demonstrated weakness and left a vacuum to be filled by others. Putin simply said one thing and did something else. He used manufactured and false pretexts as justification for engaging in aggressive, pre-planned actions. Moreover, he was following an historical pattern of Russian behavior, the elements of which include an autocrat or despot in power, repression of its people by the elimination of their freedoms, a militaristic bent, and a strong suspicion of foreigners and western values.[2]

But, shocked Americans were—and, as usual, not fully prepared. The invasion was immediately characterized as the start of a new Cold War.[3] Most Americans still do not understand why or how the threats to our country's safety and security have increased significantly as a result of the developments in Ukraine. It is imperative that they become educated immediately.

*   *   *

For several reasons, Putin could have had little doubt about the likely weakness of any NATO or U.S. response to a Russian invasion of Ukraine. Little or no action had been taken by NATO to *deter* the invasion and several actions taken—or not taken—by Western leaders had made Europe vulnerable to such aggressive conduct.

For nearly two decades, the leaders of Western Europe and the U.S. had refused to act like leaders, especially on matters of national security. They had collectively refused to acknowledge the new and emerging realities. They had avoided meeting serious problems head-on, content to kick the can down the road, to delay disaster until it occurred on some successor's watch. They had straddled fences, engaged in devious obfuscation in order to pander to their political bases and avoid educating their publics on the hard truths of the limited options available to prevent or resolve the serious problems. What actions were taken had usually been meaningless. Their capacity to deter aggression like the one being prosecuted by Russia had been greatly diminished.

They had been aware of Russia's security concerns and had "vacillated over how to deal with Putin as he resorted to increasingly aggressive steps to reassert Moscow's dominion over Ukraine and other former Soviet republics."[4] Indeed, there is more than a little reason to believe that had the U.S. and its European allies "not succumbed to hubris, wishful thinking, and liberal idealism and relied instead on realism's core insights, the [war in Ukraine] would not have occurred."[5] During that period, Western leaders either forgot that Russia was the largest country in Europe and a nuclear power or they ignored Putin's concerns about the closeness of NATO forces to Russia's border in the knowledge that NATO had no intentions whatsoever in attacking Russia. "What really mattered, of course, was what Russia's leaders thought [NATO's intentions] were or might be in the future."[6]

Aside from what Russia's leaders were thinking about NATO's intentions, they could easily see that the elements of NATO's deterrence of Russia's aggressive ambitions were in a downward spiral. Since the end of the Cold War, the member nations of NATO had slowly disarmed, continually reducing their relative military strength even as Russia was modernizing and increasing its own. Germany, one of NATO's largest and most important members, was not even seriously attempting to meet the Alliance's goal of each member spending at least two percent of its GDP on defense. Moreover, Putin effectively had Germany in his pocket. For years, German Chancellor Angela Merkel had supported broad cooperation with Russia. Germany's self-imposed policy of weakness "reflected a consensus in Berlin that mutually beneficial trade with the European Union would tame Russian geopolitical ambitious."[7] Over time, Germany became addicted to Russia's natural gas and crude oil. Lip service had been paid to the idea of developing solar, wind and other energy alternatives in order to avoid both nuclear energy and total dependence upon Russia, but the implementation of any such plan lay far in the future. For the present, Germany could not imagine the imposition of sanctions on Russian oil and gas.

Another element of NATO's failure to deter Putin's aggressive plans was the impotence of the Alliance's previous responses to Russia's actions in Georgia, Syria, and Crimea and the ineffectiveness of many of the Western economic sanctions that had been imposed on Russia over several years. In March, President Biden would declare that "economic sanctions are a new kind of economic statecraft with the power to inflict damage that rivals military might," but the facts are that sanctions involving currency markets, strategic technologies, corporate supply chains and foreign assets are of limited value, especially against a large power like Russia and they take months to have any serious effect.[8] With its expertise in illicit financial activities, Russia has developed sufficient sanctions-evasion techniques to permit Putin to simply shrug his shoulders at many of the Western efforts, temporarily tighten his country's belt, and continue as before. Western countries had filed the expected protests and criticized Putin's actions, but they had soon accepted each of these as a fait accompli.

Putin probably saw a unique but closing window of opportunity for an invasion of Ukraine. Time was working against him. The Ukrainian armed forces were quickly growing in strength. Ukrainian society was rapidly becoming more westernized and separated from Russia. If he invaded during the winter months, the European countries would be very reluctant to impose sanctions against Russia because it could literally cut off its oil and gas exports to them and they had no immediate energy sources for heating. Moreover, any sanctions that were imposed were very unlikely to have any severe effect immediately.

There were additional reasons for Putin to believe that the timing was right for an invasion. The attention of U.S. and European leaders was diverted by the Covid pandemic, economic problems, Iran's accelerated efforts to develop nuclear weapons, North Korea's development of Intercontinental Ballistic Missiles, China's illegal efforts to expand its jurisdiction over islands and shipping lanes in the Pacific, and perhaps most importantly, the absence of strong, capable leaders in Western countries. A strong NATO response to an invasion would require strong American leadership and at least three of America's last four Presidents, to different degrees and in different ways, had demonstrated that the last thing they were likely to do, was to take action that involved a significant risk of the U.S. becoming involved in a European war, especially a conflict which did not involve a NATO member. Each in their own way, had contributed to the inability of the United States to effectively deter the war which exploded upon the consciousness of the world on February 24, 2022.

*　　*　　*

Putin and President George W. Bush first met in June 2001, six months after Bush's inauguration. By that time, the new President's worldview was well known and certain parts of it would certainly have been received unfavorably by the Russian President. In a campaign speech a year before his election, Bush had sought to demonstrate that despite his lack of experience in foreign affairs, he had clearly defined and energetic, if not aggressive foreign policy principles that would guide his presidency. He rejected isolationism as a "shortcut to chaos" and promised "a distinctly American internationalism" that would be more than "management of crisis." These would include active American involvement around the world to promote democratic principles and to protect the world from rogue dictators. He noted that Russia was undergoing a transition that required the U.S. to encourage the forces of democracy, promote genuine democratic institutions, and to check undemocratic impulses within Russia.[9] We can only speculate what Putin thought about Bush's promise to affect matters within Russia and the new President's subsequent naïve comment after their first meeting that "I looked the man in the eye and found him very straightforward and trustworthy….I was able to get a sense of his soul," a remark that Bush must have regretted by 2008, if not sooner.

During Bush's fifth year in office and only 4½ years after the terrorist attacks of 9/11 2001, a growing number of Americans felt that the U.S. "should mind its own business internationally and let other countries get along the best they can on their own." This surprising rise in isolationist sentiment was a minority viewpoint, but it was shared by 42% of the public.[10] It was becoming increasingly clear that one of the main pillar's of Bush's policy of global engagement—the need to promote democracy around the world—had not struck a chord with the public. The President warned against the trend in his 2006 State of the Union Address. "Our enemies and our friends can be certain," he declared, "the United States will not retreat from the world, and we will never surrender to evil. America rejects the false comfort of isolationism."

By the time that Barack Obama entered the White House, in 2009, Vladimir Putin had been in control of Russia for eight years. His foreign policy views had been expressed many times and, in many forums, and his foreign policy in action had been the subject of news headlines for years. Whatever Russia's military capabilities were at that time, Obama was on notice of Putin's intentions. Nevertheless, during his 2008 campaign for the White House, Obama promised to end the war in Iraq and to withdraw from the Middle East irrespective of any serious consideration of America's national security interests there. He wanted to avoid the use of military force and to focus on more popular domestic issues. During his two terms of office, Obama not only failed to improve America's ability to deter aggressive action by the Russian President, he started and led an American retreat from international engagement. By his several demonstrations of weakness, his lack of political will, and his consistent willingness to give domestic politics a greater priority than the Nation's security, he undoubtedly contributed significantly to Putin's confidence that he could engage in brutal and criminal actions in Ukraine without significant consequences.

The feckless leadership of the inexperienced American President regarding Afghanistan and his withdrawal of tens of thousands of American troops in the middle of a war there and after enormous sacrifices by the U.S. Armed Forces, was a clear demonstration of his practice of following public opinion rather than leading it.[11] In December 2009, Obama rejected the recommendation of his senior military advisors on a plan for the withdrawal of American troops from Afghanistan, but he listened intently to Nancy Pelosi, the Democrat Speaker of the House of Representatives, who complained to him that "serious unrest" existed among House Democrats about the idea of spending more on the war in Afghanistan instead of on social issues at home. As justification for his decision, Obama was quoted as saying 'I can't lose the whole Democratic Party.'"[12]

Perhaps the most obvious example of his own weakness, an example that would have been of particular interest to Putin as he measured America's willingness to back up its threats and policies with force, involved Syria's use of chemical weapons against its own people in the civil war there. In an August 20, 2012, press conference at the White House, Obama declared in no uncertain terms that further Syrian use of chemical weapons would be "a red line [for the U.S.] and that there would be *enormous consequences* if we start seeing movement on the chemical weapons front or the use of chemical weapons."

On August 21, 2013, U.S. intelligence agencies eliminated any remaining doubt that Obama's red line had been crossed.[13] Twenty days after the attack, Obama delivered a televised address in which he declared that "If we fail to act, the Assad regime will see no reason to stop using chemical weapons. As the ban against these weapons erodes, other tyrants will have no reason to think twice about acquiring poison gas and using them. Over time, our troops would again face the prospect of chemical weapons."

To the world's amazement, and for no obvious reason, Obama backed down and ignored his own red line. While he was frantically searching for a face-saving excuse for not taking military action, Russia suddenly threw an unexpected lifeline to him. Obama quickly agreed to permit Assad to remain in power—one of Russia's key objectives so that it could retain its new influence in the Middle East—if Syria gave up its chemical weapons. There was, of course, little or no possibility during the middle of a shooting war of conducting a rigorous search for a hidden chemical arsenal to verify that it was, in fact, no longer in the possession of Syria. As it turned out, Assad remained in power and continued to use chemical weapons.

Obama's Secretary of Defense at the time said that Obama's failure to act dealt a severe blow to the credibility of both Obama and the United States.[14] If Obama was unwilling to strike Assad's Syria after the worst chemical attacks in decades and his own promise to take the kind of decisive action in response that would involve "enormous consequences," he would certainly be unwilling to intervene against an aggression by Russia. His second Secretary of Defense later wrote that when the President…draws a red line, it is critical that he act if the line is crossed and that Obama's refusal to take action sent "a message of weakness to the world."[15] Obama's first Secretary of Defense offered a similarly broad perspective and noted that Obama's embarrassing failure to act "was being watched in Moscow and Tehran in Beijing and Pyongyang and elsewhere. ***The rest of the world must know," he continued, "that when the President of the United States draws a red line, that it is dangerous, if not fatal, to cross it."[16] Hillary Clinton, who served as Obama's Secretary of State reportedly said "If you say you are going to strike you have to strike. There's no choice."[17]

Referring to Obama's "high-minded case for action" against Syria's use of chemical weapons, an editorial writer for *The Wall Street Journal* observed that the President had immediately disavowed it "for the least high-minded reason. It was politically unpopular." He added that "Mr. Obama and his advisers will never run out of self-justifications for their policy in Syria. They can't outrun responsibility for the consequences of their lies."[18] A few months later, Russia invaded the Crimea region of Ukraine.

A distinguished news journal would later observe that "Mr. Obama…failed to understand, throughout his Presidency, that the 'nature of power in foreign affairs' still includes military might. Mr. Putin clearly thinks so. Mr. Obama did enormous harm to American power and interests in eight years, and the price is still being paid."[19]

* * *

Events after President Obama left office could only have reinforced Putin's belief that the political leadership of the United States and other NATO countries lacked the *political will* to resist his aggressive ambitions. In an address on July 6, 2017, newly elected President Donald Trump, who had also entered office with no foreign policy or national security experience, no experience at any level of government or in the Armed Forces, and no experience in leading vast and complex organizations in which many were opposed to his personal views, appeared at first to understand that point. "[T]he defense of the West," he said, "ultimately rests not only on means, but also on the will of the people to prevail. The fundamental question of our time is whether the West has the will to survive."

Over subsequent months, however, signs were detected of a populist pushback against the "internationalist" foreign policy legacy of previous decades and the rules-based international order which, for all of its imperfections, had resulted in America's victory in the Cold War, an era of sustained, if uneasy peace among major states, and spreading global prosperity. Trump lacked a clearly defined worldview or philosophy on national security and foreign policy matters. His policy positions were ever evolving. His supporters insisted that he was not an isolationist, but he appeared to be drawn to disengagement from international matters and to wish an end to the responsibilities of world leadership, but without a loss of any of the power that comes with it.

Of concern to many in his Administration, the bellicose President preferred to make decisions which were often uninformed, improvisational, impulsive, and based upon his "gut" instinct, rather than on advance preparation, deep study, and the recommendations of far more experienced advisors.[20] He exaggerated facts and held the unreasonable belief that political pizazz and his personality were more important than careful attention to the details and desired outcomes of negotiations with more experienced foreign leaders involving complex national security matters on which they held contrary opinions.

Multiple anonymous intelligence officials, analysts who prepared his intelligence briefings and the briefers themselves, reported that Trump displayed "willful ignorance" when presented with intelligence analyses; that they had made futile attempts to retain his attention by using visual aids; and that he had reacted angrily when he was given intelligence assessments that contradicted political positions he had taken in public.[21] It was also widely reported that contrary to Churchill's concept of statecraft in war, which prevented him from ever overruling his most senior military advisers when they unanimously disagreed with one of his proposed actions, Trump, like President Lyndon Johnson, often did not even consult with senior commanders about one of his sudden decisions which affected American troops.

By the last year of Trump's presidency, both his abrasive personality and character, as well as his already strained relationship with the most senior U.S. military leaders had deteriorated to a level which made it very difficult for them to work together. On December 27, 2018, for example, it was reported that during a visit to U.S. troops in the war zone of Iraq the previous day, President Trump had undermined military discipline and morale by impugning the competence and character of several military leaders by telling the troops that he had lost faith in their Generals.[22] Churchill followed the principle that commanders in the field should feel "that between them and all forms of public criticism the Government stands like a strong bulkhead.... [Y]ou will not get Generals to run risks unless they feel that they have behind them a strong government. They will not run risks unless they feel that they need not look over their shoulders or worry about what is happening at home, unless they feel they can concentrate their gaze upon the enemy."[23] By his comments, Trump had raised many doubts about his fitness to serve as the Nation's Commander-in-Chief.

His own Secretary of Defense would later write that "Trump seemed unable to think straight and calmly;"[24] that he was "idiosyncratic, unpredictable, and unprincipled;"[25] that he "expected 100 percent political loyalty first and always" from Generals and Admirals;[26] that in a May 31, 2020, meeting with Vice President Mike Pence, the Secretary, the U.S. Attorney General, the Chairman of the Joint Chiefs of Staff, and others to discuss the civil disturbances and protests that had erupted in the District of Columbia and across the U.S. after the May 25 murder of George Floyd by a Minneapolis policeman, President Trump asked why U.S. troops couldn't just shoot the protesters ("Just shoot them in the legs or something");[27] and that when those in attendance at the May 31 meeting attempted to explain the legal and policy reasons why that could not be done, Trump became angry and yelled "You are losers. You are all f_____losers!"[28]

Of greater concern was his reluctance to strongly confront the continuing threats, naked aggression, political subversion, and disruptive actions of Russia. On March 1, 2018, Putin had used his annual address to the Russian Parliament to boast about Russia's resurgent military strength. He stood in front of a screen on which a computer-generated video showed multiple nuclear warheads streaking through space before showering down on what appeared to be an outline of the State of Florida, where Trump had a home.

President Trump's reluctance to challenge Russia's aggressions was particularly apparent at his July 16, 2018, Helsinki Summit meeting with Putin. The most that could be said for his performance at that meeting was that except to his most ardent supporters, it was a national embarrassment. He failed to confront Putin and to hold Russia accountable for its invasion and occupation of Crimea and its support of separatists in Eastern Ukraine. Substantial evidence also existed that since 2007, Russia had hacked into the computer servers of government, industrial, or financial institutions in Estonia, Lithuania, Ukraine, Bulgaria, Georgia, and others countries, but there was no evidence that those developments were discussed. In Syria the Russians were still working with Iran to prop up the brutal Assad regime, which had used poisonous gas on its own people, and to establish military bases there which could threaten the southern flank of NATO and Israel, but there were no reports that subject received attention.

An additional concern at the Summit meeting was Trump's lukewarm support at best for NATO. His own National Security Advisor would later say that Trump "barely knew where Ukraine was," that "In a second Trump term…he may well have withdrawn from NATO," and that "Putin was waiting for that."[29] Trump's position had clearly weakened the U.S. deterrence of aggression, and it is self-evident that "deterrence weakened is an invitation to instability, miscalculation, provocation and worse."[30] It is not an overstatement to say that by the time President Trump left office, he had significantly reduced America's influence over international developments that were affecting America's security. A full year after Russia's brutal invasion of Ukraine, the former President's strong isolationist beliefs had not changed.[31]

* * *

Even though Trump was not elected to a second term and even though the U.S. remains a member of NATO, President Biden's performance on national security matters must have given Putin even more reason to feel unconcerned about the likely Western response to a Russian invasion of Ukraine. One of his first actions was to discard "a powerful geopolitical advantage–America's energy independence–by canceling the Keystone XL pipeline, halting leases for drilling on federal land and waters, restricting access to capital for oil and gas companies and piling on regulatory burdens."[32]

In May 2021, the Biden Administration also waived sanctions against the Russian-owned company overseeing the construction of Russia's Nord Stream 2 gas pipeline to Germany without any concessions by Russia. President Trump had imposed the sanctions because the pipeline would have given Russia huge political and strategic leverage over the countries receiving the gas, and by bypassing Ukraine, would have deprived that country of transit revenues and made it more vulnerable to Russian aggression. The CEO of the company was a longtime ally of Putin and a former East German Stasi intelligence officer.[33] Biden took the action for no apparent reason other than a political show of reversing Trump's policy and it received bipartisan criticism from Congress.

Biden's sudden withdrawal of all U.S. troops from Afghanistan and his surrender of that country to the Taliban was also a serious strategic failure. At the time, only a comparatively few American troops remained in the country, but they provided critically important support to Afghanistan's security forces, including around-the-clock reconnaissance, timely on the ground intelligence, training, operational planning, the capability of calling in air strikes, and the opportunity to gain the trust of the Afghan forces and to provide confidence to them when the immediate future looked dim. The withdrawal also violated President George Bush's pledge after the terrorist attacks of 9/11 that the United States "will make no distinction between those who carried out the attacks and those who harbor them." The disastrous, chaotic, and incompetent manner in which the American withdrawal was handled and Biden's own unrealistic talk about how he hoped "to keep terrorist dangers in Afghanistan in check through 'over the horizon' air strikes"[34] could only have given Putin even more confidence.

While the U.S. would subsequently enjoy momentary success on July 31, 2022, when the CIA conducted a drone strike in central

Kabul which killed al Qaeda leader Ayman al Zawahiri, the revelation that he and his family had moved from the border of Pakistan to an affluent part of Kabul so soon after the Taliban returned to power after the American withdrawal, confirmed a recent UN report that the Taliban and al Qaeda remain closely connected. The tactical success of a single attack on an individual in Afghanistan in a year, was no guarantee at all that the U.S. would be able in the future to detect and track al Qaeda and Islamic State training sites and other safe havens at which terrorist attacks could be planned and from which they could be executed before another U.S. "over the horizon" strike could be made.

Biden exacerbated the problem by demonstrating his ignorance of important foreign and national security factors. On September 21, 2021, he addressed the UN General Assembly. Claiming that the U.S. had ended 20 years of conflict in Afghanistan, that it was closing a "period of relentless war," and that "we've turned the page," he promised "a new era of relentless diplomacy" which will be "squarely focused on what's ahead of us, not what was behind." He was wrong on several counts. First, the U.S. did not end the war. We merely departed from Afghanistan, leaving a power vacuum behind. Shortly thereafter, the Taliban ended the war by filling the vacuum and forcibly taking control of the country from the Afghan Government, thereby raising the possibility of future terrorist attacks by groups based there. Second, the very abrupt nature of the U.S. withdrawal left several Americans and many people from our NATO allies stranded there. Third, the withdrawal and its results once again raised a question among America's friends, potential friends, and its adversaries of the United States' staying power, its credibility, and its trustworthiness. Finally, the use of bold language like " 'turning the page' on an era of 'forever wars'" is, what one respected historian of the wars in the Middle East has called "misleading in an age in which the actions of terrorist groups cannot easily be foreseen; militant insurgencies are long-lasting; and the military actions Washington orders in response are carried out principally by local forces, backed up by U.S. advisors and airpower, and take time."[35]

Biden's public declaration ruling out the use of American military forces in Ukraine, a comment that he first made at a news conference on January 19, 2022, could only have added fuel to the fire that Putin was planning. The comments removed a critical element of deterrence, namely, artful deception—the ability to amplify the perception of risk to an adversary by using ambiguity to conceal possible future action. When he was asked why the imposition of sanctions on Russia for invading Ukraine would work, especially in light of the fact that previous sanctions had not had any significant effect on Russian behavior, Biden replied that precisely how Putin would be held accountable depended "on what he does." If he mounts "a minor incursion," he said, "there are differences within NATO about what countries are willing to do. "He did not define what would be considered a "minor incursion" and thereby left an implication that even America might not respond. A former Prime Minister of Australia would subsequently say that Biden's comment "probably sealed" Ukraine's fate.[36] The White House Press Secretary issued an ambiguous "clarifying statement" about Biden's statement, but significant damage had already been done.

Over the next several weeks, the White House staff had to make so many "clarifications" about Biden's jarring and undisciplined misstatements, or what one editorial writer called his "verbal incontinence," that European leaders openly expressed concern about the damage being caused. Polling data reflected the American public's worries about his credibility, his lack of strong leadership, and even his mental soundness. When Biden declared on March 27 that Putin "cannot remain in power," suggesting that the U.S. objective was not just to assist Ukraine, but to bring about regime change in Russia, one respected observer felt compelled to state the obvious: "…to call for the ouster of an autocratic and bellicose leader of a nation with nuclear weapons…is the kind of thing that can trigger wars that could result in the annihilation of much of humanity."[37]

*   *   *

It had been clear for some time that the meeting between Vladimir Putin and China's Xi Jinping in Beijing on Friday, February 4, 2022, the first day of the Winter Olympic Games there, was unlikely to be a mere social affair relating to the Games. It was their first meeting in nearly two years. The huge Russian military buildup on its border with Ukraine was in its eleventh month. In December, Russia, which had long been India's main arms supplier, had signed an agreement for additional weapons exports from Russia, and an agreement which extended military technical cooperation with India until 2031. Putin was eager to retain India as its largest market for weapons exports, and to expand economic ties in the energy sector to offset the impact of current and likely future sanctions.

The meeting between the two most powerful and most aggressive autocrats had, in fact, been scheduled for an announcement of a sweeping and detailed five-thousand-word agreement between their two countries to form a strategic partnership for the express purpose of changing the balance of power that had defined the global order since the Cold War ended, and to challenge the United States as a world power, NATO as a cornerstone of international security, and liberal democracy as a model for the world.[38] The agreement pledged collaboration on space, climate change, the Internet, and Artificial Intelligence. More ominously, the Director of the Kissinger Institute on China and the United States described it as "a pledge to stand shoulder to shoulder against America and the West, ideologically as well as militarily."[39] The reason for the timing of the meeting and announcement soon became very apparent.

When Americans awakened on the morning of Thursday, February 24, 2022, the news on the radio and television stations was much more than troubling. Early broadcasts reported that around 5:00 a.m. in the center of Kyiv, the capital of Ukraine, explosions from missile strikes could be heard. As the hours passed, the news became worse.

Early that same morning, Vladimir Putin had announced the start of a full-scale war in a highly bizarre and untrue, but threatening rant on television which was full of tortured logic and false historical analysis. He made the absurd claims that he had annexed the Donetsk and Lugansk regions of Ukraine earlier in the week because he had to stop "the genocide of millions of people who live there and who pinned their hopes on Russia;" that he had initiated the war because the law and order policies of the United States had "created…the curse of international terrorism and extremism;" and that after the end of the Cold War the U.S. and other Western countries had tried to "finish [Russia] off, and utterly destroy [Russia]."

Most critically, Putin warned that "today's Russia remains one of the most powerful nuclear states," that "it has a certain advantage in several cutting-edge weapons," and that "whoever tries to impede us, let alone create threats for our country and its people, must know that the Russian response will be immediate and lead to the consequences you have never seen in history." The comments could not be easily dismissed as mere bluff. In 2020, Russia had published an ambiguous document by the title of "The Basic Principles of the State Policy of the Russian Federation on Nuclear Deterrence." In a break with Soviet-era policy, the document indicated that the country has lowered its threshold for using tactical nuclear weapons and that it might use modern precision missiles which are accurate to a radius of just over 30 feet, to carry out limited strikes—all on the gambling assumption that the West would not respond with strategic nuclear weapons which could only have Doomsday results.[40] Putin's remarks were immediately interpreted as a serious threat to use nuclear weapons on any country that actively opposed Russia's actions in Ukraine, and perhaps, any future actions Russia might take in the Baltic States or other NATO countries which had been an enforced part of the Soviet Union before they gained their independence at the end of the Cold War, and which had borders close to Russia.

Expressing concern about Putin's mental health, former U.S. Secretary of State Condoleezza Rice characterized Putin's speech as a "deepening delusional rendering of history." Officials in other NATO countries soon made similar comments. In a midday speech, President Biden stated the obvious when he declared that "Putin [had] larger ambitions that Ukraine;" that he wanted to, in fact, "reestablish the Soviet Union."

Over the course of the first 24 hours after the invasion, the approximately 190,000 troops which Russia had massed around Ukraine's borders attacked Ukraine on a wide front from Belarus to the north, Russia to the east, and Russian-controlled Crimea in the south. The outcome of the invasion appeared to be foreordained because of the huge numerical, weapons, and equipment advantage of the invading forces and the fact that Ukraine was fighting alone, but by nightfall, and over the next several weeks, any hope that Putin had that Russia's "shock and awe" attack would result in the immediate cessation of all Ukrainian resistance, had evaporated. Short of weapons and everything else, the Ukrainians had shown remarkable courage and resilience and were still fighting. By the end of the fourth day of the invasion, thousands of Ukrainian civilians had taken up arms to fight in the streets to defend their capital, and the Russians could not claim control of either the air or any major Ukrainian city.

Many questions were unanswered and would remain so for some time. How long could the small Ukrainian Armed Forces hold out against the overwhelming military force of Russia? Would the new economic sanctions against Russia announced during the day and over subsequent days by a tough talking President Biden significantly influence Russia's actions or, as many were already predicting, prove to be tepid and ineffective?[41] The Russian Foreign Ministry shrugged off the sanctions imposed by the West, saying that "Russia had proven that with all the costs of the sanctions, it is able to minimize the damage." Would the partisan differences in American politics, separating internationalists and neo-isolationists, and Republicans and Democrats, now give way to a unified American resistance to the naked aggression? Only days before the invasion a group of far-left and far-right members of Congress had been pressuring Biden to relax tensions with Putin and even to make concessions to him.

Declaring that "This [invasion] is not just about Ukraine" and that "Putin only understands strength," former Vice President Mike Pence and members of Congress were expressing amazement that despite the invasion, the U.S. was still purchasing Russian oil; that the Biden Administration had taken no action to block Russia from *Swift*[42], an international payments network of banks; that no action had been taken to stop Russian exports of oil and gas to international customers; and that no action had been taken to increase U.S. oil and gas production.

Despite the huge unknowns and dangers, certain consensus conclusions were being voiced within hours after the start of the invasion. One respected analyst spoke for many when he characterized the invasion as "a criminal war of premeditated and unjustified aggression" by which Putin "aims to topple the U.S. from its global position, break the post-Cold War world order, cripple the European Union and defeat the North Atlantic Treaty Organization."[43] "The larger meaning of Russia's Ukraine invasion," declared the Editorial Board of one publication, "is that the world has entered a dangerous new era. Or perhaps it's more accurate to say the world has returned to its pre-World War II state in which the strong take advantage of the weak, and authoritarians are on the march."[44] A return to a world without a rules-based order, where only force and power matters, was a possibility frightening to contemplate.

* * *

As the days passed, the Biden Administration continued to declare to the world that no American military forces would enter Ukraine. In his State of the Union Address on March 1, 2022, the President had emphasized the point: "But let me be clear: Our forces are not engaged and will not engage in the conflict with Russian forces in Ukraine." An important element of deterrence had just been eliminated.

In many quarters, however, concern was rapidly mounting about the possibility of a war that would directly involve the United States. Noting that the U.S. had "mobilized American ground forces, air squadrons, and ship deployments to protect NATO countries, including Poland, Romania, Latvia, Lithuania and Estonia," Biden had continued. "Our forces are not going to Europe to fight in Ukraine," he said, "but to defend our NATO allies in the event that Putin decides to keep moving west. ***The United States and our allies will defend every inch of territory that is NATO territory with the full force of our collective powers. Every single inch."

Squeezed between Russia, Belarus and the Baltic Sea, the thinly populated Baltic states of Estonia, Latvia, and Lithuania were particularly vulnerable. Since Russian troops were already in Belarus, on very short notice they could cut the Baltic states off from the other NATO countries thereby preventing them from receiving reinforcements by land. That could be accomplished merely by capturing the narrow 40 mile stretch of land on the Poland-Lithuania border known as the Suwalki Corridor. The Corridor separates Belarus from the Russian enclave of Kaliningrad, a pinprick of territory that remained part of Russia after the collapse of the Soviet Union and which is now the headquarters of the Russian Baltic Fleet.[45]

Most Americans knew very little about the Baltic states. Fewer still fully understood the implications of our NATO Treaty commitment under Article 5, the commitment which the President had emphasized in his March 1 address: *The Parties agree that an armed attack against one or more of them in Europe or North America shall be considered an attack against them all.* Suddenly, they were being forced to look at the dangers to American security as they are, not as they hoped they were.

*   *   *

Even though Putin's conduct as President of Russia was widely known, and even as horrible scenes of the brutal Russian bombardment of hospitals, schools, residential and other civilian areas, the destruction of major cities within Ukraine, and reports of looting by undisciplined Russian troops were appearing on televisions and social media devices all over the world and European countries were radically reversing previously-held positions on national security matters, Americans remained divided on how we should deal with the crisis there and the question of the extent to which the U.S. should be engaged there and around the world.

Recognizing that the invasion of Ukraine presented a clear danger to their own security, European countries were taking unprecedented steps, including the imposition of hard-hitting sanctions, to punish Russia for its aggression. The new German Chancellor, for example, announced an increase in German defense spending to 2 percent of that country's GDP, a long-standing NATO policy requirement for its members, long honored primarily in the breach[46]; he stopped the important—to Russia—Nord Stream 2 pipeline[47]; and he announced that Germany would send anti-tank weapons and Stinger missiles to Ukraine. Even historically neutral countries, such as Sweden, Switzerland, and Finland joined the sanctions on Russia.

Not surprisingly, most Democrats in Congress either supported President Biden's response to the Russian invasion or remained silent. But the voice of progressive, Left-Wing isolationism, what one analyst has described as "a newer, less-noticed strain of America-first ideology,"[48] was still being heard. That voice was coming from unthinking people who want no foreign entanglements, who refuse to recognize, much less acknowledge, any threats to our security that would support the arguments of other Democrats and Republicans for increases in spending on national defense. They want those funds spent only on Left Wing priorities. One member of the U.S. House of Representatives objected to any increase in defense spending by declaring "We must put human rights and dignity first."[49] Apparently, she was unaware that freedom isn't free; she didn't see any connection between Russia's use of brutal force to crush a weak, independent sovereign nation and America's security; she was unaware of Russia's intentional massacres of civilians in Ukraine's hospitals, residential and other areas and the resulting humanitarian nightmare; she had no knowledge of history or President Washington's admonition that in order to preserve peace we must be prepared for war; and she was far more interested in pandering to her domestic political supporters, than in acting like a responsible official in the U.S. Government—which is a government that exists for all of the people.

Republicans broadly agreed that President Biden was not demonstrating sufficiently strong leadership or imposing sufficiently severe sanctions on Russia, but they were divided on specifics. Some objected to any American involvement in the support of Ukraine at all. What was called the "populist isolationist" or Far Right Wing of the Party was well represented. In a radio interview the day after Putin invaded and annexed the Ukrainian regions of Donetsk and Hugansk, former President Trump described Putin's actions as "genius" and "pretty savvy."[50] A senior editor of *American Conservative* magazine reportedly declared that "Ukraine is a corrupt country. Come and get me." *Compact* magazine released a declaration signed by 33 people which called for "de-escalation" and "good faith" peace talks, an absurd statement that ignored the obvious reality that Putin was escalating the brutality of the war every day and refusing to negotiate seriously with Ukraine. The propagandist host of a television "news" show asked "Why should we take Ukraine's side? Why wouldn't we have Russia's side?"[51] A retired Army Colonel appeared on television to argue that no sanctions should be imposed on Russia and no military aid should be given to Ukraine. When the program's host sought clarification and asked whether the Colonel was saying that the U.S. should "just let Russia take that portion of Ukraine that they want to take," he replied "Yes, absolutely."[52] The Russian state media soon flooded their programs with clips of the retired Colonel's remarks.

A leading Conservative who is an historian and the author of an award-winning biography of Winston Churchill felt it necessary to publicly chastise such thinking. "There are some in our movement," he wrote, "who enjoy being contrary for its own sake—out of perversity or a desire for attention—regardless of the cost to the wider movement...." He continued. "Now is not the time to continue fighting the struggles that seemed to matter before February 24. Just as many of the America First isolationists quickly and patriotically came around to the overwhelming need for the U.S. to join in the struggle against Japan and Germany—and thus largely escaped the contempt of history that would otherwise have been their lot—so [the critics of Ukraine's President, Volodymyr Zelensky] on the right should heed the courage of a people who are battling a more massive and naked display of barbarism by a great power than most people alive can remember."[53] Even an America-First Conservative who served in the Trump Administration wrote that the movement had taken a dangerous turn and was regressing "toward extreme isolationism, producing a self-described antiwar movement that preaches peace while callously ignoring [Russia's] war crimes."[54]

The Republican tradition of what was referred to as the conservative internationalism espoused by Presidents Ronald Reagan, George H. W. Bush and George W. Bush, was represented by Trump's Vice President Mike Pence, who declared bluntly that "there is no room in the Republican Party for apologists for Putin." The Republican U.S. Senate Minority Leader also strongly condemned the invasion and declared that it was imperative that the U.S. respond to it with strength. A Reuters/Ipsos poll conducted on March 8, 2022, found that 63 percent of the Republicans polled believed that the war in Ukraine involved America's interests and they rejected the view that what was happening there was "none of our business."[55]

It remained to be seen if America could achieve greater unity on something as important as our leadership of NATO on a matter that was as dangerous to all of the Free World, including the United States, as the brutal and irrational war by Russia on a weak but remarkably courageous democracy. One thing was certain; not one of America's three most recent Presidents had given the nation's security greater priority than domestic politics; not one had consistently acted with political courage to explain hard truths and to speak with boldness and clarity to Americans of all political persuasions in order to educate them on why and how it is necessary for us to take immediate steps to improve our ability to protect the freedom that we have taken for granted for too long.

...no arsenal, or no weapon in the arsenals of the world, is so formidable as the will and moral courage of free men and women.

President Ronald Reagan
Inaugural Address
January 20, 1981

*Russia will use all the instruments at its disposal to   counter a threat against its territorial integrity
—this is not a bluff.*

Russian President Vladimir Putin
September 21, 2022

The price of freedom is extremely high, but it is incomparably higher for those who first surrender and then try to regain it than for those who always protect it with all their might. ***We are fighting together to ensure that war is never again seen by any aggressor as a means of achieving aggressive goals.

Volodymyr Zelenskyy
President of Ukraine
July 26, 2022

XI.

THE WILL AND MORAL COURAGE OF FREE MEN AND WOMEN

A hundred days after Russia's unprovoked invasion of Ukraine, Vladimir Putin's war had not been proceeding as he had planned. While still asserting that he had initiated a preemptive attack because it was the only way to prevent what he claimed was a planned assault by NATO on Russia, a preposterous claim which was supported by no evidence other than the fact that some of the NATO nations were improving their defensive capabilities and modernizing their armed forces as he had Russia's over several years.

Russia is several times larger than Ukraine, it is a nuclear power, it has modern armed forces which greatly outnumber Ukraine's, its arsenal of weapons is more sophisticated than Ukraine's and much larger, and its economy is much larger. And yet, Ukrainian troops supported by the local population were fighting with remarkable will, moral courage and surprising effectiveness, often with improvised weapons. The Ukrainian people were demonstrating incredible resilience and an astonishing will to remain free from the yoke of Russian control. Ukraine's President, Volodymzr Zelenskyy was proving to be a highly capable wartime leader. Britain's Prime Minister likened Zelenskyy's decision to remain in his capital after the Russian attack to Churchill's decision to stay in London during the Blitz. But, he said, Zelenskyy's decision was even braver because, unlike Churchill in 1940, who could walk around bomb sites in relative safety, Zelenskyy "knew that squads of killers were hunting for [him].... And when one world leader offered [Zelenskyy] a way out, [he] replied 'I need ammunition, not a ride.'[1]

Putin had ordered the Russian troops to make a lightning strike with the objective of quickly reaching the Ukrainian capital of Kyiv, which is located in the northern part of the country, decapitating the Government within a few days, and replacing it with a puppet regime completely subject to his control. To that end, he had sent "hundreds of helicopter-borne commandos—the best of Russia's 'spetnaz' special forces—to assault and seize" the lightly defended Hostomel airfield on the outskirts of the city. The idea was to use the airfield as a base to which additional Russian troops and armored vehicles could be flown in within striking distance of the capital.[2] Putin had obviously assumed that since Ukraine was not a member of NATO, the response of the Western European countries would be tepid, that any support of Ukraine that might be provided would be too little and too late, and that the Ukrainian Government would quickly be overwhelmed and forced to surrender.

There were reasonable grounds for that particular assumption. Many western leaders reported that at the time, a consensus existed among the U.S. and its European allies that "there was nothing they could to prevent the inevitable. Their intelligence services predicted a Russian takeover of Kyiv and a collapse of the Ukrainian state within days."[3] Only two days before the Russian invasion, Dmytro Kuleba, Ukraine's Foreign Minister, met with President Biden and senior Administration officials at the White House. By then, the U.S. had already closed down its Embassy in Kyiv and evacuated all American personnel. Kuleba later recalled that he felt like a patient surrounded by doctors presenting him with a diagnosis of stage-four cancer.[4]

As a result of the fierce resistance of the Ukrainian forces in the capital region against enormous odds, however, the Russian forces stalled. They were unable to capture either Kyiv or the northern city of Kharkiv, and they were forced to retreat back into Belarus and Russia. It was reported that Russia had suffered thousands of casualties, the loss of an estimated quarter of its deployed weapons systems, and that desertions and insubordination among its troops were exacerbating its problems. Only a month after the invasion began, Russia announced that it would shift its focus and its forces to the separatist Donbas area of eastern Ukraine where the wide-open landscape would permit it to use its heavy artillery advantage to grind out territorial gains.

Other unexpected developments also began to occur. As brutal images of devastated Ukrainian cities and towns, of Russian atrocities, both intentional and indiscriminate attacks on schools and hospitals, and the deliberate bombing of civilian began to circulate around the world, public opinion throughout Europe and the U.S. was outraged. The human carnage was on display for all to see. War crimes were clearly being committed on an industrial scale by Russian forces.

One of Putin's most important delusions in planning the invasion of Ukraine, was the assumption that the NATO response, like its earlier responses to other Russian aggressions, would not be significant and that as a result, the Alliance would lose all credibility and remain only as a badly weakened shell of its former strength. After all, in November 2019, French President Emmanuel Macron had called NATO "brain dead." President Trump admitted that he had threatened not to defend NATO against Russia, i.e., to abandon U.S. allies by ignoring Article 5 of the NATO Treaty.[5] In short, nothing that NATO had done over the previous decade deterred the Russian dictator.

Suddenly, the member nations of NATO had coalesced into a much more cohesive group than they had been for several years. They were being joined by non-NATO countries in imposing new and more biting economic sanctions on Russia and in sending heavier and increasingly sophisticated weapons to Ukraine. Even though Russia was using energy supplies to Europe as a weapon, e.g., by cutting off gas supplies to Poland and Bulgaria, Germany, which for two decades had relied completely upon Russian energy and had no contingency plans for securing other sources, was racing to obtain new sources. The European Union, which had already banned all coal imports from Russia starting in August, was now proposing an imminent ban of Russian oil. In bipartisan votes of 368-57 in the U.S. House, and 86-11 in the U.S. Senate, Congress approved $40 billion of additional assistance to Ukraine.

The only dissenters in the U.S. Congress were a conspicuous faction of Republican isolationists. Republican Senate Leader Mitch McConnell stated the obvious when he declared that "America's support for Ukraine's self-defense is not mere philanthropy. It is in the U.S. national interest. Ukraine's brave defense with U.S. help has weakened Vladimir Putin, which means he is less able to make trouble elsewhere. Every Russian tank destroyed by the Ukrainians is one that won't threaten an American soldier." Other voices expressed a warning which appears as one of the principal tenets of this book: isolationists imagine "a world in which America can ignore what rogue powers do, send flowers to the victims, and the U.S. won't be affected."[6]

Slowly at first, but steadily, the West also began to supply Ukraine with better weapons and many forms of logistical support. In mid-May, Finland, a neutral country whose nonalignment had deep historical roots, and which had remained out of NATO even at the height of the Cold War in order to avoid provoking Moscow, announced that it was now applying for membership. A senior official at the Finnish Foreign Ministry observed that "Russia is much more unpredictable than we ever thought. It is much more willing to take risks and even take heavy losses, and it's also capable of mobilizing 150,000 men on the border of a neighboring country without general mobilization." The official further expressed great concern about Russia's "loose talk of using weapons of mass destruction."[7] The Alliance was expected to approve Finland's application with alacrity, a development that would, with the stroke of a pen, more than double Russia's border with NATO by adding 830 miles and join the well trained and well equipped Finnish Armed Forces[8] to those of the other NATO members. Many people still remembered Churchill's reference to the Finnish Army in January 1940 when it fought not only with gallantry, but with great effectiveness against the much larger and more powerful forces of the Soviet Union. "Superb, nay, sublime," he said. "In the jaws of peril, Finland shows what free men can do. The service rendered by Finland to mankind is magnificent." Shortly after the Finnish announcement, Sweden, another previously nonaligned country, announced that it would also be applying for NATO membership.

Historians also remembered the prescient remarks of Churchill in a similar situation some 73 years earlier. At a March 1949 dinner in New York hosted by Henry Luce of *Time*, he reflected once again upon Soviet leaders. By that time, his "Iron Curtain" warnings had been vindicated. "These men in the Kremlin," he said, "how is it that they have deliberately united the free world against them? …It is, I am sure, because they feared the friendship of the West more than they do its hostility. They can't afford to allow free and friendly intercourse between…those they control and the rest of the world. They daren't see it develop. I believe that their motivation is self-preservation—not for Russia—but for themselves. Of course, going out of office in Russia isn't quite as easy a business as it may be here…You lose the election, you may lose your life. It's very high stakes they play for…and I'm sure that self-preservation for themselves lies at the root of this strange, extraordinary, unreasonable policy."

* * *

By the one hundredth day of the war, Ukrainian confidence was also growing. In the north, beyond Kharkiv, the country was engaged in counteroffensive operations to disrupt Russian supply lines into the Donbas region. But it had also suffered major setbacks, most notably in the southern port city of Maruipol, and in the east where Russian forces were using their great advantage in heavy artillery to take control of parts of the strategically important Ukrainian city of Severodonetsk, an area which borders Russia and which was once Ukraine's industrial heartland The war was being described as a war of attrition, a bloody slog with no end in sight. The Ukrainian Defense Minister agreed that the war was entering a protracted phase. Its Military Intelligence Chief said that the country would continue fighting until Russian forces were evicted from all Ukrainian territory, including Crimea and all other areas seized by Russia 2014. "This is a war of all Ukrainians," he declared, "and if someone in the world thinks that they can dictate to Ukraine the conditions under which it can or cannot defend itself, then they are seriously mistaken."[9] President Zelensky warned that Moscow could not win the war on the battlefield and that it could only end with a diplomatic agreement "reached at the negotiating table."[10] The comments of the Ukrainian officials could not be dismissed as mere braggadocio. They were likely part of an effort to communicate to Putin that a protracted war by Russia involving urban fighting against a country fighting for its life, would involve unacceptable costs to Russia measured in casualties, blows to its economy, and eventually, loss of public support at home.

There remained too many unpredictable factors to clearly foresee how the war would end and what the ending would look like. Putin clearly retained the intention and will to achieve his original goal of annexing the entire Ukrainian State and he could afford a considerable loss of public support at home. It was not clear whether all of the promises of military and economic aid to Ukraine already made by Western European countries would be fulfilled and whether all of the necessary additional aid would be provided in the future if the war was too protracted. To date, the support of those countries had been lackluster compared to that of the U.S. and the United Kingdom. Several of the countries were already incurring high fuel prices and inflation and Putin was squeezing the world food supply by blockading Ukrainian ports and its exports of wheat and other agricultural products.

The hesitant Western military effort was still being characterized as suffering from a sense of disbelief, "a widespread incredulity about the seriousness of the threat" now presented by Russia, a threat which was leading to "unsteady leadership."[11] But the fact was that even the U.S. aid was not inexhaustible. For its own security it would soon need to re-supply its stocks of the weapons and ammunition which had been given to Ukraine. Most observers also doubted that the beleaguered Biden Administration would be able to convince Congress to pass many more highly expensive aid bills for Ukraine.

France's President had already observed that the outcome of the war might include territorial concessions to Moscow by Ukraine[12] and he subsequently said in an interview that Russia should not be humiliated. Italy proposed autonomy for Ukraine's Crimea and Donbas region. In a speech to the World Economic Forum in Davos, Switzerland, former Secretary of State Henry Kissinger spoke in support of his balance of power philosophy by calling on Ukraine to accept its territorial losses to Russia in 2014, including Crimea and the Donbas region, all in order to avoid defeating or marginalizing the larger power. He argued that rival great powers have "rights" and "interests" that must be respected.[13] He did not explain the legal basis of Russia's claim of "rights" to the territory of another sovereign country; or what would prevent Russia from starting other wars in the future in all or other parts of Ukraine—Putin's original objective in this war—or in the territory of other independent nations, all on the same basis of a claimed "right" or "interest;" or why such concessions by Ukraine would not encourage other powerful dictatorships to engage in the same kind of brutal aggression on the same basis; or why the Free World should ever reward the ambitious initiators of war for engaging in the kinds of unprovoked brutality and industrial scale aggression as that being committed by Russia against Ukraine.

President Zelensky rejected the ideas of concessions, comparing them to the failed efforts in the 1930s to appease Nazi Germany. But the fact that the ideas had been proposed suggested that if the Ukrainians continued to be "successful" and became too "ambitious," pressure from Western Europe to limit their advance might carry the implicit message that future support would be conditioned upon Ukrainian acceptance of a limitation. To his credit, the Republican Leader of the U.S. Senate declared that the end state of the hostilities should be whatever Kyiv—not Western Europe—concluded it should be. One astute observer expressed a broader perspective about the future. The eruption of the Russian-Ukrainian War, he said, i.e., of the greatest war in Europe for the last 70 years, "is only one indicator pointing toward what begins to look like a great unraveling of the tapestry of world order that Americans and their allies have been weaving since 1945."[14]

Concern was growing about the long-term prospects of continued support of Ukraine by European countries. Supply-chain disruptions and energy price hikes related to the imposition of sanctions on Russia and Russia's stoppage of gas supplies were already starting to affect industrial production. The inflation and its effect on the cost of living was already being felt. Regrettably, the leadership qualities and political will of several European leaders remained suspect. Not one had the steel of Churchill. As of May 31, for example, Germany, Europe's largest economy, and a country with a population of more than 83 million, had sent less military aid to Ukraine than Estonia, a tiny country with a population of just over one million.[15]

Concern was also increasing about President Biden's continuing caution and ambivalence on the war and his continuing tendency to telegraph U.S. plans and strategies to Russia, a practice certain to remove whatever deterrent effect remained against future Russian military operations. The Editorial Board of one respected journal declared that "Sometimes, it's hard to tell if President Biden and his strategists want Ukraine to win its defensive war against Russia, or merely to survive to sign a truce with more of its former territory under Russian control."[16]

This issue was moving to the front as Russian forces continued to expand their control of Severodonetsk. The battle there was highlighting the central role of heavy artillery, in which Russia had a great advantage. The long range, firepower, and large number of its artillery pieces gave Russia the ability to strike Ukraine's forces from within Russia's borders. The fall of the city would contribute greatly to Russia's goal of controlling Donbas.

For months, the Ukrainians had been asking unsuccessfully for artillery systems which have a range of at least 75 miles in order to blunt the Russian advantage, but Biden had refused the requests on the ground that if Ukraine fired munitions that reached into Russia, the risk of an escalation of the war would increase unacceptably. On the face of it, Biden appeared to be frightened by the usual Putin threat of "unpredictable consequences" if the U.S. continued to provide the kinds of weapons to Ukraine that would permit the embattled country to have a fighting chance of stopping the brutal and devastating Russian invasion. Ukraine had no choice but to announce that its forces would not strike targets inside Russia, but after the announcement was made, Biden only agreed to provide weapons with a range of about 48 miles, not weapons with a much longer range of 180 miles. The decision confirmed Biden's ambivalence about the war and his lack of attention to the concept of deterrence, and the principle of not telegraphing one's plans to an adversary.

*   *   *

Meanwhile, fears that Putin had greater ambitions were continuing to grow. On June 9, 2022, he effectively communicated the idea that Ukraine was just his first territorial target. At an exhibition honoring Peter the Great, Russia's first emperor, Putin compared himself to the empire-expanding czar and declared that when Peter took from Sweden the area that is now St. Petersburg, "he was merely returning what is ours, and strengthening it.... Taking back and reinforcing. That's what [Peter] did. And it looks like it fell on us to take back and reinforce as well."[17] It was reported that Vladimir Medinsky, Putin's aide, was even more explicit in remarks at the same exhibition, lamenting the fact that Russia's territory has greatly diminished from the days when it controlled one-sixth of the world's surface, an area which now includes 16 independent nations, and that this territorial retreat "is not forever."[18]

Mikhail Kasyanov, who had served as Putin's Prime Minister was quoted as saying that "Putin simply does what he can get away with, like a hooligan. If he is allowed to conquer some territories and Europe and the U.S. end up swallowing that fact, he will simply keep going forward." Marat Gelman, a former adviser to Putin, asserted that at least some Russian citizens were asking "why the great army that [Putin} has been expanding and financing… cannot deal with the Ukrainian resistance" and that as a result, Putin "needs to turn everything into a new dimension, where he is at war not with Ukraine, but with the entire world." There is a danger, he said, that Putin "will choose another victim."[19]

It was not surprising that several European leaders, especially the leaders of the now independent NATO countries which were formerly a forced part of the Soviet Union, were very concerned that a potential cease-fire or other kind of settlement which left Russia in control of a significant part of Ukraine, with a capacity to regroup, to rebuild its temporarily depleted armed forces, and to prepare for new offensives, would end up putting those nations in Putin's crosshairs.[20] If that should be Putin's plan, he would probably attack the tiny Baltic states of Estonia, Latvia, and Lithuania first on the assumption that there would be no interest in the American public to risk a war directly with Russia over those nations even though they are part of NATO. It is likely that Putin would also wait to make such an attack until after the 2024 Presidential Election in the U.S. in the hope that a more isolationist administration would come to power and be even more reluctant than Biden to block Putin's expansionist plans.

A month before Russia's imminent invasion of Ukraine, one astute national security analyst asserted that "the argument over isolationism has been overtaken by events. The world as it is in front of our faces makes clear that isolationism from the left or right is an absurdity. Like it or not, we're in it up to our frazzled neurons."[21] That may be, but by June 2022, it was clear that President Biden was far more worried about his own political standing and that of his party at home, than he was about Ukraine and that until the mid-term congressional elections in November, he was going to continue to "resist doing much more than sticking U.S. thumbs in any of the globe's leaking dikes...."[22]

Five months after the Russian invasion, the armies on both sides of the conflict were exhausted and Ukraine had blunted Russia's offensive in the Donbas region and temporarily stabilized the situation there. Western estimates were that around 20,000 Russian troops had died in Ukraine by that date, but it was clear that the much more powerful Russian Army intended to continue its brutal war of attrition.

On July 26, President Zelenskyy was honored by the International Churchill Society with its highest award for his "steadfast attachment to fundamental principles, his indifference to the pressures and expediencies of the moment, and his unbending determination [which] is not only saving his country, [but] also helping to save Europe." In accepting the award via a video link, Zelenskyy spoke in words that clearly demonstrated "the will and moral courage of free men and women" to which President Reagan referred in 1981. "The price of freedom is extremely high," Zelenskyy said, "but it is incomparably higher for those who first surrender and then try to regain it than for those who always protect it with all their might. ***We are fighting together to ensure that war is never again seen by an aggressor as a means of achieving aggressive goals."

By mid-September, the sacrifices and remarkable resilience and spirit of the Ukrainian people had clearly demonstrated the truth of Napoleon's famous maxim that in war, the moral power (morale) is to the material (weapons, equipment and manpower) as three to one.

They had also resulted in serious battlefield losses by Russia. A fast-moving Ukrainian counter-offensive into Russian-occupied territory recaptured more than 3,500 square miles in the north-eastern Kharkiv region. It was reported that after spending weeks capturing the region, Russia had suddenly lost more than 10 percent of the territory it had taken over since invading Ukraine. The surprising reversal came after several months of stalled advances by Russian forces.

When it invaded Ukraine on February 24, Russia had relied primarily on the 200,000 troops which formed the largest part of its professional land forces. After suffering tens of thousands of combat losses, it subsequently attempted to replace the losses by reliance upon mercenaries, such as those provided by the shadowy Wagner Group,[23] which recruited prisoners in Russian penal colonies, by forcibly drafting male residents of Ukraine's Donetsk and Luhansk regions and by forming regional "volunteer" battalions. Since late June, none of those efforts had proved sufficient to stop the Ukrainian counter-offensive.

Ukraine's stunning success was due in great part to its adoption of the command-and-control process used by the U.S. and most other NATO nations in which junior Commanding Officers have the authority and discretion to make battlefield decisions based upon current facts on the ground. This process was permitting highly mobile Ukrainian units to use surprise and quick movement to take advantage of unexpected opportunities without having to seek permission from higher authorities. In contrast, Russian forces, which preferred attrition warfare, i.e., the use of large formations to wear down the outnumbered Ukrainians, were still relying upon the old Soviet command structure in which their troops were more often than not required to seek authority from higher levels and not given freedom to use their initiative.

There were also other contributing factors. An important one was Russia's inability to gain control of the skies. It initially had success in attacking Ukraine's air defense systems, but by early March, Ukraine had somehow managed to solve the problem. As increasing numbers of Russian planes and helicopters were being shot down and the combat air support of its ground troops was being greatly reduced, those troops became much more vulnerable to attacks from Ukrainian aircraft, drones, and artillery.

A related factor was Ukraine's use of rocket launchers supplied by the West, such as the highly mobile *HIMARS* systems.[24] Those munitions permitted Ukraine to destroy Russian air defense systems and logistics bases with great precision. Russia's forces were also reported to be exhausted, as well as inadequate. There were other reports of poor morale among the Russian forces, who, during their retreat, had abandoned hundreds of tanks, self-propelled howitzers, other armored vehicles, and stores of ammunition in their chaotic rush to safety. When the abandoned weapons were added to the weapons captured by Ukrainian forces, the total "turned Moscow into by far the largest supplier of heavy weapons for Ukraine, well ahead of the U.S. or other allies."[25] Russian casualties were also high. The U.S. Department of Defense estimated that as many as 80,000 Russian troops had been killed, wounded, or captured since the invasion in February.

In addition to the changed military situation, Russia's economic campaign against Europe, namely its reduction and even cessation of natural gas supplies, had not resulted in a reduction of European support for Ukraine. But, the winter months were approaching and a possibility still existed that large swaths of European industry might be forced to close because of energy shortages and, in a worst case, rolling blackouts for consumers.[26]

On September 21, a beleaguered Vladimir Putin announced in a nationally televised speech that he would mobilize 300,000 Reservists to supplement the Russian troops already in Ukraine. He also hinted yet again that he would consider a nuclear attack on Ukrainian forces. He had already ordered a campaign of cruise missile strikes on Ukraine's civilian infrastructure, including dams and power stations. The partial call-up of Reservists, which had to date been disproportionally from minority groups, was clearly designed to avoid a full mobilization, which would include the sons of Russian elites living in Moscow and St. Petersburg and "average Russians in [other] major cities in the street and at the workplace,"[27] because such a step would be very unpopular, because it would be inconsistent with Russia's propaganda narrative to its public that the war with Ukraine was going well and was resulting only in victories, and because if average Russians were forced to participate in the war, the public's broad support for the conflict might quickly disappear. To the surprise of many, the mere announcement of the mobilization—Russia's first such effort since World War II—triggered a backlash in several parts of Russian society where people who had previously tuned out the war in Ukraine as a foreign conflict, now found it coming to their homes. The mobilization also resulted in the exodus from Russia of tens of thousands of potential conscripts, large numbers of which were part of the country's educated professional class who had the resources to flee, e.g., scientists, economists, lawyers, IT workers, etc.[28]

It appeared that the Reservists would not have any immediate effect on the battlefield situation since many, if not most of them would be former conscripts who would require training, and not battle-hardened former military professionals. It was also doubtful that the forcibly mobilized Reservists would be highly motivated combatants.

In an obvious additional attempt to stop Ukraine's momentum, puppet officials in the Russian occupied and controlled parts of the Donetsk, Luhansk, Kherson and Zaporizhzhia regions of Ukraine suddenly scheduled votes on the question of whether Russia should "annex" those areas. The sham referendums were designed to confer a veneer of legitimacy and sovereignty over provinces that Russia only partially controlled and where Ukrainian troops were advancing.[29]

The outcome of the referendums was pre-ordained since Russia had used coercion and threats, including the use of soldiers going to homes forcing people to vote at gunpoint, and it had invested huge resources consolidating its rule in those areas since it "annexed" Crimea in 2014. Once the "annexations" occurred, Putin planned to describe any effort by Ukraine to liberate those regions as an attack on Russian territory, thus justifying in his mind a major escalation of the war. He apparently also hoped to deter the West from sending more weapons to Ukraine. On September 27, President Zelensky delivered a virtual address to the United Nations Security Council. "Another attempt to annex the territory of Ukraine," he said, "will mean that there is nothing to talk about with this president of Russia." The warning of continuing battles was clear. It was very difficult to see how and when the war might end.

Meanwhile, a Wall Street Journal-NORC poll found that 89 percent of Ukrainians opposed any peace deal with Russia that would cede any territory conquered by Russia since the invasion. The courageous Ukrainian President announced that despite Ukraine's own mounting casualties, the Russian destruction of its cities, and its widespread killing of innocent civilians, he would not even agree to a cease-fire that would allow Russia to keep captured Ukrainian territories because it would only give Moscow a badly needed opportunity to replenish and rearm for the next round of fighting and encourage a wider conflict.[30]

* * *

As the Russian military situation in Ukraine continued to deteriorate, Vladimir Putin continued his saber-rattling threats to use tactical nuclear weapons, conveniently disregarding his joint statement with President Biden at their June 2021 meeting that "A nuclear war cannot be won and must never be fought." The continuing threats were obviously designed to weaken or even eliminate the resolve of the West to continue its support of Ukraine. In his usual fumbling way, Biden did not discuss Putin's threats in a frank address to the American people. Rather, in comments to political donors at a Democrat cocktail fundraising party, he referred to what he characterized as the first "prospect of Armageddon" since the October 1962 Cuban Missile Crisis.

Tensions were further increased after an explosion on October 8 damaged a section of Russia's new 12-mile Kerch Strait Bridge which connects the Russian mainland with Crimea, the Ukrainian territory which Russia unlawfully annexed in 2014. The bridge had been built in defiance of international law and had opened in 2018. It had since become critical to Russia's war effort as a way to ferry heavy weapons, ammunition, fuel and troops to Ukraine's southern regions which Putin had just "annexed."

On October 9, it was announced that Russia and Belarus, which borders Ukraine, had agreed to form a regional military force. Belarus had already permitted Russia to use it as a base to which tens of thousands of Russian troops had been deployed for the invasion of Ukraine. Russian warplanes had also been taking off from Belarusian bases. On October 10-11, Russia escalated the war by bombarding several parts of Ukraine's electrical grid and other civilian infrastructure with some 84 cruise missiles and Iranian-supplied drones. President Zelensky promptly asked the G-7 (the group of seven leaders of large world economies) for additional aid in the form of improved air defense systems and longer-range missiles, undoubtedly reminding them that wars are not won by courage alone.

As these events were taking place, one analyst expressed the view that by "the standards of classic 'realist' theory, defending Ukraine isn't in America's core national interest. But during the past century, Americans have embraced a broader view of U.S. foreign policy. Experts and ordinary citizens alike care about defending a peaceful world order in which dictators don't change boundaries by force of arms and don't suppress people's desires for self-government."[31] Regrettably, it was also reported that "factions in the West, on the right and left, [still believed] Ukraine should be left to its fate without Western aid, and they will blame Ukraine for having the nerve to defend itself against a brutal dictator."[32]

The limited education of the members of those factions apparently did not include any study of history. If it had, perhaps they would have been aware of a courageous and incisive comment by Prime Minister Winston Churchill. In July 1940, Britain had been fighting Hitler for more than ten months. France had surrendered and Germany stood triumphant in Europe. Her armies controlled the Continent from Norway to the borders of Spain, from Poland to the Atlantic. An invasion of Britain by Germany was a high priority of Hitler and a very real possibility. The North Africa Campaign, also known as the Desert War, between Britain and the Axis Powers, had just commenced. The Battle of the Atlantic, i.e., the devastating attacks by German U-Boats against all ships sailing to the island nation, lay in the future.

In a BBC broadcast from London on July 14, Churchill spoke words which, but for the distance of time and personality, might today be thought to be those of Ukraine's Prime Minister: "And now it has come to us to stand alone in the breach, and face the worst that the tyrant's might, and enmity can do. We are fighting by ourselves alone, but we are not fighting for ourselves alone." Whatever the limits of their education, the "factions" in America who oppose U.S. support of Ukraine should consider whether they wish to live in a world where large, strong, ambitious, authoritarian nations feel free to ignore both international law and moral and other restraints to engage in nuclear blackmail and warfare to steal from the weak whatever they may wish.

Most Americans were only dimly aware of the severity of the present and growing dangers to our security. They were still absorbed in the continuing tensions associated with the Covid Pandemic, rampant inflation, the culture war, unchecked crime, the endless flow of thousands of illegal migrants crossing our borders, inept presidential leadership, the national debate on abortion, the hyper-partisanship and inability of both Houses of Congress to resolve major problems, and the other cares of daily life.

These circumstances were not unlike those described by Churchill in an essay published eight years before the commencement of the conflict that became World War II. Noting that "the great mass of human beings [were] absorbed in the toils, cares and activities of daily life [and were] only dimly conscious of the pace at which mankind [had] begun to travel," he expressed great concern about the absence of competent national leaders. "Great nations are no longer led by their ablest men," he said, "or by those who know most about their immediate affairs, or even by those who have a coherent doctrine. Democratic governments drift along the line of least resistance, taking short views, paying their way with sops and doles, and smoothing their path with pleasant-sounding platitudes. Never was there less continuity or design in their affairs."[33]

Now, 91 years later, the same feeling was being expressed for many by an informed observer who was worried about a deterioration of American pride in concepts like rigor and excellence." Noting that President Biden's order to immediately withdraw all U.S. forces from Afghanistan had not been a departure, but rather "a collapse, all traceable to the incompetence of diplomatic and military leadership," she declared that "we are losing old habits of discipline and pride in expertise…." She continued with the anguished observation that "I've never seen a country so in need of a hero."[34]

America's need, however, was not for something as simple as the mythical "man on a white horse," but rather eyes which are open to the real facts which underlie the real and growing worldwide dangers described here and the same kind of will, moral courage, and staying power to take whatever actions and to make whatever sacrifices may be necessary to deter further aggressions by China, Russia and other authoritarian powers, as the people of a weak country like Ukraine have shown in battling Russia.

> *China has entered a new era…and must take Center Stage in the world.*
> Chinese President Xi Jinping
> October 18, 2017

> *China is engaged in a whole-of-state effort to become the world's only superpower by any means necessary.*
> FBI Director Christopher Wray
> July 7, 2020

> *…the Chinese people will never allow any foreign forces to bully, oppress or enslave us. Anyone who dares to try that will have their heads bashed bloody against a Great Wall of steel forged by over 1.4 billion Chinese people.*
> Chinese President Xi Jinping
> July 2021

> *China is engaged in a "a coordinated campaign on a grand scale" that represents "a strategic contest across decades. We need to act."*
> Ken McCallum
> Director-General of the United Kingdom's
> MI5 domestic counter-intelligence
> and domestic security agency
> July 6, 2022

XII.

CHINA: THE EARLY AND RECENT WARNING SIGNS

For many years, the United States has been aware of the increasingly dangerous security threat posed by the Peoples Republic of China (PRC). U.S. National Security Strategy documents have consistently employed vanilla language to refer to China as a "strategic competitor," but it is much more than that. It is an increasingly powerful state which uses its military and economic strength to compel neighboring states to acquiesce to its demands, including its unlawful territorial and maritime claims. It is a military power which has rapidly modernized its forces and "engaged in its largest ever nuclear force expansion and [weapons] arsenal diversification effort in its history."[1] According to the Director of the FBI, China is "engaged in a whole-of-state effort to become the world's only superpower by any means necessary."[2]

*   *   *

A November 2021 Report of the U.S. Department of Defense declares that the broad objective of China's National Strategy is to "surpass U.S. global influence and power, displace U.S. alliances and security partnerships in the Indo-Pacific region, and revise the international order to be more advantageous to Beijing's authoritarian system and national interest."[3] The primary means of achieving this objective are the two million military personnel who are in the Regular Forces of the Peoples Liberation Army (PLA),[4] which has for years been working to develop the capabilities to conduct joint, long-range precision strikes by land, air and maritime forces across all warfare domains, as well as space, counterspace, cyber, electronic warfare operations, and to accelerate the large-scale expansion of its nuclear forces.[5]

In 2019, China highlighted the increasingly global character that it ascribes to its military power by deciding that the PLA should take an even more active role in advancing its foreign policy objectives. This is being accompanied by an aggressive new style of coercive, nationalistic diplomacy which is referred to as Wolf Warrior

Diplomacy, in which Chinese diplomats who were previously cautious and moderate in their behavior and who used cooperative rhetoric, have now become "far more strident and assertive—exhibiting behavior that ranges from storming out of international meetings to shouting at foreign counterparts and even insulting foreign leaders.[6]

The aggressive nature of China's foreign and military policies has been matched by the bellicose words of its authoritarian President Xi Jinping, who also serves as the General Secretary of the Chinese Communist Party (CCP). In a speech to the National Congress of the Communist Party on October 18, 2017, he asserted that China has entered a "new era" and that it expects to "take center stage in the world." In March 2021, he declared that the United States is the "biggest threat" to China's security. In a speech four months later to thousands of people in Beijing who were marking the 100th anniversary of the founding of the Communist Party, he declared that "the Chinese people will never allow any foreign forces to bully, oppress or enslave us. Anyone who dares to try that will have their heads bashed bloody against a Great Wall of steel forged by over 1.4 billion Chinese people." He also vowed "resolute action" against any efforts by Taiwan toward independence and reiterated that it was the Chinese Communist Party's "historic mission" to bring Taiwan under Beijing's control. His words had the same ominous overtones as those of a former Japanese Foreign Minister, who announced on August 1, 1940, only sixteen months prior to the attack on Pearl Harbor, that Japan was establishing what it called the Greater East Asia Co-Prosperity Sphere. Japanese militarists and nationalists used the policy not only as a vehicle to free Asian nations from the colonial rule of Western powers, but also to strengthen Japan's power and advance its dominance within Asia. They also promoted the idea of Japanese superiority and used the policy as a device for the development of the Japanese race.

And who is this leader who has been described as "the autocratic, muscular-nationalist, order-obsessed strongman in charge of China?"[7] Apparently, there are few, if any, substantive and careful biographies of the man It is well known that Xi was the son of Xi Zhongxun, who once served as Deputy Prime Minister of China and was an early comrade-in-arms of Mao Zedong. The elder Xi was purged and out of favor with the CCP and the Government before and during the 1966-1976 Cultural Revolution[8] after he openly criticized the Government's actions during the Tiananmen Square incident in 1989.[9] Despite his father's fall from favor, Xi is still considered to be a "princeling."[10] In his rise to power, Xi had a reputation for prudence and following the Party line. He is said to actually believe the CCP's propaganda and historical narrative and to further believe that anyone who challenges that narrative is a criminal.[11]

In 2000, Xi became the governor of Fujian. A scandal involving the senior leadership of Shanghai, which erupted in early 2007, led to Xi becoming that city's Party Secretary and his selection as one of the nine members of the Standing Committee of the CCP's Political Bureau (Politburo), the most senior ruling body in the Party. In March 2008, he was elected Vice President of China and in October 2010, he was named Vice Chairman of the powerful Central Military Commission. In November 2012, he became the General Secretary of the CCP and in March 2013, he was elected President of China by the National People's Congress.[12]

Xi moved quickly to consolidate power during his first term as President. After many years of collective leadership, he broke Party rules and initiated a nationwide anti-corruption campaign which served as one of several means of removing or purging his political rivals. Under his aggressive leadership, China has become increasingly assertive in international matters. As part of his campaign against what he believes are morally corrupt western values, he has pursued increasingly authoritarian attacks on executives of successful companies which are not controlled by the Government; social media celebrities have been reigned in; cryptocurrency has been banned; many new regulations have been imposed on China's technology sector; and, of course, elections in China, like in all totalitarian regimes, are a sideshow. There is only one political party and a person who is "elected" has been decided upon in advance by the CCP.

A more telling example of Xi's severe authoritarian leadership on domestic matters in China is his treatment of Uyghurs and other Muslims in Xinjiang, which has caused several countries, including the U.S., Canada, and the Netherlands to accuse China of committing genocide and crimes against humanity.[13] What has been described as "an extraordinary cache of leaked photographs and documents from inside China" has reportedly made it plain, "beyond any doubt," that "millions of Muslim Uyghurs—including children and elderly people— have been badly oppressed; that in the single county of Xinjiang, "22,762 residents, more than 12 percent of the adult population, were interned in a [re-education] camp or prison during 2017 and 2018" for having been deemed to have displayed any behavior viewed as a sign of untrustworthiness, all as part of Xi's assimilation campaign. In addition to pursuing a strategy of forced labor, "reports have emerged of China forcibly mass sterilizing Uyghur women to suppress the population, separating children from their families, and attempting to break the cultural traditions of the group."[14] An unofficial tribunal of lawyers has alleged that "Chinese President Xi Jinping bore primary responsibility" for the "torture against Uyghur, Kazakh and other ethnic minority citizens in the northwest region of China known as Xinjiang."[15]

It is also believed that because of CCP controls and the absence of free elections, the most senior Chinese leaders, including Xi, are unable to relate to the lives and needs of ordinary Chinese people. They mainly see the public only through the lens of the CCP's propaganda and social media. Individual leaders are administrators and, other than Xi, rarely policy-makers. Policies made under his rule leave no doubt about either his beliefs or his priorities. Some of them have been summarized in this fashion: "China's economic and military clout have expanded rapidly; he has overseen the mass incarceration of Uyghur Muslims in the western region of Xinjiang; and Beijing has significantly stifled the free press and criticism of the Chinese Communist Party, both on the mainland and further afield. Under his watch, freedoms have been drastically curtailed in Hong Kong, an ostensibly autonomous city…. [D]uring a 2017 visit, he presided over the biggest military parade held in the metropolis since the [1997 British] handover."[16]

In a recent article, a distinguished former Prime Minister and Foreign Minister of Australia, a country in China's Pacific neighborhood, has briefly summarized Xi's governance of China with these words: "Under Xi, ideology [not pragmatism] drives policy more often than the other way around. Xi has pushed politics to the Leninist left, economics to the Marxist left, and foreign policy to the nationalist right. He has reasserted the influence and control the CCP exerts over all domains of public policy and private life." The Prime Minister has further asserted that "China's approach to foreign policy is driven not only by a rolling calculus of strategic risk and opportunity, but also by… a turbo-charged belief that history is irreversibly on China's side…." The Prime Minister concluded his article with these words: "The United States should realize that China represents the most politically and ideologically disciplined challenger it has ever faced during its century of geopolitical dominance."[17]

The leadership of China is "opaque when it comes to identifying opposition to Xi," but Xi's future will not be decided by the Chinese people. Power struggles are fought within the Communist Party behind closed doors.[18] The Chinese political elite remains what it has been for many decades, a "self-contained, rigid, disciplined, and monopolistically intolerant hierarchy" interested almost exclusively in its bureaucratic self-interest.[19] During the March 2018 session of China's National People's Congress, a provision of the constitution that set term limits for the country's President and Vice President was abolished and Xi was unanimously elected to a second term as President. Undisputed facts indicate that he is determined to gather in his own hands, even more authority over China than that which was possessed by Mao Zedong.

* * *

China's actions have been speaking louder than the words of its leader. In 2015, Xi initiated China's most ambitious and most consequential military reforms in many decades. He greatly increased the PLA's budget. He directed the creation of Special Operations forces. He supported the rapid growth of China's cyberwarfare capabilities to the extent that today they are widely considered to be state-of-the-art, giving China the tools to launch cyberattacks that would "disrupt critical infrastructure in the U.S., including oil and gas pipelines and rail systems."[20] He modernized the PLA's organizational structure with the objective of ensuring that its individual military services could work together with the kind of force multiplying jointness that has characterized the U.S. Armed Forces since 1947. He increased efforts to attract more qualified people into the PLA.

In early 2014, China sent dredgers and construction crews to the Spratly Islands in the South China Sea to reclaim land and construct buildings and necessary infrastructure. The work proceeded rapidly. In 2015, China denied that it had any intention of militarizing the South China Sea, but by early 2016, most of the seven Spratly artificial islands were completed and "China then added military infrastructure : 72 aircraft hangers, docks, satellite communication equipment, antenna array, radars, hardened shelters for missile platforms, and the missiles themselves."[21]. In 2022, the U.S. Navy Admiral who was the Commander of the U.S. Indo-Pacific Command observed that "The function of those islands is to expand the *offensive* capability of the PRC beyond their continental shores. They can fly fighters, bombers plus all those offensive capabilities of missile systems."[22] Three of the outposts in the Spratly Islands are now "full-fledged military bases that {also} host airfields, surface-to air and anti-ship missiles." The Parcel Islands, which are located further north, have also now been developed and militarized. A Chinese bomber has landed there.[23]

China has defied international law by using its military and economic power to seize the disputed islands, an area covering 1.4 million square miles in international waters, all in an effort to advance its new claim of territorial sovereignty over nearly all of the South China Sea and to make it very difficult, if not impossible, for other nations to operate in that area. It has accomplished this without any effective response from the U.S. or its allies, thereby effectively accomplishing a *fait accompli*.

The South China Sea is a major international trade route through which trillions of dollars in trade passes each year. Some 50 percent of all global oil tanker shipments pass through it.[24] Its waters are also deep in fish stocks and rich in oil and natural gas deposits. The islands which China has militarized are claimed by a number of other countries, including the Philippines, Taiwan, Vietnam, Brunei, and Malaysia. China's activities in the South China Sea were challenged in a proceeding before the Permanent Court of Arbitration in The Hague pursuant to the 1982 United Nations Convention on the Law of the Sea. In a landmark decision on July 12, 2016, a five-judge tribunal of the Court ruled unanimously in a 501 page Award that the Chinese activities were unlawful. China ignored the ruling and continued its land reclamation and militarization activities unabated. China's Vice Foreign Minister dismissed the Court's ruling as "a scrap of paper."

The world's oceans are, of course, critically important to America's national security and economic strength. They "connect global markets, provide essential resources, and link societies together. By value, 90 percent of global trade travels by sea, facilitating $5.4 trillion of the annual commerce of the U.S. and supporting 31 million American jobs. Undersea cables transmit 95 percent of international communications and roughly $10 trillion in financial transactions each day."[25]

China's efforts to project its military power from bases outside of its territorial limits are not limited to the South China Sea. It set up its first overseas military base in 2017 in Djibouti on the east coast of Africa. That facility is now capable of docking an aircraft carrier and nuclear submarines and it is located only 6 miles from the largest American base in Africa, which is home to 4,500 U.S. troops. The Middle East is also a target of China. In the spring of 2021, it was reported that U.S intelligence agencies had discovered that China was secretly building a military facility at a port in the Arab Emirates, one of America's closet Mideast allies. After several rounds of meetings between U.S. and UAE officials, the construction was halted. Elsewhere, China has built commercial port facilities in Pakistan and Sri Lanka that could be used by its rapidly expanding Navy.

A major part of China's efforts to expand its influence and its network of bases around the globe is its Belt and Road Initiative. The Initiative is a strategy adopted in 2013 to convert economic influence into economic coercion. It involves large loans to foreign governments for infrastructure development. It has flooded countries in Asia, Africa, Europe, and Latin America with tens of billions of dollars in loans pursuant to the $1 trillion Initiative. More than 70 countries have been involved. The Initiative is a Chinese push for dominance in global affairs through the use of "debt-trap diplomacy," in which China extends excessive credit to a country with the intention of cultivating and corrupting the leadership of the country and extracting political or other important concessions from the debtor country when it becomes unable to honor its debt obligations. In late 2017, for example, China forced Sri Lanka to hand over control of its Hambantota port facilities for 99 years to satisfy its debt.[26] China is also rapidly expanding its nuclear arsenal, developing missiles, and building a capability to project military power by sea. In September 2021, it was reported that it was rapidly constructing nearly 300 hardened underground silos in its western desert to house its *Dongfeng*-41 Intercontinental Ballistic Missile, which can carry multiple nuclear warheads and has the range to hit the continental U.S. In 2022, the U.S. Department of Defense estimated that over the last two years, China has doubled the number of its nuclear warheads to 400. The commander of the U.S. Strategic Command described the scope and scale of the activities to be a "strategic breakout by China."[27] While it continues to rapidly accumulate a broad range of military assets, China refuses to accept U.S. offers to enter into arms-control talks. That alone is a cause for concern.

It is also developing a capability not found in Western navies: a capacity to control the sea from the land. It now has the means to launch Intermediate Range Missiles from Western China or Medium

Range Ballistic Missiles from Eastern China to attack the U.S. Navy's Battle Groups of aircraft carriers and other surface ships. At least one analyst has concluded that "The U.S.'s planned Naval Modernization efforts are far behind what will be needed to avoid being outflanked by China" in an armed conflict between the two countries.[28]

In July 2021, the *Financial Times* reported that China had successfully tested a nuclear capable Hypersonic Missile that circled the globe, and then dropped a hypersonic glide vehicle that glided all the way back to China to strike a designated target. Hypersonic weapons travel in the upper atmosphere at speeds of more than five times the speed of sound, or about 3,853 miles per hour. Unlike Intercontinental Ballistic Missiles which travel in a predictable arc and can be tracked by long range radars, a hypersonic weapon maneuvers much closer to the earth, making it more difficult for radars to track and for U.S. defensive systems to destroy. During the previous five years, the U.S. had conducted nine hypersonic tests while China had conducted hundreds.[29] None of the U.S. tests had been successful. The successful Chinese test was a Wake-Up Call for U.S. military leaders, especially in the context of the earlier discovery of hundreds of new missile silos in the Chinese desert. The former Vice Chairman of the U.S. Joint Chiefs of Staff expressed the belief that the Chinese could soon have the capability to launch a surprise nuclear attack on the U.S. "They look like a first-use weapon," he said. "That's what those weapons look like to me."[30]

More news about the dangers of a rapidly growing Chinese Navy was reported in June 2022. Satellite imagery showed that after several years of work in the Jiangnan Shipyard in Shanghai, China had launched the *Fujian*, its third Aircraft Carrier. The ship will use a new electromagnetic catapult technology similar to that which is used only on the most recent American Aircraft Carrier. Evidence suggested that China had plans to build at least six carriers.[31] Analysts believe that the *Fujian* is a key component in Xi Jinping's ambition to ensure that China is a military power which is capable of projecting offensive force over great distances and going toe-to-toe with all Western navies.[32] In November 2021, it was reported that China had built models in a western desert which had the dimensions of a U.S. Aircraft Carrier and other U.S. warships and that the mock-ups were presumably designed for target practice.[33]

In October, yet another startling and dangerous development was made public. The United Kingdom's Ministry of Defense reported that for several years, the PLA has been recruiting veteran Western pilots into a program that is designed to train Chinese pilots and thus to dramatically improve China's ability to fly planes from its Aircraft Carriers in the event of a war with the U.S. The program, which dates back to the early 2010s, has targeted former military pilots from the U.K., Norway, France, the U.S. and other countries who have "experience flying F-35s, America's most advanced stealth fighter," which is used on our Aircraft Carriers and which would fight the Chinese J-20, its stealth fighter, in the event of an armed conflict.[34] The program has also targeted former pilots who have knowledge of other very sensitive subjects, such as the way the West develops new aircraft, sensors, and advanced weaponry. Pilots who have entered the program have been sent to China for several months each year to train the Chinese pilots in courses such as "Advanced Fighter Tactics," "Fighter Weapons Instruction," and "Electronic Warfare and Tactics." For their work for only a few months a year, they have made "hundreds of thousands of dollars."[35]

This news was particularly disconcerting because China already had what was considered to be the largest Navy in the world with 355 ships compared to the U.S. Navy's 297 ships. China's Navy can be quickly expanded by the use of its large Coast Guard fleet. Its naval shipbuilding program has been building warships at an astonishing rate. In 2010, the U.S. Navy had 68 more ships than the Chinese Navy. According to a member of the U.S. Congress, by July 2021, it had 63 fewer ships, a swing of 131 ships in only 10 years.[36] The Chinese program put more vessels to sea between 2014 and 2018 than the total number of ships in the German, Indian, Spanish, and British Navies combined.[37] Many of the new ships were amphibious assault ships and landing craft that have no defensive purpose, but would be needed for an invasion of Taiwan.

Even more worrisome was the fact that for budgetary reasons, the Biden Administration was planning to have a fleet of only 280 ships by 2027, while China's Navy was expected to grow to 460 ships by 2030.[38] To put these matters in perspective, it is important to remember that just prior to the fall of the Berlin Wall and the dissolution of the Soviet Union, the U.S. Navy had 594 ships, and that America, like Great Britain, is fundamentally a maritime nation which relies upon the safety and security of the world's shipping lanes for the importation of critical materials; while China, arguably the world's strongest land power, is working hard to become self-sufficient in key commodities such as energy, food and minerals, and is seeking to dominate shipping lanes that have long been protected by the U.S. Navy.

It was further reported that China was expanding its network of overseas bases to Cambodia and the Soloman Islands in the South Pacific. It had been reported in 2019 that China and Cambodia had entered into a secret agreement which would permit the Chinese Navy to use a facility at Cambodia's Ream Naval Base on the Gulf of Thailand. The Solomans are not far from America's ally Australia and are near important commercial shipping lanes.[39] In December 2021, it was reported that China was attempting to establish its first permanent military presence on the Atlantic Ocean in the tiny Central African country of Equatorial Guinea. Such a development would raise the prospect that Chinese warships would be able to rearm and refit at a location opposite the East Coast of the U.S., giving China a critically important offensive capability.[40]

*   *   *

While China is clearly engaged in a massive effort to continue to rapidly modernize its armed forces in ways that will permit it to surpass the military power of the United States, there is also substantial evidence to suggest that it has concluded that economic and technological power may be more important than military power in establishing the worldwide power which it desires.

In a remarkable speech on July 7, 2020, Christopher Wray, the Director of the FBI, discussed in considerable detail the wide range of espionage and other unlawful tools being used by China in the U.S. in "a whole-of-state effort to become the world's *only* superpower." "The Chinese Communist Party," he said, "believes that it is engaged in a generational fight to surpass our country in economic and technological leadership." For years, it has been generally recognized in the U.S. that China is guilty of the theft of intellectual property, but the scope of its illicit activities and their effect on our national security is not understood. China does not want to engage in the time-consuming hard work of innovation; it seeks to make great leaps in cutting-edge technologies by targeting American "research on everything from military equipment to wind turbines to rice and corn seeds."

Wray urged the American people to understand that "China uses a diverse range of sophisticated techniques–everything from cyber intrusions to corrupting trusted insiders," and they have "pioneered an expansive approach to stealing innovation through a wide range of actors—including not just the Chinese intelligence services, but state-owned enterprises, ostensibly private companies, certain kinds of graduate students and researchers, and a whole variety of other actors…." The Chinese Government also uses the personal data of millions of Americans, which its hackers steal, to identify people for secret intelligence gathering. It uses social media platforms, "the same ones Americans use to stay connected or find jobs, to identify people with access to our government's sensitive information, and then targets those people to try to steal it."

One particularly egregious Chinese activity is a clear violation of U.S. sovereignty and in some cases, the constitutional rights of its victims. It has been reported that in 2015, the Chinese Government launched a campaign to repatriate overseas "fugitives" by any means. Chinese police officers have entered the U.S. and at least 120 other countries on covert missions to intimidate Chinese natives living here into returning to China. Beijing claims that more than 10,000 people have been repatriated.[41]

After describing other unlawful techniques employed by China, Wray's conclusion became very apparent and must be understood by all Americans, whatever their politics: "The greatest long-term threat to our nation's information and intellectual property," he said, "and to our economic vitality, is the counterintelligence and economic espionage threat from China. It's a threat to our economic security–and by extension, to our national security."

On July 6, 2022, Wray and the Director-General of MI5, Britain's counter-intelligence and domestic security service agency, conducted a rare joint news conference. China is engaged in "a coordinated campaign on a grand scale" that represents "a strategic contest across decades," the Director-General said. "We need to act." The same day, the U.S. National Counterintelligence and Security Center issued a bulletin which declared that the Chinese Government's efforts can threaten "the integrity of the U.S. policy-making process and interfere in how U.S. civil, economic, and political life functions." In a rare speech only three months later, the Director of Britain's

Government Communications Headquarters, the equivalent of the U.S. National Security Agency, expressed his own concerns. Calling the matter "the national security issue that will define our future," he said that China was aiming to use an array of existing and emerging technological means, including digital currency and satellites, to control markets and people, extend surveillance and censorship, and export its authoritarian system around the world.[42]

A few days later, a congressional investigation reported findings that showed "a sustained effort by China, over more than a decade, to gain influence over the [U.S.] Federal Reserve" banking system by using talent recruitment programs, which often included cash and offers to Fed employees of lucrative appointments at Chinese research institutes, all as part of China's efforts to obtain classified or proprietary information. U.S. counterintelligence officials said that the Chinese offers amounted to incentives to steal U.S. secrets.

A late but important first step to stem the tide of U.S. technology transfers to China was taken by the U.S. Commerce Department in October 2022 when it imposed new U.S. export control rules that prohibit U.S. citizens from supporting China's advanced chip development. Microchips are used widely in Chinese military weapons. The new rules apply to an array of chips and chip-making technologies. Remarkably, it was reported that at least 43 of the most senior executives working with or for Chinese semiconductor companies were U.S. citizens. Almost all of them "moved to China's chip industry after spending years working in Silicon Valley for U.S. chip makers or semiconductor equipment firms."[43] Ironically, previous efforts by the U.S. Government to get U.S. technology companies involved in addressing high priority national security problems, had not been noticeably successful.

* * *

Analysts who take the long view of geopolitical developments, such as a former Secretary General of NATO, recognize that the threat from China is about more than military hardware; that "From trade to technology, China is trying to rewire the postwar multilateral system to serve its own interests."[44] They also recognize that there may be another reason why China and Russia have moved so quickly in recent years to improve their relations and cooperation and have now entered into a strategic partnership that is, in all but name, a military alliance. That reason may be the time factor.

President Biden had hoped to steer relations with China toward "stable and manageable competititon."[45] But, it was not until May 27, 2022, that Secretary of State Anthony Blinken laid out the Administration's China policy, sixteen months after Biden entered the Oval Office. Blinken's speech reflected what has been called Biden's "liberal internationalism"[46] and his desire to defend the global order which the U.S. and its allies have built since the end of World War II. Few Americans would disagree with that objective but, a statement of American principles, no matter how lofty the objective may be, is no substitute for a clear statement of *actions* that must be taken to protect critically important U.S. interests, particularly, a rapid and broad buildup of all of its military capabilities. That is why the time factor must be considered.

There are several plausible reasons why China and Russia have moved so quickly to form their new "partnership." During the Obama and Trump Administrations, the two countries may not have felt sufficiently strong militarily to confront the U.S. and NATO. It is also possible that Trump was too unpredictable, and that in any event Putin hoped to do business with him in a second Trump Administration. For the reasons I have previously discussed, Xi Jinping may now have concluded that Taiwan is not Ukraine; that because the island is isolated it has no NATO neighbors from whom it could quickly expect massive aid; that Biden is too feckless and the American people are too focused on other problems at the present to support the use of America's combat power in the defense of Taiwan; and that if China does not subjugate Taiwan before the end of Biden's term of office, it may be faced with a much stronger American leader.[47]

There may also be other reasons why China and Russia may have decided to confront the U.S. and its allies sooner, rather than later. One view is that the leaders of the two countries recognize that "their power disadvantage relative to the U.S. and its allies will *worsen* unless they move soon, making victory increasingly unattainable;" that the U.S. Armed Forces "will require time to restructure and refit away from counterterrorism and toward high-intensity state-on-state great power conflict; that national cohesion across the West is too strained to support a war in defense of Taiwan; and that certain "internal pressures [are] building within Chinese and Russian societies" that make the future less predictable.[48]

Russia's war in the Ukraine is now more than a year old. The degree of China's future support of Russia in that war remains to be seen. On June 15, 2022, Putin and Xi conversed by telephone for only the second time since Russia invaded Ukraine nearly four months earlier. The public readouts of the conversation which were released by their respective governments diverged. The Chinese readout neither criticized nor endorsed Russia's invasion of Ukraine. Three days earlier at the conference in Singapore discussed above, the Chinese Minister of Defense had declared that "China has never provided material support to Russia" regarding Ukraine.

Even if the Minister could be believed, it was also fact that in the communiqué that was released after the meeting of Putin and Xi on February 4, the two leaders vowed that the "friendship between the two States has no limits" and that "there are no 'forbidden' areas of cooperation; that in a poll conducted by the Pew Research Center two months after Russia's invasion of Ukraine, Americans expressed acute concern about the new partnership between China and Russia, with nine-in-ten U.S. adults saying that it is at least a somewhat serious problem for the U.S., and a 62 percent majority saying that it is a *very* serious problem;[49] that Beijing had accused the U.S. of being the leading instigator of the situation in Ukraine; that China has expressed understanding for what Russia terms as threats to its national security, and that in the telephone call between the two leaders, "Xi reiterated his support for Russia in terms of security and sovereignty."[50]

Whether China will risk a war with the U.S. on any issue within the near future may well depend upon how eager Xi Jinping is to attempt to exploit whatever perception he may have of China's current relative advantages. One respected student of the conflict between China and the United States posed the following rhetorical question in the Preface of a book he wrote on the matter: "What is this book's Big Idea?" He answered the question this way. "When a rising power threatens to displace a ruling power, alarm bells should sound: danger ahead. China and the United States are currently on a collision course for war— unless both parties take difficult and painful actions to avert it."[51]

China has implemented a strategy...that aims at the heart of the United States' maritime power. It seeks to corrode international maritime governance, deny access to traditional logistical hubs, inhibit freedom of the seas, control use of key checkpoints....

Advantage At Sea
U.S. Maritime Strategy
December, 2020

Yes. That's the commitment we made.

President Joe Biden's reply to a reporter's question of whether the U.S. would respond militarily in the defense of Taiwan
May 23, 2022

Those that play with fire will perish by it.

Chinese President Xi Jinping
July 28, 2022

The complete unification of the motherland must be realized, and it will be realized.

Chinese President Xi Jinping
October 16, 2022

XIII.

CHINA: TAIWAN AND OTHER ACTS OF AGGRESSION

In recent years, as he has consolidated his power as China's supreme leader, Xi Jinping's actions and his rhetoric have become increasingly aggressive. This has been apparent in his unlawful seizures of the disputed territory in the South China Sea and China's One Belt One Road initiative, but nowhere more so than in connection with the relationship between China and Taiwan. In his July 1, 2021, speech at the celebration of the founding of the Communist Party, he emphasized that it is the Party's "historic mission" to bring Taiwan under Beijing's control and he vowed "resolute action" to "utterly defeat" any efforts toward what he called "Taiwan independence." At the opening of a Communist Party congress on October 16, 2022, he reiterated his previous threats: "The complete unification of the motherland must be realized, and it will be realized."

On October 1, 2021, China's National Day, a record 149 military aircraft, including nuclear-capable bombers and fighter jets, crossed into Taiwan's Air-Defense Identification Zone.[1] The U.S. State Department called the flights provocative and destabilizing and declared that they risked miscalculations and "undermine regional peace and stability." The U.S. Secretary of Defense said that "it sure looks a lot like rehearsing" for operations against Taiwan. The Admiral who was the head of the U.S. Indo-Pacific Command agreed with that assessment and added that it was a part of a coercive campaign to intimidate the people of Taiwan.[2] On October 9, Xi called for "reunification" of Taiwan with China and declared that "Those who forget their heritage, betray their motherland and seek to split the country will come to no good."

When the news broke at about the same time that U.S. Marines and Special Forces troops had been training Taiwanese troops, Beijing hawks, speaking through the *Global Times* newspaper, called the presence of U.S. troops on Taiwan "a red line that cannot be crossed" and warned that in the event of war in the Taiwan Straits, "Those U.S.

military personnel will be the first to be eliminated."[3]

When Taiwan celebrated its own National Day on October 10, 2021, its President Tsai Ing-wen declared that the country would not act rashly, but she stressed that "there should be absolutely no illusions that the Taiwanese people will bow to pressure. We will continue to bolster our national defense and demonstrate our determination to defend ourselves to ensure that nobody can force Taiwan to take the path China has laid out for us."[4]

And what is that path? And how did the dangerous situation in the Taiwan Straits, which are international waters, reach this point? For now, Xi Jinping seeks unification based on the Shanghai Communiqué of 1972 and under the same "one country, two party systems" framework which Beijing promised the former British colony of Hong Kong in the Sino-British Joint Declaration of 1984. The 1972 Communiqué between the U.S. and China recognized that Taiwan and China are both part of "one China," but the U.S. has always interpreted it as including an implicit endorsement of the de jure fiction that while China may "control" Taiwan, Taiwan's de facto independence must be maintained. In the 1984 Declaration, China also promised Hong Kong 50 years of self-governance starting on July 1, 1997, the date on which sovereignty of the island was transferred from the United Kingdom to China.

Very sadly, China did not wait even 25 years before it blatantly violated the promises to Hong Kong. In 2020, it imposed a sweeping new "national security" law on Hong Kong which has eviscerated its political freedoms. Since then, opposition politicians have been arrested, the Chinese Communist Party has taken control of Hong Kong's judicial system, independent news outlets have been shut, and other similar actions have been taken, all in the name of "national unity." An authoritarian government clearly is in Hong Kong's future. One can easily understand if Taiwan is unwilling to rely upon China's "promises."

China has also issued threats about Taiwan on matters unrelated to military matters. On May 23, 2022, President Biden announced a new 13-nation Indo-Pacific Economic Framework which includes Japan, South Korea, India, Australia, New Zealand, and much of Southeast Asia. Even though Taiwan is a technological powerhouse as well as a leading democracy, it was not invited to join the new economic cooperation pact because of a concern that it could anger Beijing. Instead, a week later, the U.S. announced a new and separate bilateral trade pact with Taiwan. A spokesman for the Chinese Embassy in Washington promptly declared that "China firmly opposes all forms of official interactions in any name or form between Taiwan and countries having diplomatic ties with China." He urged the U.S. to "immediately stop elevating relations with Taiwan in essence, stop any form of official interaction and contact with Taiwan and stop sending any wrong signal to 'Taiwan independence' forces."[5]

It is well known that China has been building a military force designed to overwhelm Taiwan's defenses with an amphibious and aerial invasion that includes amphibious assault ships and landing craft, neither of which are needed to defend China. It has also been reported that the force it is building is designed "to prevent the U.S. from rapidly reinforcing Taiwan with air and naval assets," that China has "a long-range missile force that could cripple U.S. bases and airfields in the region," and that those missiles "would also attack U.S. warships, including aircraft carriers, if they move within range to deploy U.S. fighters to defend the island."[6] There is thus no reason to doubt the prediction of Taiwan's Minister of Defense that China will be ready to attack Taiwan by 2025. The Chairman of the U.S. Joint Chiefs of Staff informed Congress on September 29, 2021, that "the Chinese are clearly and unambiguously building the capability to provide [the option to invade Taiwan] to… [China's] national leadership."[7]

The attempts by China to intimidate Taiwan into unifying with the mainland and to force other nations into its sphere of influence continues through a series of bloodcurdling threats, the massive buildup of its military power, the self-inflicted reduction of America's military power which is currently planned for the mid-2020s, and a range of dangerous military provocations. In February 2022, a Chinese ship directed a laser at an Australian maritime patrol aircraft, which was flying in international air space. On May 24, 2022, while President Biden was visiting Tokyo to meet with the leaders of Japan, India and Australia to discuss China's regional assertiveness, two Chinese H-6 bombers and two Russian TU-95 bombers flew over the Sea of Japan. They were subsequently joined by two additional Chinese bombers and two Russian jet fighters which entered South Korea's Air Self-Identification Zone.

*   *   *

Many Americans know little or nothing about Taiwan or how its dispute with China arose. A few historical facts relating to the current tensions between the two antagonists, and how those tensions involve the United States and the West, are useful to an understanding.

The great majority of Taiwan's 23 million people are ethnic Chinese. In 1683, Taiwan came under the loose administration of the Manchu Dynasty and in 1887, it became a province of imperial China. After the Sino-Japanese War of 1894-95, the Manchu Dynasty ceded the island to Japan, which ruled it for fifty years.[8] During World War II, China, then named the Republic of China (ROC), was led by Chiang Kai-shek and his Nationalist Party, the Kuomintang, or KMT. The ROC was an ally of the U.S. throughout the War. In early 1943, President Roosevelt decided that after the War, Taiwan should be returned to China and it was the ROC Army that took control of Taiwan from the Japanese after the war ended.

Matters deteriorated after Mao Zedong's Communists defeated Chiang's Nationalists in the Chinese Civil War and declared the establishment of the PRC. Chiang and his government retreated to Taiwan in 1949. It is significant that the PRC has never governed Taiwan. Until the 1990s, the leaders of both the ROC on Taiwan and the PRC on the Mainland asserted that Taiwan was part of the territory of the state called China. They disagreed over which government—the ROC or the PRC—was the government of China.[9]

When the KMT moved to Taiwan, Chiang Kai-shek imposed an authoritarian regime. The democratization of the island began with a shift from has been called "the hard authoritarianism of the 1950s and 1960s to a softer authoritarianism of the 1970s." A respected student of Taiwan's history has characterized its democratization as "a really interesting case of political change" because it "occurred peacefully. It occurred gradually. And it occurred in a Chinese society."[10]

The increased democratization that began in the 1980s included a series of constitutional amendments. The first popular elections for the legislature were authorized. New political parties were established. The freedoms of expression and assembly became widely exercised. Particularly interesting was a change in political self-identity. In 1992, an Election Study Center began conducting surveys that asked the public whether they were Chinese, Taiwanese, or both. In 1992, 25% said they were Chinese; some 17% said Taiwanese; the remaining 46% said both. By 2021, 63% of the respondents said

Taiwanese, some 31% said both; only 3% said Chinese.[11]

Today, Taiwan's economy and democracy are both strong. The Taiwan Semiconductor Manufacturing Company has emerged over the past several years as the world's most important producer of the sophisticated micro-computer chips which are in the billions of products which have built-in electronics, including vehicles, iPhones, and personal computers. More than seventy percent of the world's most advanced chips are now manufactured in Taiwan.

While democracy is in decline in many parts of the world, Taiwan's elections are clean, political rights are protected and the principle of democracy has broad public support. Its democratic system has been recently described as "vibrant and competitive" and it has "allowed three peaceful transfers of power between rival parties since 2000." Protections for civil liberties are "generally robust."[12] In a 2021 annual survey by the *Economist Intelligence Unit (EIU)*, an independent research and analysis business within the London media company that publishes *The Economist* magazine, Taiwan ranked as the eighth-strongest democracy in the world.[13]

*   *   *

In December 1954, the Sino-American Mutual Defense Treaty was entered into by the U.S. and the ROC (Taiwan). The Treaty was intended to secure Taiwan from a potential invasion by the PRC. It supported the ROC in its assertion that it was the only legitimate government of the whole of mainland China. In 1979, however, the U.S. and the PRC established diplomatic relations and in an act of dubious constitutional validity, President Jimmy Carter unilaterally nullified the Sino-American Mutual Defense Treaty.

After the breaking of full diplomatic relations between the U.S. and the ROC, the Taiwan Relations Act was passed by Congress. That Act does not guarantee that the U.S. will intervene militarily if the PRC attacks or invades Taiwan. It does, however, declare that "It is the policy of the United States…to consider any effort to determine the future of Taiwan by other than peaceful means, …a threat to the peace and security o the Western Pacific area and of grave concern to the United States …[and] to maintain the capacity of the United States to resist any resort to force or other forms of coercion that would jeopardize the security, or the social or economic system, of the people of Taiwan."

The Act further states that the U.S. "will make available to Taiwan such defense articles and defense services in such quantity as may be necessary to enable Taiwan to maintain sufficient self-defense capabilities."

For decades since that Act became law, American foreign policy regarding Taiwan has been based upon the concept of "strategic ambiguity," a policy which implies that the U.S. would intervene with its Armed Forces to defend Taiwan from China without actually making an official commitment. In April 2022, Abe Shinzō, the former two-time Prime Minister of Japan, argued for a change in the policy. "The policy of ambiguity worked extremely well," he said, "as long as the U.S. was strong enough to maintain it, and as long as China was far inferior to the U.S. in military power. But those days are over." That policy, he continued, "is now fostering instability in the Indo-Pacific region by encouraging China to underestimate U.S. resolve, while making the government in Taipei unnecessarily anxious."[14]

On May 23, 2022, President Biden added to the confusion regarding America's commitment to Taiwan. During a visit to Tokyo, he was asked by a reporter whether the U.S. would respond militarily in the defense of Taiwan if China attempted to take it by force. He answered with a blunt "Yes. That's the commitment we made." He had made another similar public statement in the last year.[15] It was not clear whether he meant to say that the U.S. would provide defensive weapons as it was doing in Ukraine, or that U.S. troops would be actively involved in combat operations to defend the island. Did he make the statement intentionally, or was he confused, or was his comment merely the latest instance in his history of verbal gaffes? As before, a White House staffer subsequently said that the U.S. policy on Taiwan had not changed.

U.S. policy on Taiwan was cast into further confusion by another Biden gaffe four months later. In an interview with CBS's "60 Minutes" program that aired September 18, 2022, the program's host asked the President whether U.S. forces would defend Taiwan if it was attacked by China. Biden replied: "Yes, if in fact, there was an unprecedented attack." Since he had emphasized several times that U.S. military forces would not fight Russian troops on Ukrainian soil, the host pressed him on whether the situation would be different in the event of an attack on Taiwan. "So, unlike Ukraine, to be clear, Sir, U.S. forces—U.S. men and women— would defend Taiwan in the event of a Chinese invasion?" the host asked. "Yes," Biden replied. Once again, a White House official subsequently found it necessary to declare that U.S. policy on Taiwan had not changed.[16]

At a conference in Singapore on June 10,[17] U.S. Defense Secretary Lloyd Austin informed the Chinese Defense Minister that the U.S. stance of recognizing, but not endorsing China's claim of sovereignty over Taiwan, was unchanged. In a speech to the conference, Austin declared that the U.S. commitment to the Indo-Pacific is "the core organizing principle of American national security policy," that it is "our priority theater of operations, the heart of American grand strategy," and "our center of strategic gravity." He further declared that "the rules-based international order matters just as much in the Indo-Pacific as it does in Europe." He also warned that Chinese ships and aircraft were acting with increasingly belligerent [and implicitly unacceptable] behavior and he specifically criticized an incident which had occurred on May 26. A Chinese J-16 fighter aircraft had maneuvered alongside an Australian P-8 maritime surveillance aircraft which was conducting a routine mission in international airspace. The Chinese plane had released flares and then positioned itself in front of the P-8 where it sprayed a bundle of chaff which had entered the P-8's engine.[18] The Australian Defense Ministry said that the dangerous maneuver had posed a safety threat to the Australian aircraft.

If President Biden's May 23 statement was intended as an expression of political will for the purpose of deterring China from attacking Taiwan, as some believed,[19] there were undoubtedly many others, including the leaders of China, who were not convinced that the statement was a "credible deterrent," i.e., a threat of unbearable retaliation" against China in the event of an invasion. It also left unanswered the question of whether the U.S. even has the means, i.e., the military capability to back up the statement. On that question, opinion is divided.[20]

The U.S. would have to deal with several major problems if it intervened in an armed conflict between China and Taiwan. They include the realities of distance, numbers, and economics. If China landed forces in Taiwan it could easily replenish and reinforce those forces across the narrow Taiwan Strait in an effort to seize control of Taiwan quickly. The U.S. would have to mover reinforcing ships, aircraft, other military units, munitions and other supplies for both its own forces and those of Taiwan thousands of miles. Some steps have been taken to position more U.S. forces within striking distance of China, but they are insufficient. On December 8, 2022, it was announced that Australia had agreed to permit the U.S. to build a staging ground in its norther territory at which munitions and fuel can be stored. Plans also include an upgrade to an existing Air Force base which will give it the capability of accommodating six U.S. B-52 bomber which carry nuclear weapons.

The numbers problem involves the great and increasing numerical advantage that China has in combat ships, vessels which would be critical in a U.S. defence of Taiwan. Historical evidence shows that in naval warfare, the side with the most ships almost always defeats a smaller fleet of superior quality ships. A study of 28 naval wars (or wars with significant and protracted name combat) dating back to the Peloponnesian Wars indicates that "25 were won by the side with the larger fleet."[21] Some assessments contend that by the end of this decade, China's fleet will reach 460 ships as the U.S. fleet, which is committed to missions all over the world, sinks to perhaps only 260 ships.[22] Moreover, a war against China's larger fleet would take place "on China's home turf, within range of the PLA's air and rocket forces."[23]

A third reality is the current weakness of the U.S. defense industrial base. As I have already noted and discuss again in Chapter XVII, it will take time to revitalize it. China has been on a crash program of military modernization for several years.

Because of new doubts about the reliability of the U.S. and a "[loss of] some confidence in American staying power in the region as a consequence of President Trump's unpredictable demands and President Biden's messy withdrawal from Afghanistan,"[24] Japan, Australia and South Korea, the U.S. partners in the Pacific, have taken modest stops toward rearmament. But their combined military power will not soon be significant. When it is, it is not likely to have much of an impact in helping the U.S. deter China from invading Taiwan. As one penetrating analyst put the matter: "Hedgehogs do not attack a dragon, and the dragon knows it."[25] There was also evidence that China had been closely monitoring the West's response to Russia's war in Ukraine so that if it decides to use military force against Taiwan, it will be able to copy some of the techniques employed by Russia to insulate its economy from injury by the predictable sanctions imposed by the international community.

Four months after Russia's invasion of Ukraine and the announcement of the new Russia-China partnership, isolationist sentiment among both Republicans and Democrats appeared to be rising in the U.S. Nevertheless, the American public generally also appeared to be more in favor of intervention if China invades Taiwan than it had been in nearly four decades. An October 2021 poll by the Chicago Council on Global Affairs found that while the idea of defending Taiwan was supported by only 28 percent in 2015, that support had almost doubled in 2021 to 52 percent. A majority of Americans said that they supported using U.S. troops to defend any ally—not just Taiwan—from an invasion, even if the invasion was being made by a major or nuclear-armed world power.[26] It remained to be seen if this state of opinion remained steady after the full nature of the new Russia-China partnership became more apparent.

*   *   *

China's increasing aggressiveness was also being manifested in a less noticed region of the world: the Arctic. Like the rest of the world, the Arctic was drawn into both World War II and the Cold War. German weather stations broadcasted reports to the Luftwaffe and the Kriegsmarine. German U-boats hugged the edge of the ice pack as they lay in wait for the critically important Allied merchant convoys on the northern runs. In the late 1940s, the Arctic skies began to be filled with "the contrails of long-range bombers, and later, the tracks of Intercontinental Ballistic Missiles, making the far north the strategic frontier of the Cold War."[27] In 1955, a series of radar stations—the Distant Early Warning system, or the DEW line, were constructed.

China's recent malign activities in the Arctic were preceded in August 2007 by an aggressive attempt by Russia to expand its territory there. It dispatched two mini-submarines on a 2.5-mile descent to the ocean floor under the North Pole as part of an effort to claim rights to the seabed which could be rich in oil and gas. The subs planted a Russian flag on the floor. In 2001, the United Nations had rejected a claim by Moscow to the ocean bid. Similarly, several nations objected to the 2007 operation as a brazen land grab. Canada's Foreign Minister declared that "This isn't the 15th Century. You can't go around the world and just plant flags and say, 'We're claiming this territory.'" But the world was on notice that the Arctic Region was very likely to be the venue for future land grab attempts by Russia and other ambitious countries.

The rapidly melting polar ice cap, which is the result of the Global climate change, is leaving the once impossible Arctic Ocean ice-free for longer periods, and the increasingly navigable Arctic waters have created new vulnerabilities for the North American continent and increased the possibility of future confrontation between nations which are located in or near the Arctic Region, and Russia and China, whose interests and values differ markedly from most of them. Those two countries already have more ice-breaking ships and Arctic ports than the U.S. While interest in the Arctic Region is not limited to littoral states, China has been rapidly increasing its presence in the Region declaring itself a "near-Arctic state." Its near-term Arctic focus appears to be on liquefied natural gas (LNG). It is speculated that the Region may contain as much as 30% of the world's undiscovered supplies of LNG.

China's longer-term interest is shorter shipping routes. The maritime shipping distance from Shanghai to Hamburg is approximately 4,000 miles shorter via Canada's Northwest Passage[28] than the southern route through the Strait of Malacca and the Suez Canal. To that end, China has been building icebreakers and taking other actions to build new shipping routes through the Arctic via a joint Chinese-Russian initiative called the Silk Road Economic Belt and Maritime Silk Road, which was launched in 2018. It is worth noting that in August 2012, a Chinese icebreaker became the first vessel to traverse the Northwest Passage even though China has not recognized Canada's claim of sovereignty over the Passage.[29]

In December 2020, the U.S. Navy, U.S. Coast Guard and U.S. Marine Corps published a new maritime strategy.[30] Noting that the U.S. is a maritime nation and that the world's oceans play "a vital role in America's national security and prosperity," the strategy declared that "China has implemented a strategy and revisionist approach that aims at the heart of the United States' maritime power. It seeks to corrode international maritime governance, deny access to traditional logistical hubs, inhibit freedom of the seas, control use of key chokepoints, deter our engagement in regional disputes, and displace the United States as the preferred partner in countries around the world."[31] The maritime strategy further declares that "China's aggressive actions are undermining the international rules-based order, while its growing military capacity and capabilities are eroding U.S. military advantages at an alarming rate, and that "we must maintain our critical military advantages."[32] On June 20, 2022, the Canadian Defense Minister declared that since Russia's invasion of Ukraine, "the threat environment has changed," that development has required Canada "to devise and develop [a] new chapter in continental defense," and that most of Canada's focus would be on the Arctic. She then pledged that Canada would spend $30 billion over the next two decades to help detect and track military threats from China and Russia in the arctic.[33]

Ten days later, the leaders of the NATO countries met in Madrid. For the first time ever, America's closest Indo-Pacific allies–Japan, Australia, South Korea, and New Zealand attended the annual meeting. At the meeting, the NATO leaders released an updated "Strategic Concept," the mission statement of the organization for the next decade. For the first time ever, the Europe centered alliance recognized the security threat posed by China. After acknowledging that "The Russian Federation is the most significant and direct threat to Allies' security and to peace and stability in the Euro-Atlantic area," the statement candidly addressed the systemic threats posed by China.

"The People's Republic of China's (PRC) stated ambitious and coercive polices," the Strategic Concept declared, "challenge our interests, security and values. The PRC employs a broad range of political, economic and military tools to increase its global footprint and project power.... The PRC's malicious hybrid and cyber operations and its confrontational rhetoric and disinformation target Allies and harm Alliance security. The PRC seeks to control key technological and industrial sectors, critical infrastructure, strategic materials and supply chains. It uses its economic leverage to create strategic dependencies.... It strives to subvert the rules-based international order, including the space, cyber and maritime domains. The deepening strategic partnership between the People's Republic of China and the Russian Federation and their mutually reinforcing attempts to undercut the rules-based international order run counter to our values and interests."[34] It was reported that current and former officials in the countries which attended the Madrid meeting, all democracies with market economies, see their security as entwined.

*   *   *

A major new crisis in U.S.-Chinese relations erupted early in the week of July 19, 2022, when news of a possible trip to Taiwan by Speaker of the House Nancy Pelosi was regrettably leaked. President Biden contributed to the crisis when, after a reporter asked him what he thought about such a trip, he replied that "the military thinks that the trip is not a good idea right now." Apparently sensing U.S. equivocation about the trip, a Chinese Foreign Ministry spokesman escalated tension by declaring that "Should the U.S. side insist on making the visit, China will act strongly to resolutely respond to it and take countermeasures. We mean what we say."

While the proposed visit would have symbolic significance, it was obvious that no new, significant foreign policy changes would be made and, in deference to the constitutional separation of powers between the Executive and Legislative Branches of the Government, the Biden Administration made no overt effort to prevent the trip. From the viewpoint of many Americans, the trip had a reasonable basis since Taiwan was a major trading partner of the U.S., and in 1997 the then Speaker of the House, Newt Gingrich, had visited Taiwan, as had several Members of Congress over the years, including some during the current year.

In a July 28 telephone conference between Biden and Chinese President Xi Jinping however, Xi ratcheted the tension to a higher level by telling Biden that the safeguarding of China's "national sovereignty" was the "unbending will of 1.4 billion Chinese people." In an obviously patronizing tone, he further warned Biden that "those that play with fire will perish by it." By that time, the U.S. could not afford to cancel the yet to be officially announced trip by Pelosi, or to otherwise permit China to dictate or block the travel destinations of U.S. officials. If it did, "China would notice that its bullying threats succeeded, and so would U.S. allies in Japan, South Korea, India, Australia and others in the Asia-Pacific region that worry about U.S. staying power."[35]

On August 2, still without any formal announcement, Pelosi landed in Taiwan in defiance of the Chinese warnings. The following day she met with the Taiwanese President and some of the island's legislators. She also issued a statement declaring "America's unwavering commitment to supporting Taiwan's vibrant democracy." Even though Pelosi had conspicuously failed to invite any Republican members of Congress to accompany her on the flight, some 26 Republican members of the U.S. Senate issued a statement which declared that Pelosi's visit to Taiwan was consistent with the long-standing U.S. policy of One China, which acknowledges—but does not endorse—Beijing's claims regarding Taiwan.

In addition to issuing several threatening declarations criticizing Pelosi's trip, China responded to it with an unprecedented showing of military force. Several Chinese Su-35 fighter aircraft flew over the dividing line in the Taiwan Strait which separates China from Taiwan. On August 4, China commenced several consecutive days of live-fire military exercises in six large maritime zones and their air space which encircle the island. The detailed coordinates of the zones announced by China indicated that they were in the vicinity of major Taiwanese ports. That fact confirmed previous speculation that China was positioning its forces as it would to blockade the island if a war developed, or if it decided to make a pre-emptive attack.

For years, U.S. military planners had assumed that if China did attack Taiwan, the attack would involve an amphibious invasion in which Chinese troops and weapons would be transported over the 100-mile-wide Strait, an operation which would be much more difficult than Putin's invasion of Ukraine and with which China has no experience. Recent wargames conducted by Washington Think-Tanks had indicated that the U.S. and Taiwan could defeat such an operation, but at great cost in lost ships, aircraft, and human casualties.[36]

The circumstances would be much different if China decided to quarantine Taiwan rather than to conduct amphibious landings. China's purpose would be to prevent Taiwan, which is dependent upon imported energy, from receiving the oil and natural gas which is required for its factories, power plants, and homes; to cut off the U.S. and the rest of the world from the 90 plus percent of the cutting-edge semiconductors that are manufactured in Taiwan; and to give China leverage in a crisis by forcing Taiwan's Government to submit without the risks that would be involved in an airborne and amphibious invasion and the subsequent street by street combat against an island fighting for its life. An article in English language in the state-owned Chinese newspaper *Global Times* quoted an alleged "mainland military expert" as saying that China's military exercises "should be viewed as a war plan rehearsal;" that "in the event of a future military conflict, it is likely that the operational plans [that were being rehearsed in the military exercises; would] be directly translated into combat operations."[37] When a reporter asked the Biden Administration about a U.S. response to the unprecedented and very aggressive Chinese actions, or at least a comment, the White House spokesman offered nothing more than the weak response that "We are monitoring the situation."

* * *

Within days, an increasing number of American security analysts were predicting a Chinese attack on Taiwan within the near future, perhaps within 18 months. It was reported that the CIA has concluded that Xi Jinping has ordered the PLA to be prepared to invade Taiwan no later than 2027. Noting the historical tendency for rising states to become more aggressive as they become more fearful of impending decline, and referring to Germany in 1914 and Japan in 1941 as examples, two informed observers asserted that because Xi's China was being fueled by a dangerous mix of strength and weakness, including soaring power ambitious and "profound economic demographic and strategic problems, it will be tempted to use its burgeoning military power to transform the existing order while it still has the opportunity."[38] The obvious danger, they alleged, is that "thanks to a mixture of inertia, distraction and simple denial," Washington was not racing to address the many security problems. President Biden's policies are complicating U.S. efforts to deter China. Noting that it took the U.S. six years to revamp its defense industrial base before World War II; that Biden had recommended that Congress cut the Defense Budget; and that what investments have been made "don't expand shipbuilding capacity or ensure that missile stockpiles remain high," military analysts have expressed concern that "China is likely to conclude that the U.S. views Sino-American competition as economic and political, not military, at least in the short term."[39] Biden had apparently not read the words of President Theodore Roosevelt in his December, 1904 Annual Message to Congress: "It is not merely unwise, it is contemptible," he said, "for a nation, as for an individual, to use high-sounding language to proclaim its purposes, or to take positions which are ridiculous if unsupported by potential force, and then to refuse to provide this force."

* * *

Before China had even completed its war exercises over and around Taiwan, informed critics were screaming that "The U.S. [was] running out of time to prevent a cataclysmic war in the Western Pacific;"[40] that in the near-term, China was likely to gamble big to reshape the balance of power before its window of opportunity closed;[41] that "A Sino-American war [could] escalate rapidly because it [would] involve technologies that work best when used first, including cyberattacks, hypersonic missiles and electronic warfare" and that "The side that is losing might decide to use low-yield nuclear weapons to turn the tide or force its opponent into submission."[42] The critics could not then know that only a few months later, China would take advantage of a U.S. vulnerability in its network of ground-based radar stations to aggressively expand a Chinese intelligence gathering capability. The incident, which the U.S. House of Representatives would unanimously later characterize as a "brazen violation of U.S. sovereignty," would be a large Chinese balloon carrying high altitude spying equipment the size of three buses, such as an array of antennas capable of intercepting U.S. communications and large solar panels for powering intelligence sensors. The balloon would spend at least a week over U.S. territory, including a one period of time where it would loiter over U.S. missile sites in Montana.

One foreign policy commentator observed that "What [was] utterly reckless about America's longtime China policy [was] not any single incident… [but rather] the strategic passivity and incompetence that blinded a generation of American political leaders to the growing threat of greatpower war in the Western Pacific;" and that "For many years China [had] moved toward a more assertive posture toward Taiwan as American diplomacy became more erratic and unpredictable—and as the U.S. and its allies allowed their overwhelming military superiority in the region to fade slowly away."[43]

The immediate problem was that "thanks to a mixture of inertia, distraction and simple denial," America's political leadership in Washington were collectively refusing to acknowledge the new national security realities.[44] They were still not taking the urgent action required to address the problem.[45] The U.S. Defense Budget has loads of money for future capabilities that might materialize in the 2030s, but that won't help win a war over Taiwan in this decade, wrote other commentators. "The fact that China faces an ugly long-term trajectory won't be much consolation if Beijing thrashes Washington and Taipei in the coming fight for dominance of the Western Pacific."[46] One Editorial Board stated the reality of the situation and the current weakness of our deterrence posture, by referring to future U.S. plans to build a new bomber this way: "The only military assets that change Beijing's calculus today are the ones that are ready to drop weapons tonight."[47] By late 2022, the U.S suffered another blow to its ability to deter a war with China when it was learned that as a result of its efforts over several years to modernize its nuclear forces, China now has more land-based intercontinental-range ballistic missiles than the U.S. The U.S. Defense Department has predicted that by the 2030s, and for the first time in U.S. history, America will confront two countries, namely Russia and China, who are major nuclear powers and who may well become adversaries, if not enemies.

The consequences to America if Taiwan should fall under the control of China were generally being described in stark terms. One analyst put the matter this way: "Allowing the island to fall would give the Chinese Navy unrestricted access to the open oceans, as well as effective dominance in the sea lanes of the western Pacific, through which more than three trillion dollars' worth of goods passes each year. It would also signal to America's democratic allies in the region—including South Korea, Japan and the Philippines—that the U.S. could not protect them. ***If Taiwan falls, we are in a different world, where the tide of authoritarianism becomes a flood."[48]

A worldwide alarm has now been sounded. When danger is announced so loudly, action must be taken at the risk of losing what may become unrecoverable. One scholar has described the threat posed by China in this fashion: "We now face a new period of superpower antagonism, this time with a foe much wealthier than the Soviet Union, but also one with no true ideology beyond brute nationalism. A *Pax Sinica*, should it come, promises to be the stuff of nightmares. America's foreign policy faces its most daunting challenge yet."[49]

> *States like [Iran, North Korea, Iraq], and their terrorist allies constitute an axis of evil, arming to threaten the peace of the world. By seeking weapons of mass destruction, these regimes pose a grave and growing danger. They could provide these arms to terrorists, giving them the means to match their hatred. They could attack our allies or attempt to blackmail the United States. In any of these cases, the price of indifference would be catastrophic.*
>
> **President George W. Bush**
> **State of the Union Address**
> **January 29, 2002**

> *If that was the last resort, yes.*
>
> **President Joe Biden's reply to a television interview question of whether he would use military force to prevent Iran from obtaining a nuclear weapon**
> **July 13, 2022**

> *The only thing that will stop Iran is knowing that… if they continue to develop their nuclear program, the free world will use force. You have said many times, Mr. President, that big countries do not bluff.*
>
> **Israeli Prime Minister Yair Lapid**
> **July 14, 2022**

XIV.

IRAN: NUCLEAR ARMED TERRORIST?

In 1979, the regime of Mohammed Reza Shah Pahlavi, the Shah of Iran, a strategic American ally since 1953, was collapsing under the pressures of what was becoming an Islamic revolution. The Shah had alienated many Iranians by his efforts to modernize the country in the 1960s and by his tyrannical style of governance. At the same time, many Iranians had become followers of the Ayatollah Ruhollah Khomeini, an elderly and obscure radical Islamic nationalist cleric who had been living in exile in Paris and Iraq.

U.S. relations with Iran began in the early 1950s when a newly elected Prime Minister declared his intent to nationalize Iran's oil industry, the majority of which had been controlled by British corporations. Cold War tensions were high and a power struggle ensued between the Shah and the Prime Minister. Concerned that the Prime Minister was moving Iran into the Soviet Union's sphere of influence, the U.S. and Britain supported a coup d'etat in August 1953 which gave the Shah unchallenged power. He established a pro-Western, secular, anti-communist government, but his secret police brutally repressed opposition to his rule.

In late December 1978, as developments in Iran were becoming worse each day, then President Carter's National Security Advisor informed Carter that the "disintegration of Iran would be the most massive American defeat since the beginning of the Cold War, overshadowing in its real consequences the setback in Vietnam."[1]

In early 1979, conservative Islamists forced the Shah into exile, leaving a caretaker government of managers and technocrats in control. In February, the Ayatollah Khomeini returned to Iran, was instantly installed as the country's new political and religious leader and began to whip popular discontent into rabid anti-Americanism. On April 1, Iran declared itself to be a theocratic republic guided by Islamic principles. Large numbers of the Shah's supporters were soon being executed daily after mock trials.

On May 5, 1979, Khomeini issued a decree which resulted in the establishment of an Islamic Revolutionary Guard Corps, a force that was designed to among other things, support revolutionary movements around the world. Sixteen years later, a political party and militant group named Hezbollah was founded in Lebanon. It is well known that the group opposes Israel and Western involvement in the Middle East and that it receives substantial financial support and training from Iran's Islamic Revolutionary Guard Corps. It is widely seen as a proxy for Iran. The U.S. has designated Hezbollah a terrorist organization.

The same may be said of Iran's support of Hamas, a group located in Gaza which seeks to establish an Islamic state throughout Palestine. When it was founded in 1988, its charter committed it to an armed struggle to destroy the State of Israel. The military wing of Hamas soon began sending suicide bombers to attack Israeli targets.

In November 1979, after it was learned that the Shah, now in Mexico, was dying from cancer, Carter permitted him to come to the U.S. on humanitarian grounds for medical treatment and refuge. The action outraged Muslim fundamentalists in Iran. Not long thereafter, in an egregious violation of international law, a mob of approximately 3,000 militant Iranian students who were loyal to the Ayatollah, some of whom were armed, stormed the American Embassy in Tehran, seized 66 Americans, who were mostly diplomats and employees of the Embassy, and three additional members of the U.S. diplomatic staff who were at the Italian Foreign Ministry. The students demanded the return of the Shah to stand trial, an apology from the United States, and the return of money and property located outside of Iran. Even after the U.N. Security Council demanded an end to the crisis in an unanimous vote, Khomeini refused all appeals to release the hostages, but weeks after the Embassy was stormed, he began to release non-U.S. captives, and all female and minority Americans, citing these groups as among the people who were oppressed by the U.S. Government.[2] One hostage was subsequently released for health problems, but 52 men and women remained in captivity.

Carter called the hostages "victims of terrorism and anarchy" and declared that "The United States [would] not yield to blackmail." As time passed, however, and diplomatic efforts failed to obtain the release of the hostages, the situation became humiliating and foreign leaders began to tell Carter that America's international standing was being damaged by his excessive passivity and failure to take effective action.[3]

In April 1980, Carter finally authorized a rescue operation. On April 24, eight helicopters flew from the aircraft carrier U.S.S. *Nimitz* (CVN-68) to a remote road which was being used as an airstrip in the Great Salt Desert of Eastern Iran. Severe dust storms disabled two of the helicopters which were flying with radio silence. The following morning the remaining six helicopters joined several C-130 *Hercules* transport aircraft at a landing site and refueling area. A third helicopter was then found to be unserviceable. Since a minimum of six was considered essential for the operation, the commander recommended that the mission be aborted. Carter approved the recommendation. As the remaining helicopters were being repositioned for refueling, one collided with a C-130 tanker aircraft and crashed, killing eight servicemen and injuring several more.[4]

In November 1980, Ronald Reagan was elected the Nation's 40th President. On January 20, 1981, just as he completed his twenty-minute Inaugural Address, the hostages were released. They had been held in captivity for 444 days, the longest hostage crisis in recorded history,[5] living in "deep uncertainty and fear, subjected to…beatings, threats of bodily harm and execution."[6] The former American Embassy building, which had served as a prison for the hostages, subsequently became an Islamic cultural center and museum and a symbol of the Iranian Revolution.

Thus, it was that the hostage crisis brought the United States directly into conflict with militant, political Islam for the first time.

*   *   *

Over the next two decades the U.S. attempted to engage with Iran, but little success was achieved. Two developments in 1989 would have important consequences thirty-three years later. First, Ayatollah Khomeini, who remained Iran's supreme leader, divided the world into three parts. He asserted that the West and the East were led by infidels. The third part was the Muslim-led but Western-harassed Third World. That same year, he exploited a deep vein of Muslim anger at the importation of Western values into Iran by issuing a "fatwa"[7] against author Salman Rushdie calling for Rushdie's death in response to his novel "The Satanic Verses," which Khomeini characterized as "blasphemous against Islam." Khomeini's edict was "the first time a Muslim militant had the audacity to apply an Islamic punishment deep inside the West."[8]

In 2002, international concern about Iran's nuclear activities increased dramatically. An exile group revealed that Iran had secretly built a facility in Natanz which was capable of enriching uranium for use in nuclear weapons as well as in civilian nuclear power reactors. After the terrorist attacks of 9/11 2001, the Bush Administration had placed a high priority on fighting terrorism and countering nuclear proliferation. There was great concern that these two dangers might merge into an ominous threat of nuclear terrorism. It was thought that two other countries which sponsored terrorist groups, namely North Korea and Iraq, were also pursuing nuclear weapons. President Bush sought to dramatize this risk in his State of the Union Address on January 29, 2002, in which he called the three states "an axis of evil" and warned Americans that "the price of indifference" to the threats posed by the three countries "would be catastrophic."

In October 2003, hope was raised when the foreign ministers of Britain, France and Germany and Iranian officials in Tehran issued a statement in which Iran agreed to cooperate fully with the International Atomic Energy Agency (IAEA) and to voluntarily suspend all enrichment activities. The statement was codified in the Paris Agreement, which was signed on November 4, 2004. The following year, however, Iran's newly elected President Mahmoud Ahmadinejad accused the Iranian diplomats who had negotiated the Paris Agreement of treason and he restarted Iran's nuclear activities.

Nevertheless, the Administration did not cease its efforts to engage the regime. In August 2005, it supported an international campaign which offered Iran a choice: economic aid and engagement or economic pressure. No agreement was reached and Iran's support of extremist groups continued to grow. Still, Bush continued what has been described as a "two clocks" strategy. It had two elements. First, the U.S. tried to push back the time when the Iranian regime would have a clear path to a nuclear weapon. Second, the Administration attempted to bring forward the time when public pressure would either cause the regime to change its nuclear policy by suspending enrichment or transform it into a government which was more likely to make the strategic choice to deal with the international community.[9]

In 2007, the U.S. Director of National Intelligence released the judgments of a National Intelligence Estimate which confirmed that Iran had a covert program to develop nuclear weapons. The program included covert nuclear weapon design, weaponization (including combining a nuclear warhead with a ballistic missile delivery system) and uranium enrichment-related work. That year and the next the United Nations, and then the European Union, imposed new economic sanctions against Iran.

* * *

By the time that Barack Obama entered the White House, American public opinion about Iran had been colored by several years of destabilizing activities by that country. As I noted in Chapter VII, in 1987-88, it had been necessary for the U.S. and six European allied countries to engage in naval and air operations to protect oil tankers from Iranian attacks in the Persian Gulf. Over the next several years, multinational maritime operations had been commenced to increase security in the Strait of Hormuz, a vital oil checkpoint in the Persian Gulf, and in other key waterways. At that time, some 30 percent of the world's seaborne oil supplies flowed through the Strait, which has an international shipping lane that is only two miles wide. Oil from Persian Gulf countries then accounted for 18 percent of the total U.S. crude oil imports. From time to time, as many as 13 Iranian Islamic Revolutionary Guard Corps Fast (attack) Boats would begin to swarm and come dangerously close to U.S. ships. Those activities continue to this day.

By early 2015, it had become clear that Iran was pursuing two objectives which posed a serious threat to U.S. allies in the Middle East and to the national security interests of the U.S.: a rapid development of nuclear weapons and an expansion of the Shiite Islamic revolution for the purpose of obtaining a conventional military domination of the Arab World. Iranian-backed Houthi rebels had seized control of the Government of Yemen, which had supported U.S. drone attacks on al Qaeda in the Arab Peninsula. In Syria, the Iranian leadership was in the process of saving the regime of Bashar al-Assad and his war against moderate, U.S.-supported rebels by sending in troops, weapons, and money, and by pushing their Lebanese proxy, Hezbollah to give additional support.

By the fall of that year, the Iranian problem had become worse. Desperate for some kind of foreign policy achievement, President Obama pushed through the UN a Security Council resolution which he had signed along with the leaders of France, Germany, Russia, China, and Britain, which approved a deal with Iran regarding its nuclear weapons program. Regrettably, the agreement (which was referred to as the Joint Comprehensive Plan of Action, or JCPoA) was, in the eyes of most people badly flawed even though it was believed at the time that "No international agreement in a generation [matched it] in strategic significance and geopolitical gravity."[10]

Obama knew that the agreement would not come close to receiving the two-thirds vote of approval in the U.S. Senate which the Constitution requires for all treaties. A majority of Congress, including all Republicans and some Democrats in the Senate, opposed the deal. A Pew Research Center Poll disclosed that the American public opposed the deal by a staggering 28-point margin. So, he refused to follow the constitutional requirement and signed the agreement using only his own limited executive powers. He was obviously hoping that the UN resolution would enshrine the JCPoA in international law, prevent any vote by the U.S. Senate, and tie the hands of any future President who might wish to withdraw from the agreement.

There were several reasons for the opposition to the JCPoA. Most importantly, it only placed temporary limits on Iran's nuclear activities. After 10 to 15 years, the agreement's physical constraints on fissile material production and most of its verification and enforcement provisions would expire. At that point in time, Iran would be permitted to expand its nuclear capabilities for the purpose of producing fissile material for nuclear weapons.[11] Like too many others, Obama apparently assumed naively and incorrectly that the Government of Iran was a responsible state and could be trusted when its leadership declared that it was developing nuclear power only for peaceful purposes.

By its terms, the deal removed all economic sanctions on Iran— the world's greatest exporter of terrorism—thus freeing up $100 billion in frozen Iranian assets, tripling the country's oil exports, and encouraging foreign investments. The deal legitimized Iran's nuclear program and by characterizing it as peaceful, made the country entitled to receive international financial assistance. The agreement also failed to address such matters as Iran's growing ballistic and cruise missile arsenal and its support for proxy militias in other countries in the region. It ended Iran's isolation even though the country's leader had declared that Israel would be wiped out within 25 years.

* * *

President Trump had strongly criticized Obama's agreement with Iran during his 2016 Election campaign. After he entered the White House, he reluctantly certified that Iran was complying with it, but he continually called for it to be renegotiated, In October 2017, he promised to work with allies to close the obvious loopholes, address the proliferation of Iran's missiles and other weapons, and "deny the regime all paths to a nuclear program." At the same time, newly acquired intelligence indicated that Iran had repeatedly lied to UN weapons inspectors about its previous nuclear activities.

In April 2018, it was becoming increasingly apparent that Trump was considering withdrawing the U.S. from the JCPoA. Critics argued that such a move would damage U.S. credibility, but the absence of Senate ratification made it only an Executive Branch or political agreement by a previous President, which was not legally binding on the current President. Hoping to prevent such a development, the President of France and the Chancellor of Germany travelled to Washington the same week to plead with Trump not to withdraw, to inform him that they believed that the current agreement was better than no agreement and that their countries remained committed to the deal even if the U.S. should decide to leave it.

Left unstated was the fact that European companies were benefiting from new commercial dealings with Iran. Trump was already unpopular in Europe, and it was obvious that a U.S. withdrawal risked a transatlantic rift between the U.S. and its European allies, who would be joined by Russia and China, the other signatories to the agreement. Nevertheless, on May 8, Trump withdrew the U.S. from the JCPoA, calling it "defective at its core." He declared that the U.S. would reimpose "the highest level of economic sanctions" on several of Iran's industries and that "any nation that [helped] Iran in its quest for nuclear weapons" might also be strongly sanctioned. But he also renewed his offer to negotiate a better agreement.

Tensions between the U.S. and Iran continued during the final two years of the Trump presidency. In April 2019, Trump designated the Islamic Revolutionary Guard Corp (IRGC)—a branch of the Iranian Army—a Foreign Terrorist Organization (FTO). It was the first time that the U.S. had designated part of another country's government as an FTO. Between May and October of that year, Iranian Fast Boats again attacked oil tankers in or near the Strait of Hormuz. In January 2020, the U.S. killed Qasem Soleimani, the Commander of the IRGC's elite Quds Force, with a drone strike. In November and December 2020, Iran moved to boost its uranium enrichment to 20 percent—far above the concentrations permitted by the JCPoA. It also vowed to expel International Atomic Energy Agency (IAEA) inspectors if the sanctions on its banking and oil sectors were not lifted within 60 days.

*   *   *

During the 2020 Presidential Election campaign, Joe Biden repeatedly pledged to reenter the JCPoA, but he indicated that it needed to be updated and broadened. He also said that if elected, his administration would continue sanctions on Iranian state institutions and senior officials for human rights abuses, support for terrorism, and the development of ballistic missiles. In an Op-Ed for CNN on September 13, 2020, he declared that as President he would "make an unshakeable commitment to prevent Iran from acquiring a nuclear weapon." In an interview with CNN a month after the Election, the President Elect declared that "The bottom line is that we can't allow Iran to get nuclear weapons." In remarks at the Munich Security Conference a month after he entered the White House, now President Biden urged "careful diplomacy" on the threat of nuclear proliferation, but he recognized that the U.S. "must also address Iran's destabilizing activities across the Middle East."

In June 2022, it was reported that Iran's nuclear program had entered dangerous new territory because the country "now possesses enough highly enriched uranium for a nuclear bomb. That material," the report said, "enriched to 60 percent, would need to be further enriched to roughly 90 percent—so-called weapons-grade uranium—before it could be used in a nuclear weapon. But that process, known as 'breakout,' will now take just weeks due to Iran's advances since 2019...."[12] The U.S. Special Representative to Iran noted that "Iran's capabilities have reached a point where Tehran "could potentially produce enough fuel for a bomb before we could know it, let alone stop it."

After seventeen fruitless months of trying to convince Iran to engage in meaningful negotiations on the nuclear issue, President Biden wrote in a July 9, 2022, Op-Ed that "My Administration will continue to increase diplomatic and economic pressure until Iran is ready to return to compliance with the 2015 nuclear deal."[13] Within days, the head of the IAEA declared that Iran's nuclear program was "galloping ahead."

Meanwhile, after years of focusing on Iran's nuclear program and targeting Iranian agents and proxies in places like Syria, Israel had concluded that Iran's nuclear program shouldn't be addressed in isolation from its much broader strategic objective of becoming the dominant or hegemonic power in the Middle East, a key element of which is the destruction of Israel. As a result, the Israeli campaign to thwart Iran's nuclear, missile and drone programs with a series of covert operations began to target a broader range of key targets within Iran itself, including individuals associated with its nuclear program, IRGC members who were engaged in kidnapping, assassinations, and other subversive activities in foreign countries, military bases, and weapons storage facilities.[14]

One analyst observed in July 2022 that in addition to the well-established fact that when the leader of a nation is in political trouble at home, he usually searches for foreign policy victories, another obvious reason that the Biden Administration was letting the periodic talks with Iran drag on so long was "the unappetizing consequences of admitting their failure. The definitive end of the Iran deal would almost certainly force the Administration to choose between accepting a nuclear-armed Iran and initiating a confrontation likely to culminate in another American war in the Middle East. Both courses of action entail unpredictable but large risks and costs."[15]

It was in this context that President Biden traveled to Israel on July 14, 2022. In an interview with an Israeli television channel that was recorded before he left Washington, Biden said that he would keep Iran's Revolutionary Guard Corps on the U.S. Foreign Terrorist list even if that killed any chance of renewing the 2015 Iran nuclear agreement. More importantly, he was asked if his past statements that he would prevent Iran from obtaining a nuclear weapon meant that the U.S. would use force against Iran. Biden replied "If that was the last resort, yes."[16]

In his own welcoming remarks to Biden the next day, Israeli Prime Minister Yair Lapid immediately went to the heart of the critical issue under discussion. "This year, with Russia's unjustified invasion of Ukraine," he said, "with the Iranian nuclear threat becoming more dangerous, and with the threats of terrorism worldwide, we are all reminded of something: To protect freedom sometimes force must be used. Nobody wants that, but neither can we shy away from it…. Words will not stop them Mr. President. Diplomacy will not stop them.

The only thing that will stop Iran is knowing that if they continue to develop their nuclear program, the free world will use force."

In words that suggested that he was thinking both of Obama's humiliating "red line" bluff in connection with Syria's use of chemical weapons and the incompetent way in which Biden had abandoned Afghanistan to the Taliban by suddenly rushing to withdraw the few remaining U.S. troops there, the Prime Minister indirectly addressed the unspoken issue of U.S. credibility. "You have said many times, Mr. President, that big countries do not bluff. I completely agree. It should not be a bluff but the real thing. The Iranian regime must know that if they continue to deceive the world, they will pay a heavy price."

Americans were reminded of the need to see Iran's nuclear push in a global context. The crisis with Tehran had come at an extremely beneficial moment for Russia and China. A real risk existed that as the economic consequences of Russia's war against Ukraine began to seriously affect Western economies and the threats facing America continued to grow, the cohesion at home and in U.S. alliances abroad would weaken.

Sure enough, almost as if on cue, two significant events occurred. First, within days of the meeting between Biden and Israeli leaders on the Iran nuclear issue, North Korea completed preparations for its seventh nuclear test and accused the U.S. of "dangerous, illegal, hostile acts" for conducting routine military exercises with South Korea. Second, in reaction to the visit to Taiwan of Speaker of the U.S. House Nancy Pelosi, China engaged in the dangerous live-fire military exercises around Taiwan which are described in the previous chapter. Those exercises disrupted commercial air and sea traffic and effectively imposed a temporary blockade around the island. Meanwhile, the war in Ukraine initiated by Russa continued unabated.

It was obvious that with respect to Iran, America's political leaders would have to "move beyond finger pointing and blame games over the fate of the JCPoA. Republicans [could] say justly that...Obama's decision to sign something as consequential and controversial as the Iran nuclear deal without the bipartisan support needed to get a treaty ratified in the Senate was a historic mistake. Democrats [could] reasonably riposte that...Trump's unilateral withdrawal made everything worse."[17]

Very regrettably, several developments over the previous 14 years had badly weakened America's credibility. Now, the man that would serve as the country's Commander-in-Chief until at least 2024 had repeatedly said that Iran would not be permitted to build nuclear weapons. Most informed Americans undoubtedly shared the view expressed by one foreign policy scholar. If the Biden Administration failed "to hold that line," he wrote, "the consequences for American power [and American honor he might have added] in the Middle East and globally would be profound and perhaps irreversible. If America [attacked] Iranian nuclear facilities and [found] itself stuck in yet another Middle Eastern quagmire, the effects at home and abroad [would] also be dire. China and Russia would take advantage of America's Middle East preoccupation to make trouble elsewhere, and U.S. public opinion would be further polarized."[18]

* * *

Suddenly, the number of options available to the U.S. had decreased dramatically. President Biden's comments about the use of force were typically vague, but the strong implication was that he meant military force since cyberattacks and covert intelligence operations were very unlikely to seriously interfere with Iran's nuclear program. If diplomacy was dead and the threat of military force did not appear sufficiently credible to Iran's leaders to deter them from rushing to "breakout," what kind of deterrent, if any, was left?

There were several other problems. A military operation would encounter many obstacles. First, the international community might not detect an imminent breakout in sufficient time to respond militarily to stop it. Some U.S. officials were of the opinion that Iran would need a "matter of weeks" to produce enough material for a bomb, but outside experts had estimated that it could be done in about ten days.[19] Second, there might be less than absolute confidence in the intelligence information upon which an order to make a preemptive attack on Iran would be based. It has been argued that "After Iraq, when flawed intelligence on Saddam Hussein's [Weapons of Mass Destruction] programs was central to the Bush Administration's case for preventive war, the United States would simply not get the benefit of [any] doubt. And doubt there would be in the absence of hard evidence of weaponization."[20] Third, over the years Iran had dispersed the sites of its covert nuclear facilities and placed many of them deeply underground. Fourth, the most likely weapon of choice for the U.S. would be the

Massive Ordinance Penetrator, a precision-guided 30,000-pound bomb which is purportedly, the weapon most capable of reaching the deeply buried Iranian nuclear facilities. That weapon would be carried by B-2 bombers based in Missouri. The flight time to Iran would likely be over 30 hours. The mission might well span several days since it would be necessary to target command-and-control facilities and radar and air defense sites, as well as Iran's dispersed nuclear infrastructure, making it what one analyst has called "the most telegraphed punch in history."[21] Finally, the proximity of the bombed Iranian nuclear sites to population centers might pose a radiological risk of unpredictable scope to thousands of Iranians.

* * *

In August 2022, the U.S. was shocked by two new Iranian provocations. On August 10, a Criminal Complaint was unsealed in a Federal Court alleging that an agent working on behalf of Iran's Islamic Revolutionary Guard Corps' Quds Force, the elite unit responsible for Iran's foreign operations, had attempted to assassinate John Bolton one of former President Trump's National Security Advisers, and a former U.S. Ambassador to the United Nations and senior State Department Official, by offering to pay an individual in the U.S. $300,000. The court document further alleged that the Iranian agent had also intended to assassinate another former U.S. Government official, purportedly Mike Pompeo, the former Secretary of State, Director of the CIA, and Member of Congress.[22]

Two days later, a 24-year-old New Jersey man rushed to the stage at the Chautauqua Institution and stabbed Salman Rushdie multiple times in front of a horrified crowd. In a brief interview, apparently while he was in jail, the man praised the late Ayatollah Khomeini and discussed his dislike of Rushdie. It was reported that a semiofficial Iranian foundation had posted a bounty of over $3 million for Rushdie's death.[23]

* * *

In the fall of 2022, President Joe Biden was confronted by a mine field of complex and very dangerous national security problems that would have severely tested the leadership skills, the political strength, and the will power of the best of America's previous Presidents. Tragically, neither Biden nor either of his immediate predecessors approached even the bottom tier of that grouping.

In the Ukraine, Russia's war of aggression was continuing and despite the high number of casualties, including hundreds if not thousands of innocent civilians, and the brutal destruction of cities, towns, and Ukraine's economy, there was no evidence that either belligerent was ready to negotiate. In October, it became clear that Iran was now Russia's most important ally, an active supporter of Putin's war against Ukraine, and a regional power with ambition to project at least its military power and influence beyond the Middle East. Russia had fired hundreds of low cost but sophisticated Iranian-produced drones, or unmanned aerial vehicles, at power plants and other parts of Ukraine's civilian energy infrastructure. One type of Iranian drone which was equipped with an expensive warhead, had a range of more than 1,500 miles. It was reported that since 2015, Iran and its proxies had carried out drone attacks on several other countries. Russia also announced in late October that more than 80,000 of the 300,000 new troops which had very recently been mobilized by Putin were already deployed to Iran.

As the conflict there dragged on, Russia's manipulation of oil and gas supplies to the coalition of European countries which were supporting Ukraine was challenging the coalition's unity amid fears in those countries that they would not be able to stockpile sufficient energy supplies for the winter months. German Chancellor Olaf Schultz, who had initially demonstrated great courage at the beginning of the war, was now continuing his recent vacillation in the delivery of weapons to Ukraine.

As the U.S. approached the important mid-term Congressional Elections, it was not at all clear that Biden would be able to convince Congress to maintain the current levels of political and military support and economic aid to the embattled Ukrainians and their needs were not expected to decline in the coming months.[24] Moreover, many Americans were more concerned about the immediate effects of inflation, an economy that was at least on the edge of a recession, border security, increasing crime, and other domestic matters, than with less tangible threats to the nation's security.

The confrontation with China over Taiwan had also suddenly become a dangerous and pressing security problem. To the surprise of many, a recent war game conducted by a U.S. Think Tank had concluded that the U.S. and Taiwan would be able to successfully defend the island from a Chinese amphibious invasion across the 100-mile Taiwan Strait, but at the cost of shattering Taiwan's economy and incurring the destruction of major units of the U.S. Fleet and other elements of its Armed forces, damage that "would take years to rebuild, with repercussions for America's global power."[25] Moreover, as previously discussed, there was considerable new evidence that China had learned from Russia's early setbacks in its invasion of Ukraine and had now changed its strategy to rely less upon an amphibious invasion and more upon a slow squeeze of the island that could develop into a blockade.

Decades of neglect had left the U.S. Navy too small to meet its global obligations, particularly in the vast expanses of the Pacific Ocean and particularly if America was required to fight and sustain a long war there, or elsewhere. A large part of the problem was due to the outdated and bureaucratized contracting process used by the Department of Defense for the purchase of weapons systems and their associated ammunition. "Fighting a war and running low on bombs is a bad place to be," wrote the Editorial Board of one distinguished journal, "as the Russians are learning, and the lessons from Ukraine are worth absorbing before China makes a play to seize Taiwan."[26]

A greater danger was the lack of resolve of the Biden Administration and Congress. The Senate Minority Leader declared in late September that if the Administration didn't move faster on the production and delivery of weapons systems to Ukraine "it [would] be an indictment on the persistent unwillingness to invest in our own military stockpiles and our defense industrial base." After all, "it is not true strength and resolve that provoke the bully. It is delay and weakness."[27] That is undoubtedly true, but the majority Democrats in the Congress also bore responsibility for the problem. On September 30, 2022, the last day of the Government's Fiscal Year, Congress had not yet authorized legislation to fund the Government's operations for FY 2023, which commenced on October 1. All it could manage was a short-term funding extension at current levels until mid-December to avert a Government shut-down. There was no certainty that a more comprehensive spending bill would be approved even then.

The regular problem of appropriating funds for our national security was not new, but it was clear that it had caused a lack of total confidence among important U.S. allies in the Pacific that America was engaging in crash programs and taking all necessary actions to immediately upgrade its ability to deter a war there. In their view, Presidents from both of America's political parties had "failed to back rhetoric and diplomacy with increased deployment of hard power,"[28] what one respected scholar and practitioner of international relations has called the indispensable military "ability to crush, maim, destroy, and kill."[29]

The legs of the negotiations between the U.S. and Iran on revisions to the JCPoA were also on the verge of collapse. It was reported that European Union negotiators had offered what was described as the final text of a revised version of the deal from which President Trump withdrew in 2018. It was also reported that Iran had rejected a central element of the proposal, namely, the requirement of an investigation by the International Atomic Energy Agency of the likely breaches by Iran of its nuclear commitments dating back to the early 2000s.

The situation was made worse by a new domestic crisis in Iran. Since September 16, protests had erupted and swept across the country in reaction to the death of a young woman who was in the custody of the Morality Police for allegedly violating Iran's strict Islamic dress code. Supreme Leader Ali Khamenei declared that "I say this clearly, …these riots were planned by America and the fake Zionist regime." By the second week of October, the unrest had turned into a larger movement as urban middle class Iranians, including workers in Iran's oil and gas industry, were expressing increasing anger with the country's deteriorating economy—due in no small part to U.S. sanctions that were targeting Iran's oil industry and financial sector—and to their frustration with Iran's rigid Islamic system of governance. Observers who were closely following the negotiations expressed concern that President Biden might agree to a deal "that would ease the hundreds of billions of dollars' worth of sanctions [against Iran] in return for time-limited nuclear pledges Tehran might not allow anyone to verify."[30]

The dangers of a rejection of the text by either side were succinctly described in an Op Ed: "Mr. Biden," the author wrote "would have to decide how to redeem his pledge that Iran will never be allowed to obtain nuclear weapons. Israel would probably ask the U.S. again for the bunker-buster bombs it would need to attack Iran's underground nuclear facilities. The deepening entente between Iran and Russia would make the President's options even less palatable because Moscow could choose to help Tehran respond to an Israeli or American air strike."[31]

* * *

In his memoir of World War I, Winston Churchill recalled the possibility of war between France and Germany after the Agadir Crisis of 1911. The crisis was triggered when French troops were deployed in the interior of Morocco and Germany responded by sending a gunboat to Agadir, an Atlantic port of Morocco, threatening war, and stirring up German nationalists. Germany's real objective was obtaining territorial compensation for France's expansion in Morocco, but the talks of war and the possibility that France and Germany might drift into war through the "ordinary platitudes of ministerial pronouncements upon foreign affairs," caused Churchill to reflect upon such dangers in his memoir with a warning.

> *They sound so very cautious and correct, these deadly words. Soft, quiet voices purring, courteous, grave, exactly measured phrases in large peaceful rooms. But with less warning cannons had opened fire and nations had been struck down by this same Germany.... It is nothing. It is less than nothing. It is too foolish, too fantastic to be thought of in the twentieth century....*
>
> *No one would do such things. Civilization has climbed above such perils. The interdependence of nations in trade and traffic, the sense of public law, the Hague Convention, Liberal principles, The Labour Party, high finance, Christian charity, common sense have rendered such nightmares impossible. Are you quite sure? It would be a pity to be wrong. Such a mistake could only be made once—once for all.[32]*

The Agadir crisis was resolved, after the Chancellor of The Exchequer, David Lloyd George, delivered a speech in which he declared that national honor was more precious than peace. The speech was interpreted by Germany that she could not impose unreasonable terms on other countries. Germany soon backed down and the matter was settled.

When our domestic politics have reached the precarious state in which they currently reside, the situation and the shortness of time demand that serious, responsible Americans of all political persuasions force the President and Members of Congress to finally use all of their political capital to authorize and appropriate whatever funds are required to immediately improve the U.S. tools of deterrence so that both America's honor and peace could be preserved. Will they ignore the inevitable and unrelenting criticism of the idealogues in one or the other of the political parties who are likely to be inflamed by the agitations of highly politicized journalists and activist members of the "news" (entertainment) media? It would be a pity if they failed to do so, and perhaps, a mistake that could only be made once.

*   *   *

And then, there were the problems caused by the rogue nation of North Korea....

> ...our country's nuclear war deterrent is...
> ready to mobilize its absolute power
> dutifully, exactly and swiftly....
>
> North Korean leader Kim Jong Un
> July 28, 2022

> The utmost significance of legislating
> nuclear weapons policy is to draw an
> irretrievable line so that there can be
> no bargaining over our nuclear weapons.
>
> North Korean leader Kim Jong Un
> September 2022

XV.

NORTH KOREA: INTERNATIONAL OUTLAW

Early in the morning of June 25, 1950 (Korean time), ten North Korean divisions in an armored brigade of the North Korean People's Army led by tanks and some 1, 613 large pieces of artillery, crossed the 38th parallel and marched into an unsuspecting and totally unprepared South Korea. Since the U.S. had withdrawn its troops from South Korea after the partition of the Korean Peninsula, Kim Il-Sung, the leader of the North Korean puppet regime, with the support of Soviet dictator Joseph Stalin, who was convinced that the Americans would not interfere, had determined that South Korea could be quickly overrun using the same kind of blitzkrieg operation that Germany had used so successfully when it invaded Poland in September 1939. The North Koreans used the main highways in the South and the rail systems to expedite their drive, which was very successful.

At the end of World War II, the Korean peninsula had been divided into two occupation zones. The northern half of the peninsula above the 38th parallel was administered by the Soviet Union. The U.S. administered the southern half. When the two major powers were unable to agree on the implementation of a Joint Trusteeship, the Communist Democratic People's Republic of Korea (DPRK) was established in the north in September 1948. The non-Communist Republic of Korea (ROK) was established in the south.

The Korean Peninsula was clearly an important backwater in the minds of the U.S. foreign policy establishment. On the order of President Truman, and over the opposition of U.S. military leaders, all U.S. forces had been withdrawn from South Korea in June 1949. Six months later, as I noted in Chapter IV, Dean Acheson, then Truman's Secretary of State, greatly increased the risks associated with the Peninsula. In an important speech at the National Press Club on January 12, 1950, Acheson defined the American "defensive perimeter" in the Pacific as a line running through Japan, the Ryukus, and the Philippines. Critics immediately claimed that the speech gave the DPRK a "greenlight" to attempt to forcibly unify the Korean Peninsula by implicitly declaring that the

U.S. would not defend South Korea. It certainly gave an impression of American indifference to the fate of the ROK.

On June 24, Truman had flown to his home in Independence, Missouri for the weekend. He had just finished a pleasant dinner with his family when the telephone rang in the hall. Acheson informed him of the invasion. It was agreed that the Secretary General of the United Nations would be immediately notified and asked to call a special meeting of the UN Security Council. During his flight back to Washington the next day, Truman reflected upon earlier events in his generation when the strong had attacked the weak. He would later write that he remembered "how each time that the democracies had failed to act it had encouraged the aggressors to keep going ahead." Whatever American mistakes had contributed to the invasion, if it "was allowed to go unchallenged it would mean a third world war, just as similar incidents had brought on the Second World War."[1]

At a meeting with his senior military and foreign policy advisors that evening, Truman solicited their views on an appropriate response. His biographer would later write that "the last thing Truman wanted was a war in Korea, or anywhere," but that he was determined "to do what he felt had to be done...."[2] Earlier that day, he was blessed with a stroke of luck. The Security Council had voted 9-0 in favor of a resolution declaring that a breach of the peace had been committed by the North Korean action and calling for an immediate cessation of hostilities and the withdrawal of North Korean forces to the 38th Parallel. The resolution had passed only because the Soviet Union had not exercised its veto power. It was boycotting the UN for recognizing the Republic of China as "China." No one expected North Korea to comply with the resolution. Truman would be criticized for not seeking a Declaration of War from Congress, but there was little political risk in not doing so since Democrats controlled both the Senate and the House. He would later refer to the conflict as a "police action," not a war.

The U.S. had no war plan for Korea. That was but a small part of the American problem. The drop-off between the strength of the U.S. Army as it had existed at the height of the World War, its sheer professionalism and muscularity, and the shabbiness of American forces as they existed in June 1950, was nothing less than shocking. As I write this, a similar folly by America's political leadership, if not as extreme, has taken place over the three decades since the end of the Cold War.

The first American troops who were airlifted to the combat zone in Korea from Japan were undermanned, poorly trained units with faulty, often outmoded equipment and surprisingly poor high-level command leadership, [and they] were an embarrassment."[3] In addition to leadership deficiencies, other weaknesses existed whose echoes can be heard today. Army Lieutenant Matthew Ridgway, who relieved General Douglas MacArthur as Commander of the U.S. Eighth Army in December 1950 after the Chinese entered the war and MacArthur was relieved by Truman, believed that a loss of fiber had contributed to the disappointing early performance of Army troops; that because of the country's ever greater materialism, it was becoming a place where people seldom walked anymore and its men were becoming softer every year; and that our troops had become too dependent upon their machines and their technology.[4] Despite these facts and the possibility that U.S. and other UN forces might be opposed by Russian and Chinese forces, Truman did not hesitate to commit the American troops. He would later say that this decision was even more difficult than his decision to use the atomic bomb on Japan.[5]

After China entered the war, the Truman Administration wanted to bring the Chinese to the negotiating table without investing significantly more resources in the conflict. Ridgway knew that task would be a bloody one—to make the Chinese pay so high a price that victory would seem as out of reach to them as it already seemed to the Administration.

Syngman Rhee, the President of South Korea opposed peace talks and wanted the ROK Army to drive all the way to the Yalu River in order to unify the country. Kim Il-Sung also wanted to unify the country, but by driving "the enemy into the sea." As a result, the conflict soon became a grinding war "of cruel, costly battles, of few breakthroughs, and of strategies designed to inflict maximum punishment on the other side without essentially changing the battle lines."[6] On July 10, 1951, talks concerning an armistice finally began.

Eleven days prior to the 1952 Presidential Election, Dwight D. Eisenhower announced that if he was elected, he would give top priority to ending the war in Korea. He further pledged to "always reject appeasement," because a foreign policy "is the face and voice of a whole people. It is all that the world sees and hears and understands about a single nation. It expresses the character and the faith and the will of that nation."[7]

The facts on the ground were not good and the conduct of the war to date by the Truman Administration had left the incoming Eisenhower Administration with few options. Through the first months of the Eisenhower presidency in early 1953, the armistice negotiations continued without success. Having been given a mandate by American voters to end the war, Eisenhower was willing to consider all possible courses of action to do so. At a meeting of the National Security Council only three weeks after he entered the White House, he "expressed the view that we should consider the use of tactical nuclear weapons."[8] There was no doubt that "Eisenhower was deadly serious. If compelled to wage a prolonged war in Korea, he would do so with one end in sight: victory."[9]

In the end, the new President decided on a course that involved both quiet public diplomacy and military muscle-flexing. Warnings were made that American patience was exhausted, that the U.S. had made its final offer at the negotiating table, and that "in the absence of satisfactory progress in the negotiations," the U.S. "intended to move decisively without inhibition in [its] use of weapons and would no longer be responsible for confining hostilities to the Korean Peninsula."[10]

Because of his military career Eisenhower did, of course, have considerable credibility on those matters. His personal credibility was enhanced by another factor. Only three days prior to his election, the U.S. had conducted the first successful test of a Hydrogen Bomb. It was not entirely surprising, therefore, that on July 27, 1953, six months after his inauguration, the Armistice was signed by the parties. It established a "complete cessation of all hostilities in Korea by all armed forces," but it was only a cease-fire. No agreement was reached between the North and South Korean Governments to normalize relations. Consequently, today, the Korean Peninsula remains one of the world's most dangerous flash points.

* * *

What has happened to South Korea during the almost seven decades since the signing of the Armistice is a remarkable story. In the first years after World War II, its government was characterized by incompetence and corruption. But slowly at first, and then at a faster pace, it developed room to modernize, first militarily, then technologically and industrially, and finally, politically. These developments have been characterized as "an odd mix of revolution with evolution, all taking place at an unusual rate of speed."[11] It now has the world's 10th largest economy, and it is an export powerhouse and a technological leader.

By the beginning of the 21st Century, the differences between South Korea and North Korea were stark. The government in the North had a rigid authoritarian structure imposed from the top down. It was a land without debate, discussion, or choice. As a society, North Korea "was like a living organism that simply could not breathe and …as it could not breathe, it could not grow."[12] Under the harsh leadership of Kim Il Sung, it had become "one of the most xenophobic places in the world," a land "frozen in a terrible monomania, …with only one man whose thoughts could be acted upon." Kim had always been referred to as the Great Leader. He created a cult of personality. According to an author who wrote about the two Koreas, there were at least 34,000 monuments to Kim in the North. He had become an international outlaw. He attempted the assassination of critics in South Korea and kidnapped people from the South who he believed could be helpful to him. As he aged, he seemed "to have two main dreams, first to develop an atomic bomb of his own, and second, to name his son, Kim Jong Il, as his successor."[13]

* * *

At his death in 1994, the first of Kim's dreams was fulfilled when Kim Jong-il became the second Supreme Leader of Nort Korea. Like his father, he ruled the country as a repressive and totalitarian dictatorship. In addition to increasing the political power of the DPRK Army and making it the central organizer of civil society, even at the expense of a large portion of the population which had great and often desperate needs as a result of a severe famine, he demanded absolute obedience and agreement from both his ministers and officials of the Workers Party of Korea and he viewed even a slight deviation from his thinking as a sign of disloyalty. Kim was also the focus of a broadly orchestrated personality cult similar to that promoted by his father. In 2010, the British newspaper *Sunday Telegraph* reported that even though much of his country was impoverished, Kim had $4 billion on deposit in European banks in case he ever needed to flee his country.[14]

In 1994, the U.S. and North Korea entered what was referred to as an Agreed Framework, which was designed to freeze and eventually dismantle North Korea's nuclear weapons program in exchange for U.S. aid and a promise that the north would not again be invaded. Only eight years later North Korea admitted that ever since the Framework was signed, it had been producing nuclear weapons.

In December 2011, it was announced that Kim Jong-il had died and that Kim Jong-un, his 28-year-old youngest son was the new Supreme Leader of North Korea. Since then, Kim has followed the precedent established by his father and grandfather, ruling North Korea as a totalitarian dictatorship, and building the same cult of personality. Kim is universally believed to be brutal, immature, provocative, and ruthless in killing potential political rivals. He has demonstrated particularly brutal methods of purging the Government of officials and executing other people who might be a threat to his regime.

Some of the reporting of Kim's purges and executions have been difficult to verify, but the alleged facts of many others are widely believed. It is undisputed that in December 2013, Kim Jong-un's uncle Jang Song-thaek, a leading official in the government of North Korea, was arrested and executed for treachery. Many believe that Jang was executed by a firing squad, but since a confirmed favorite tactic of Kim is blowing people away with anti-aircraft guns, some believe that was Jang's fate. Many members of Jang's family, including the children and grandchildren of all of his close relatives, were also put to death. According to the South Korean newspaper *The Chosen Ilbo*, a deputy security minister in the North Korean Ministry of People's Security was executed by flamethrower for his support of Jang. It is also considered almost certain that Kim sanctioned the death of his own half-brother who was sprayed in the face with a nerve agent.[15]

* * *

Of much greater interest to most of the world is North Korea's development of nuclear warheads and various types of missiles which can carry the warheads to short, medium, and even long-range targets. As President Obama was in the process of turning the responsibilities of the Oval Office over to then President-Elect Trump, he reportedly informed Trump that North Korea would be his most worrisome problem.[16] The country conducted its first nuclear test in 2006. Under Kim Jong-un, North Korea's development of nuclear weapons, including missile delivery systems, has continued at an accelerated pace and with each test, the nuclear explosions have grown in power lending credence to the Government's claim of having developed a Hydrogen Bomb.

For over a quarter of a century, various U.S. Administrations have pursued traditional negotiating techniques and imposed economic sanctions on North Korea, but they have floundered while searching for some way to prevent its continuing development of nuclear weapons. President Obama's policy of "strategic patience," which was very similar to the approaches employed by previous Presidents, was based on the false belief "that the status quo, while less than ideal, [was] better than many possible consequences of taking [forceful] action."[17]

North Korea is not in the same situation as countries like tiny Israel, which has been surrounded for decades by immediate neighbors who have attacked it and who seek its destruction. Kim's objective is not the survival of his country, but rather the survival in power of the Kim regime, i.e., a continuation of the Kim family business in perpetuity. While it is true that because of the many provocations by North Korea over a 70-year period and at the request of South Korea, the U.S. continues to maintain approximately 28,500 military personnel in the south, there is no evidence that the U.S. or any of North Korea's neighbors seek its destruction and none have attacked it since the 1953 Armistice. Nevertheless, Kim Jong-un believes, as his father and grandfather presumably did, that nuclear weapons are his guarantee of regime survival.[18] The nuclear program also has a second purpose: to bolster the strength and image of Kim.[19]

In 2017, the U.S. intelligence community concluded that North Korea already had between thirty and sixty nuclear weapons. In his first months in office earlier that year, President Trump declared that he was abandoning Obama's "strategic patience' approach to the rogue nation. He told a member of the Senate's Armed Services Committee that he would be willing to order a preemptive military strike to destroy North Korea's nuclear capability—regardless of the huge number of casualties in the region that would likely result from such an attack—if that's what it would take to prevent North Korea from reaching the point of development which many intelligence analysts had already accepted as a fait accompli. "If thousands die," Trump reportedly said, "they're not going to die here."[20]

When North Korea responded with new threats, Trump warned that it would be "met with fire and fury and frankly power, the likes of which the world has never seen before" if it did not stop threatening the United States. In a speech to the UN a few weeks later, he declared that the U.S. has great strength and patience, but that "if it is forced to defend itself or its allies, we will have no choice but to totally destroy North Korea. Rocket Man is on a suicide mission for himself and his regime."

Suddenly, a possible opportunity appeared. After meeting with Chinese leaders, Kim delivered a speech on April 20, 2018, to his Workers' Party's Central Committee in which he took credit for North Korea's acquisition of "the powerful treasured sword" of nuclear weapons. He then suggested that it was time for his backward country to focus on economic development. Not long thereafter, arrangements were made for Kim and Trump to meet in Singapore. The historic meeting, the first between a sitting U.S. President and a North Korean leader, took place on June 12, 2018. It only lasted a few hours, but with his usual hyperbolic language Trump described it as "fantastic," with "a lot of progress, really very positive." He predicted that he and Kim would have "a terrific relationship." He fawned over the young North Korean tyrant and bestowed upon him an international legitimacy he did not deserve by declaring that "We fell in love." Trump wrote on Twitter that there was "no longer a nuclear threat from North Korea."

As I noted in an earlier book,[21] that claim was subsequently repudiated by Pentagon leaders and U.S. intelligence agencies. At the end of 2018, the independent Center for Strategic and International Studies identified a secret North Korean ballistic missile base that is a threat to U.S. security. The Center also concluded that despite a promise from Kim to denuclearize, North Korea was not dismantling its nuclear weapons facilities.

Other critics, both liberal and conservative, were also very skeptical of the rosy view of the meeting with Kim that had been painted by Trump. They asserted that the President had sacrificed much of the U.S. leverage over North Korea by making a unilateral concession, namely, by agreeing to stop U.S. and South Korean military exercises, while receiving nothing more than a vague promise from Kim to denuclearize, a promise to which they attached very little value.[22] They pointed out that there was no record of North Korea ever having honored any international agreement and that Kim, his father and his grandfather had made previous pledges (in 1985, 1994, 2005, 2007 and 2012) to end or disable North Korea's nuclear weapons program, and that in each instance, the country had broken its commitment.

Critics of Trump's meeting with Kim were not limited to the U.S. In a book written by former Japanese Prime Minister Shinzo Abe before his assassination in July 2022, Abe declared that Trump was weak and overly anxious for a deal with North Korea. The former Prime Minister said that he was very fearful that North Korea would learn of Trump's dovish tendencies. Everyone should have been fearful of the steps Trump might have taken to fulfill his reported desire for a Noble Peace Prize.

Only 17 days after the Trump-Kim summit, U.S. intelligence agencies reported that North Korea was rapidly expanding a major missile-manufacturing plant and upgrading a nuclear research facility, strong evidence that the country never intended to fully surrender its nuclear weapons and was, instead, working to continue its concealment of the exact number and location of its nuclear warheads and secret production facilities.

In November 2018, North Korea repeated the demand it had made at the Singapore Summit, i.e., that the U.S. remove all significant economic sanctions as a condition for a continuation of talks between the two countries. On February 27-28, 2019, Trump and Kim met again in Hanoi. The American position continued to be that sanctions would not be removed until North Korea was fully denuclearized. In addition to other differences between the two countries, they could not even agree on exactly what the term "denuclearization" entailed. To Trump's credit, and despite the consistent concerns of some American officials that he might agree to something contrary to America's security interests in the hope of being awarded the Nobel Peace Prize, he announced at the end of the meeting that "Basically," [North Korea] wanted the sanctions lifted in their entirety. We had to walk away from that."

On June 12, 2019, Trump announced that he had received a "beautiful letter" from Kim. He praised Kim's leadership and suggested that talks between the two countries might resume. Less than three weeks later, at the conclusion of a meeting of the G20 countries in Osaka, Japan, Trump joined the South Korean President in a visit to the Demilitarized Zone (DMZ) to meet Kim. Never one to pass up a publicity opportunity, Trump accepted Kim's invitation to briefly step across the border separating the two Koreas, thus becoming the first sitting U.S. President to enter North Korea. No serious discussions took place at the meeting and the following year then presidential candidate Joe Biden accused Trump of "coddling" dictators while making numerous concessions for negligible gain.

Since that time, North Korea has continued its development of nuclear bombs and warheads. In recent years, it has also tested missile delivery systems of several ranges, including Cruise Missiles and Ballistic Missiles. The latter are barred by United Nations Security Council resolutions because they can attain intercontinental reach. It continues to take increasingly provocative actions. It has publicly supported Russia's invasion of Ukraine. It has also engaged in very dangerous cyberattacks against the U.S. for the purposes of stealing highly classified military secrets, billions of dollars in money and cybercurrency, and inflicting extensive damage on computer networks and our critical infrastructure systems.[23] Very regrettably, the outlaw nation has also ignored all attempts by the U.S. and South Korea to revive dialogue, including the Biden Administration's offers to talk "anytime, anywhere." The isolated regime simply repeats its demand that the U.S. unilaterally withdraw its "hostile policies," i.e., its military exercises with South Korea and economic sanctions.

*   *   *

In November 2017, North Korea demonstrated its capability of firing an Intercontinental Ballistic Missile (ICBM) which has the range to strike the U.S. mainland. In October 2021, it test fired a submarine-launched ballistic missile. In January 2022, and despite the fact that he was attempting to deal with his country's battered economy, food shortages and continuing COVID 19,[24] Kim Jong Un personally attended that final test launch of its new Hypersonic Missile, which is purportedly North Korea's top priority. As I previously explained,[25] a Hypersonic Missile flies in excess of five times the speed of sound, and because it flies closer to the earth than conventional ICBMs and can maneuver in mid-flight, it is very capable of penetrating air defenses and difficult to detect with defensive radars, track and shoot down. That technology is so advanced that Russia, China, North Korea, and the U.S. are the only countries working to develop it.[26]

In February 2022, it was reported that satellite images had identified a base in North Korea's Chagang Province, close to its border with China, which is likely intended for the stationing of ICBMs. Security analysts believe that the stationing of ICBMs so close to China is intended to make any pre-emptive strike against them very difficult because of the risk of hitting Chinese territory.[27] In March, North

Korea announced that it had successfully tested the Hwasong-17, a mammoth-size ICBM which can carry "several tons of payload over an intercontinental range—enough for a single, heavy warhead, or multiple smaller ones."[28]

Speaking to North Korean war veterans on July 28, 2022, the 69th anniversary of the end of the 1950-1953 Korean War, Kim Jong Un warned that he is ready to use his nuclear weapons in military conflicts with the United States or South Korea. In fiery rhetoric, he accused the two countries of pushing the Korean Peninsula toward war. In September 2022, he declared that his country would never relinquish its nuclear weapons. North Korea's Supreme People's Assembly, the country's titular parliament, also passed a law which established a first-strike nuclear policy by authorizing the Government to launch preemptive nuclear strikes and authorized North Korea's armed forces to use nuclear weapons "automatically and immediately" in case of an imminent attack against the country's leadership or "important strategic objects" in the country. In a speech to the Assembly, Kim declared that "the utmost significance of legislating nuclear weapons policy is to draw an irretrievable line so that there can be no bargaining over our nuclear weapons."[29]

In early October, North Korea initiated what was generally recognized to be a major escalation in is tension with its neighbors and the U.S. when it conducted a test of an intermediate-range ballistic missile which flew over Japan, reportedly disrupting airports, halting trains, and frightening the population below. It was the 23rd test of the year, the most ever, and the more than 2,800 miles it traveled was the longest to date. It was a reminder that North Korea was developing missiles that could reach U.S. cities and carry multiple warheads capable of evading missile defenses. In addition to a test of the missile, the exercise was a test of international resolve in any response that might occur. In his annual national address on December 31, Kim called for an "exponential increase" in North Korea's nuclear arsenal. An independent source was projecting that the country could have as many as 200 nuclear weapons by 2027. These developments were causing speculation that in light of North Korea's practice of sharing or selling technology, it is very possible that some of its nuclear weapons will come into the possession of terrorists or other rogue states.

The U.S. now faced the unprecedented prospect of living in a dangerous new world in which not one or two, but four adversaries are rapidly increasing their nuclear capabilities. It would only be a few weeks before Russia would suspend its participation in its last remaining arms-control treaty with the U.S. The only serious response that can be made is for the major Free World countries to engage in all credible military preparations which are necessary to deter the four countries from any further aggressive actions which could increase the possibilty of another major armed conflict. Only the leaders of the Free Worlds countries can effectively educate their citizens on the nature and severity of the new threats and persuade them to support the required deterrence measures. It remains to be seen if they will.

The responsibility of Ministers for the public safety is absolute and requires no [political] mandate. It is in fact the prime object for which Governments come into existence.
Winston Churchill
November 1936

Firmness based on a strong defense capability is not provocative. But weakness can be provocative simply because it is tempting to a nation whose imperialist ambitions are virtually unlimited. ***Our best hope of persuading [potential enemies] to live in peace is to convince them that they cannot win at war.
Presidential candidate Ronald Reagan
August 18, 1980

A woke military is a weak military.
Mike Pompeo
Former Secretary of State,
Director of the CIA and U.S. Army Officer
September 27, 2022

…the U.S. military is …rated as weak relative to the force needed to defend national interests … against actual challenges in the world as it is, rather than as we wish it were.
The Heritage Foundation
2023 Index of U.S. Military Strength

XVI.

INEXCUSABLE AND UNACCEPTABLE FAILURES OF LEADERSHIP

In Chapters I through XV, I have reflected upon the range of political approaches taken by U.S. Presidents with respect to their constitutional duties as Commander-in-Chief of the Armed Forces and their Executive Powers, by and with the Advice and Consent of the Senate, to make Treaties, appoint Ambassadors and other public officials, to conduct the foreign policies of the Government, and to otherwise "preserve, protect and defend the Constitution of the United States ," which necessarily includes the safety, the freedoms, and the other security interests of the Nation's sovereign—the people of the United States. I have focused primarily upon the threats to those interests from the regional adversaries which each President had to confront, or from the Soviet Union, the only formidable global adversary during the Cold War. Threats from other than major regional powers have, of course, existed and continue to exist and I address them in this chapter. But, except for another world war, from which civilization itself might not survive, it is regional armed conflicts that have the potential to require the use of all of the U.S. Armed Forces if world war is to be avoided and America's safety and freedoms are to be preserved.

I have noted the historic complacency, apathy, inattention, "procrastination, …half-measures, soothing and baffling expedients, [and] delays"[1] relating to matters of security which seem to inevitably follow the end of wars and other armed conflicts. That pattern, which the U.S. has very regrettably followed since the end of the Cold War, is not necessarily unnatural in the U.S. or elsewhere. After all, it happened in Britain after Hitler was defeated, but before the end of the war in the Pacific, when voters rejected the continued governance of the Coalition Government headed by a political giant named Churchill and replaced it with a Labour Government. It is self-evident that when wars end, or are perceived to be about to end, most voters prefer to shift defense spending to the welcoming lights of domestic spending.

But, it is important to remember that at the time of critical need in May 1940, when previous British Governments had neither the vision to see and understand the rapidly growing Nazi danger, nor the political will to do anything about it because the public appeared to be comfortable with the appeasement policies in place and were reluctant to demand the rearmament and other decisive actions that were essential, one bright beacon of realism and hope jolted them to their senses—that same Churchill.

In a previous book,[2] and in Chapter III of this book, I told the story of the circumstances in 1936 in which the courageous future Prime Minister articulated the principle which must serve as the foundation of any successful government. I will repeat the principle of that story here. *"The responsibility of Ministers for the public safety is absolute and requires no mandate. It is in fact the prime object for which Governments come into existence."*

It is in furtherance of this principle, and because of the absolute necessity that the U.S. clearly prevail in regional wars that endanger its vital interests, that I have paid particular attention to the performance of the most recent Commanders-in-Chief of the U.S. Armed Forces in making certain that those forces can achieve victory in all conflicts in which America may ask them to fight.

*   *   *

In the fall of 2022, Americans were worried, perplexed by the multitude of the many problems and chaos which surrounded them, and in many cases, just plain mad. Domestic concerns such as inflation, crime, border security, abortion, the instability and bearishness of the stock market, and the fear of recession dominated their thinking. Barely more than 25 percent of the public held the view that the country was going in the right direction. In a September 16 Gallup Poll, voters said that the most important problem facing the country was "government/poor leadership" and they expressed concern that political leaders were not putting the Nation's interests first. Voters generally had a low opinion of the Congress and both political parties, but most of their angst and disapproval was directed at the current occupant of the White House.

In order to see the latest cause of that concern, Americans only had to consider President Biden's actions regarding the U.S. Strategic Petroleum Reserve.[4] On November 23, 2021, he had announced that the Department of Energy had been directed to release 50 million barrels of oil from the Reserve, not for the kind of foreign policy and national security crisis for which the Reserve was established, but "to lower [energy] prices for Americans." Since the U.S. consumed almost 20 million barrels of oil per day in 2021, the November 2021 drawdown was hardly likely to affect oil prices significantly even if that had been a proper objective.

Over the next several months, Biden ordered additional drawdowns, all in an obvious but vain effort to reduce gasoline prices and win votes for Democrats in the November 8, 2022, midterm elections. His is the first Administration to repeatedly draw down the emergency oil stockpile over several months in an explicit attempt to lower prices at the pump. The latest drawdown was announced only 20 days before the elections and it reduced the stockpile to its lowest volume in 40 years.

During his 2020 campaign, Biden had called for unity in America. It was the theme of his Inauguration—"America United." He made several appeals to unity in his Inaugural Address: "We can join forces, stop the shouting and lower the temperature. For without unity there is no peace, only bitterness and fury." He had barely won the 2020 Election and a major reason was that he had received the votes of Independents and disaffected Republicans because he had campaigned as a moderate alternative to the candidates from the Left Wing of his Democrat Party. After he was elected, he made a 180-degree turn. One pundit described the turn this way: "Mr. Biden's moderate, 'normal' presidency didn't last past Inauguration Day. His switcheroo to progressive standard-bearer for the [Bernie] Sanders—[Elizabeth] Warren—[Nancy] Pelosi policy goals was startling."[5]

Four weeks before the important midterm elections in Congress on November 8, 2022, a national poll found that only 40 percent of Americans approved of Biden's job performance, a rating that was close to the 36 percent rating in May and June, which was the lowest level recorded during his presidency to date.[6] Another poll gave the Biden Administration negative approval ratings for its performance on national security matters generally and on immigration matters.[7]

There were several sound reasons for the lack of approval. One that was causing worry related to the Nation's unpreparedness for any war that might be forced upon us. A week after these polls were taken, the Heritage Foundation published its 2023 Index of U.S. Military Strength. The Index is published to help Government officials understand the state of the U.S. Armed Forces and the challenges facing the Nation. It assesses "the ease or difficulty of operating in key regions based on existing alliances, regional political stability, the presence of U.S. military forces, and the condition of key infrastructure." The condition of U.S. military power is measured "in terms of its capability or modernity, capacity for operation, and readiness to handle assigned missions."[8] The assessment of the current adequacy of the U.S. Armed Forces was based on the ability of the U.S. to engage and defeat two major adversaries in two regional conflicts at roughly the same time.

The conclusion of the Index was very disturbing: "[T]he U.S. military is at growing risk of not being able to meet the demands of defending America's vital national interests. It is rated as weak relative to the force needed to defend national interests on a global stage against actual challenges in the world as it is, rather than as we wish it were." The "weak" rating was the first in the Index's nine-year history. It was the logical consequence of "years of sustained use, underfunding, poorly defined priorities, wildly shifting security policies, exceedingly poor discipline in program execution, and a *profound lack of seriousness across the national security establishment* even as threats to U.S. interests have surged."[9]

The authors of the Index acknowledged that during extended periods of relative peace and prosperity, politicians become complacent and distracted and prefer to spend on domestic programs rather than investing in defense. They further admitted the obvious fact that winning the political support to make the essential increases in defense spending was, and is likely to continue to be, difficult. But, they pointed out, "this does not change the patterns of history, the behavior of competitors [read adversaries], or the reality of what it takes to defend America's interests in an actual war," or the historical fact that the U.S. has been involved in a major "hot" war every 15-20 years.[10]

All blame for this dangerous situation could not be placed at the feet of President Biden since at least twelve years of the continuing complacency occurred during the administrations of previous presidents. Both houses of Congress and both political parties were also at fault. But, astonishingly and inexplicably, the Biden Administration had responded to Russia's invasion of Ukraine, Putin's threats regarding his possible use of nuclear weapons, and China's increasing aggressiveness and its large defense budget, which has been rapidly growing for several years, by submitting Defense Budget requests to Congress over two successive years which called for significant *reductions* in inflation-adjusted defense spending over the next decade.[11] Nearly 40 percent of the House Democrat Caucus had voted to actually cut the Defense Budget by as much as 10 percent.[12] Fortunately, for the second year in a row a majority of the members of both political parties rejected Biden's proposed Defense Budget for FY 2023. The Senate Armed Services Committee added $45 billion. The House added $37 billion. Critics were quick to point out that even the $45 billion plus-up would not change the [planned] "U.S. trajectory of managed military decline."[13]

* * *

The dangers described in the 2023 Index had greater clarity when the overall assessment of each military service was studied in three areas: capability, capacity, and readiness. The evaluation of the services individually was considered to be the best way "to link military force size; modernization programs; unit readiness; and (in general terms) the functional combat power (land, sea, air, and space) that each service represents." The most important causes of the unacceptable ratings of the respective services were as dismal as the ratings themselves.

The Army score was "marginal" because its equipment is aging faster than it is modernizing. It remains "Weak" in capacity because it has "only 62 percent of the force it should have. The Navy was dropped from a "marginal" rating in the 2022 Index to "Weak." The new Index concludes that the Navy needs a battle force of 400 manned ships to do what is expected of it today. "The Navy's current battle force fleet of 298 ships and intensified operational tempo [i.e., days at sea conducting operations] combine to reveal a service that is much too small relative to its tasks. While the navies of potential adversaries, especially China, are growing in number and capability, the U.S. Navy will shrink further to only 280 ships in 2037 "unless Congress undertakes extraordinary efforts to increase assured funding for several years."

Because the Air Force had one of the oldest and smallest inventories of aircraft in its history (the average age of its Fighter Aircraft fleet was 32 years old), was short 650 pilots, and training flights had been greatly reduced because of a lack of resources, the Index gave it a rating of "Very Weak." Although it was considered that there is a chance the Air Force "might win a single Major Regional Conflict in any theater, there was little doubt that it would struggle in war with a "peer adversary." The Index concluded that it desperately needs to "increase high-end training and acquire the fifth-generation weapon systems required to dominate such a fight."

The new Space Force was rated as "Weak" because "there is little evidence …that it is ready in any way to execute defensive and offensive counterspace operations to the degree envisioned by Congress when it authorized the creation of the Space Force. The majority of its platforms have exceeded their life span, and modernization efforts to replace them are slow and incremental." The Space Force's current visible capacity was judged to be insufficient "to support, fight, or weather a war with a peer competitor." At a time when Vladimir Putin was threatening regularly to use nuclear weapons in Russia's war on Ukraine, the Index rated America's Nuclear Capabilities as "Strong" but trending toward a rating of "Marginal" or even "Weak."

*   *   *

Another contributing factor to the "weak" strength of the Armed Forces and to the low approval rating of President Biden was one of rapidly increasing concern to those who have to actually fight in the Nation's wars. This concern related to what appeared to be the wholesale embrace by many military leaders of the "faddish woke politics"[14] ordered by inept politically appointed members of the Biden Administration, few of whom had personal military experience, much less combat experience, and who had little or no understanding of the strict standards, absolutely essential requirements, character, intelligence, and important traditions that must be met to field a fighting force that is guaranteed to win our wars. The severity of this problem was reflected in a November 2022 survey of public attitudes and an earlier survey by another respected polling organization.[15] Only 48% of the people questioned reported having "a great deal of confidence" in the U.S. Armed Forces, down from 70% in 2018. When Americans were asked what was driving the decline, they responded that it was not the ability of the military to fight and successfully perform their missions, but rather a serious concern about military leaders becoming politicized and a lack of trust in the civilians who give the orders, including civilian leaders in the Department of Defense and recent Presidents. Half of the respondents complained that so-called "woke" practices were undermining military effectiveness. Denying reality, Pentagon leaders asserted that this was not a problem.

Combat, for which all military personnel must be prepared, is unforgiving. The standards and rules which govern military personnel are, and for centuries have been, different from those which apply to civilian society at large for obvious reasons based upon hard-won experience. Military units must necessarily be characterized by their unity and cohesion, high morale, and teamwork which assures that the people in the unit will always act with one purpose – the accomplishment of their mission. This fact, which is obvious to combat veterans, but apparently not to politicians who pander to special interest groups in order to be elected, has long been acknowledged, but was perhaps most eloquently expressed by Five Star General of the Army Douglas MacArthur, the recipient of the Medal of Honor and many other combat decorations.

In his "Duty, Honor, Country" Address to the Corps of Cadets at West Point in May 1962, he put the matter this way: "The soldier, above all other men, is required to practice the greatest act of religious training —sacrifice. [T]he soldier, who is called upon to offer and to give his life for his country is the noblest development of mankind. ***You now face a new world—a world of change. And through all this welter of change…your mission remains fixed, determined, inviolable: it is to win our wars. All other public purposes…will find others for their accomplishment. But you are the ones who are trained to fight. Yours is the profession of arms, the will to win, the sure knowledge that in war there is no substitute for victory; that if you lose, the nation will be destroyed…. ***{S]erene, calm…you stand as the Nation's war-guardian, as its lifeguard from the raging tides of international conflict."

Very regrettably, for several years, at least since President Obama issued his Executive Order 13583,[16] a politicized group of military leaders have incrementally and often imperceptibly, ramped up their focus, committed time and resources, lowered certain standards, and supported discriminatory policies like affirmative action in order to achieve the constantly expanding objective of diversity and inclusion in the Armed Forces. Apparently, they have never heard of the constitutional mandate of the "equal protection of the laws," or Title VI of the Civil Rights Act which bars recipients of federal funds from discriminating by race, or the historic, deeply ingrained, and critically important tradition of military personnel refraining from any engagement on political issues. They must be unaware that 74% of the American people and a majority of all racial and ethnic groups and both political parties, oppose affirmative action policies on matters like the college admissions process.[17] They must be less interested in the U.S. having the very best warriors in its Armed Forces that can be recruited and trained, than they are in advancing an unpopular social policy of dubious constitutionality[18] which reflects their personal views. Discussions of performance based upon merit and eliteness in military units have been rarely heard by the public in recent years. That emphasis, when combined with obviously insufficient Defense Budgets, has had consequences. Military recruitment and readiness for combat have been dropping significantly.[19]

One factor causing the severe recruitment problem is the fact that more than 75 percent of Americans ages 17 to 24 are not eligible to serve and the reasons for disqualification include obesity, addiction, and criminal history. A more disturbing factor is the self-evident fact noted by the Editorial Board of one respected journal that "teenagers taught to think America is a racist or imperialistic country won't wear the uniform," and that "young people with prospects won't join a military that looks more hollow all the time."[20] The 2021 Military Family Advisory Network Survey of more than 8,600 military families concluded that even veterans were becoming less likely to recommend that their children serve in the Armed Forces.

In an address on July 20, 2022, a retired Army General described the situation this way: "Woke ideology undermines military readiness in various ways. It undermines cohesiveness by emphasizing differences based on race, ethnicity, and sex. It undermines leadership authority by introducing questions about whether promotion is based on merit or quota requirements. It leads to military personnel serving in specialties and areas for which they are not qualified or ready."[21]

After discussing several specific examples of the enforcement of the ideology, the General closed with a disturbing warning. "The American military remains a faithful and loyal servant of the Republic. Most Americans are still proud and trusting of our military. But this trust and support cannot be taken for granted. If Americans perceive that the military is being exploited for political purposes or being used for experiments in woke social policies, that support will evaporate, and the consequences will be dire."[22]

In a September 28, 2022 opinion column, former Secretary of State and Director of the CIA Mike Pompeo, a West Point graduate and former Army officer, addressed the woke issue in this fashion: "How can we ask young men and women who have decided to risk their lives for America, even die for America, to affirm that our country is inherently racist? How can we ask them to view their brothers and sisters in arms through the narrow prisms of race or gender? The clear and obvious answer is that we cannot—not without putting their lives at risk on the battlefield. A woke military is a weak military."[23] Remarkably, only twelve days later at a press conference, and in a demonstration of either severe incompetence justifying removal from office, or an intentional avoidance of a reality which is apparent in the everyday experience of large numbers of military personnel and at least half of the American public, Biden's Secretary of the Army, a political appointee, claimed that the Army was not involved in the culture wars and that she really didn't even know "what 'woke' means!"[24]

*　　*　　*

The circumstances call for a leader who possesses the several characteristics which a highly respected close observer of world leaders has recently argued is essential for successful national leadership, including the intellectual capacity for a deep-thinking analysis of important American national security interests and the threats posed to those interests by Iran, Russia, China and other entities; an analysis which does not focus on "short-term tactical advantage," or self-centered politics, but rather on strategies which transcend the received wisdom of the time; the inspired leadership to have already spoken with candor, clarity, and even hardness to effectively educate the public about the harsh realities and the national security risks at stake, without entrusting the fate of America to "poll-tested, focus-grouped rhetoric."[25] But, at a time when the nation badly needs a leader who has these qualities and who commands broad, bipartisan popular support, there is none.

In 2022, the decisions of how to respond to the rapidly increasing possibility of a war with China and to the other serious national security threats confronting the U.S., was in the hands of a very flawed American President, a man who is inclined to talk tough, but whose recent proposed Defense Budgets and other actions had demonstrated that he did not really understand either the principle that relatively high defense spending represents good value for American taxpayers because combat is always far more expensive than deterrence, or that credible deterrence, manifested by stronger military capabilities than all existing or potential enemies, is only real guarantee of peace.

Joe Biden is a President whose failings have not been a secret. Robert Gates, the Secretary of Defense in the Obama-Biden Administration has described him as a politician who "has been wrong on nearly every major foreign policy and national security issue over the past four decades."[26] President Obama himself reportedly said to a Democrat supporter "Don't underestimate Joe's ability to f… things up," and to one of the Democrat presidential candidates in 2020: "And you know who really doesn't have it? Joe Biden."[27] Obama's former Deputy National Security Advisor wrote in his memoirs that "in the Situation Room," where critically important national security matters are discussed, "Biden could be something of an unguided missile."[28] Other senior aides in the Obama-Biden Administration described Biden as someone who was undisciplined, and who routinely males gaffes by blurting out whatever was on his mind.[29] Another Biden failing are the questions about his character that have persisted over decades because of several incidents of plagiarism and obvious falsehoods[30]—a matter which has inevitably raised doubts about his promises and credibility, not only among Americans, but also among U.S. adversaries against whom he has threatened the use of force.

*   *   *

In addition to the major threats to U.S. security in 2022 which have been discussed thus far, there were other matters relating to the Nation's security which were not likely to result in a major armed conflict, but which were nevertheless of rapidly growing concern.

The first matter involved the huge, continuing problem of illegal migration across U.S. borders, particularly the Southern Border. On October 21, 2022, the U.S. Customs and Border Protection (CBP) agency released new data regarding the wave of illegal migration during Fiscal Year 2022, which ended on September 30. More than 2.7 million enforcement actions had been taken against illegal crossers at the U.S.—Mexico border, more than a million more than the 1.72 million enforcement actions which had been taken in Fiscal 2021, which was the previous record. In 2021, the illegal migrants came from 150 different countries. Some 19 percent of the illegal migrants apprehended were repeat offenders, which clearly suggested that the American Border is "so porous that migrants will keep coming even if they are arrested once or more," because "They know they'll get through sooner or later."[31] Huge numbers of the illegal migrants had been permitted to remain in the U.S. while they seek asylum or pursue other claims in a Federal Immigration Court,[32] "a process that can take years to complete amid a backlog of roughly 1.9 million pending cases."[33]

In a speech delivered only six months after President Biden entered the White House, a former Acting Commissioner of the CBP declared that: "The …reality is that by incentivizing and facilitating illegal immigration, the Biden Administration is making it easier for drugs to pour into the U.S., for human trafficking to expand, and for criminal aliens to infiltrate our society."[34] In January 2022, the former Acting Commissioner declared in an interview that "Anytime you're so overwhelmed that you can't perform the fundamental national security mission to secure our borders, the result is that every aspect of our nation's public health, public safety and national security is being impacted."[35]

In June 2022, the Republican Members of the U.S. Senate Committee on Foreign Relations issued a report in which they declared that the illegal migration crisis "presents a grave security threat to the United States and a humanitarian catastrophe for the vulnerable people involved;" that transnational criminal organizations facilitate and profit off the smuggling and trafficking of migrants by exploiting "the porous borders, rough terrain and weak law enforcement throughout the region;" and that the "lax enforcement of U.S. immigration policies here at home weakens the incentives among [foreign] governments to address challenges posed by illegal migration in their own countries."[36]

In 2006, Congress had enacted the Secure Fence Act of 2006. The bipartisan legislation had the support of 80 of the 100 members of the U.S. Senate, including then Senator Barack Obama, who said in 2005: "We …cannot allow people to pour into the United States undetected, undocumented, unchecked, and circumventing the line of people who are waiting patiently, diligently, and lawfully to become immigrants in this country;" Senator Chuck Schumer, now the Majority Leader, who said in 2009: "Illegal immigration is wrong, plain and simple…. People who enter the United States without permission are illegal aliens and illegal aliens should not be treated the same as people who enter the U.S. legally;" and then Senator Joe Biden, who said in 2006: "Let me tell you something, ...people are driving across [the] border with tons, tons—hear me, tons of everything from by products from methamphetamine to cocaine to heroin, and its all coming through corrupt Mexico."[37] Coming only five years after the terrorist attacks of 9/11, the Secure Fence Act reflected the great worry by Americans that other terrorists could easily slip across the border. It was well known that a single terrorist could carry a weapon of mass destruction across the border in something as small as a suitcase and that others could simply bring their evil objectives in their minds.

But, immediately upon assuming office, President Biden used his executive powers to make broad and dangerous changes to existing immigration policies. Since voters in the 2020 Presidential Election had only given him an evenly divided Senate and a razor-thin majority in the House of Representatives, his actions were not only a stark reversal of his previous policy position for the obvious purpose of pandering to the Left Wing of the Democrat Party, they greatly exceeded his mandate. They also appeared to many people to be primarily an effort to reverse the immigration policies of the Trump Administration as a slap against the previous president and to use illegal immigration as a political weapon to attract "much needed Democrat voters."[38]

*   *   *

It is difficult for many Americans to understand how the Middle East and particularly Saudi Arabia, relate to U.S. national security interests. Except for terrorist groups such as Al-Qaeda, 15 members of which carried out the attacks of 9/11 2001, no Middle East state has the capability, much less the will to invade the U.S. homeland.

Saudi Arabia is the largest Middle Eastern country by area, while the most populous countries in the region are Egypt, Iran (Saudi Arabia's main regional threat), and Turkey. Since the 1920s, the unwritten bilateral relationship between the U.S. and Saudi Arabia has been based on security cooperation and strong business ties, particularly in the energy sector. The "implicit understanding [was] that the U.S. would ensure Saudi Arabia's territorial integrity and the kingdom would keep oil flowing to a global economy dominated by America."[39] Despite periodic tensions over Saudi Arabia's Islamic conservatism, monarchical rule, and human rights abuses, the relationship has survived 15 U.S. Presidents, 7 Kings, an Arab oil embargo, 2 Persian Gulf wars, and the 9/11 attacks.[40]

The U.S. is often described as a nation that relies on stable oil prices to sustain a healthy economy. For several decades, the U.S. purchased Saudi oil and in turn, Riyadh became the largest purchaser of U.S. weapons. In the Persian Gulf War of 1990-1991, the U.S. led the coalition which forced Saddam Hussein out of Kuwait and prevented Iraq from taking over the Saudi oil fields.

For years, the U.S. was dependent on foreign energy for as much as 40 percent of its needs, but by 2019, it was a net energy exporter. During the Biden Administration, the U.S. – Saudi relationship turned sour for several reasons. First, as one well informed student of Saudi Arabia has noted, "thanks to President Biden's suppression of domestic energy production in an effort to boost green energy, the U.S. this year is again a net energy importer…. The White House still puts domestic politics ahead of national interests."[41] Second, the [R]elentless pursuit of a chimerical nuclear deal with Iran [Saudi Arabia's main regional antagonist]–first by the Obama Administration and now its Biden redux–has left Saudi Arabia with no trust in its former partner and protector."[42] Two other factors are the U.S. charge that Saudi Crown Prince Mohammed bin Salman, the kingdom's young day-to-day ruler, ordered the murder of a dissident journalist inside the Saudi consulate in Istanbul in 2018, a charge which the Crown Prince denies, and Saudi Arabia's military intervention in Yemen.

Presidential candidate Biden poisoned the relationship in advance of his election in a November 21, 2019, Democrat debate in Atlanta when he distanced himself from the policy of the Obama Administration in which he had served, and attempted to demonstrate a greater concern for human rights than his Left-Wing Democrat opponents, Senators Bernie Sanders, Elizabeth Warren and Cory Booker. "I would make it very clear," he said, "we were not going to …sell more weapons to [the Saudis]. We were going to …make them pay the price and make them in fact the pariah that they are." Then in a final insult, he said that there is "very little social redeeming value in the present government in Saudi Arabia."

Whatever President Biden thinks of the Saudi leadership, it is critically important to U.S. security interests that the U.S. – Saudi relationship not be ruptured. The Saudis had reportedly declared that they could support Ukraine and work with Russia at the same time.

Should that happen, the sanctions imposed by the West on Russia could be undermined and sensitive security operations jeopardized. The U.S. and Saudi Arabia continue to share "an interest in Mideast security and oil supplies. With Russia, China and Iran all plotting how to take advantage of the U.S., which they view as a declining power, it's imperative that Riyadh and Washington try to restore their relationship through quiet and wise diplomacy."[43] The exclusive attention which the Biden Administration has given to democracy and human rights in the U.S. – Saudi relationship must be adjusted. As one former U.S. diplomat put the matter, "realism must trump idealism" because "a foreign policy based on such a preference in a world defined by geopolitics and global challenges is unwise and unsustainable."[44]

At the end of 2022, few people could see that a dramatic development which would shake up the geopolitics of the Middle East lay only weeks in the future. In mid-March 2023, the same week that oil industry executives announced that U.S. oil shale production is waning and that greater dependence in the future on foreign energy sources is certain, the Shiite Muslim nation of Iran and the Sunni Muslim nation of Saudi Arabia, entered into an important agreement which was brokered by China. Among other things, the two long-time antagonists and potential enemies agreed to reestablish diplomatic relations. It was believed by many that the Saudis had decided to seek alignment with Iran rather than conflict because they didn't believe that the U.S. would honor its pledge to prevent Iran from completing its development of nuclear weapons. Overnight, the agreement decreased the already waning American influence in the region and established China as a major power broker and economic force there, all in accordance with Xi Jinping's brand of diplomacy which does not require Western-style democracy or emphasis on human rights. It was unclear what impact the agreement would have on Iran's nuclear weapons ambitions.

What was becoming clear was that even though the Saudis were still seeking new security guarantees from the U.S., in repairing the damage that he caused to the U.S.-Saudi Arabia relationship, Biden would be wise to consider the response of Churchill, a long-time anti-Communist, to the invasion of the USSR by Germany on June 22, 1941. In a radio address to his nation that night, he declared: "No one has been a more consistent opponent of Communism [and opponent of Joseph Stalin, who in his Great Purge, was believed to have executed at least 700,000 between 1934 and 1939] for the last twenty-five years. I will unsay no word I have spoken about it. But," he said, "the Russian danger is …our danger." He later remarked: "If Hitler invaded Hell, I would make at least a favorable reference to the Devil in the House of Commons."

*   *   *

On October 27, 2022, the Biden Administration released its 2022 National Defense Strategy, a congressionally mandated document which is prepared every four years. Like those issued by other recent administrations, the Strategy predictably described China as the greatest threat to America's security because, in the words of Secretary of Defense Lloyd Austin, it is "the only country with both the intent to reshape the international order, and increasingly, the economic, diplomatic, and technological power to do so." Russia was described as an "acute threat." Those two countries pose the most dangerous threats to U.S. security, the Strategy document asserted, despite continuing terrorist threats, because both states "are already using non-kinetic [cyberwarfare] means against our defense industrial base and mobilization systems, as well as deploying counterspace capabilities that can target our Global Positioning System and other space-based capabilities that support military power and daily civilian life." Words and strategy documents are fine, but this strategy document failed to address in any detail the elephant in the room, namely the total failure of the three most recent Presidential Administrations to implement or execute strategies.

In a previous book,[45] I pointed out that most senior civilian defense officials are appointees who are selected for political reasons very often unrelated to real world executive and national security experience. And yet, they are responsible for the implementation of major strategies, policies, and programs and that requires a sense of urgency and "unremitting attention and effort."[46] Whatever the abstract merit of an Administration's strategy, its actual effectiveness will only be as good as the ability of its political leaders to *execute* it and to otherwise get things done. On the basis of many years of combat experience, one of the most decorated American general officers of the last century described this principle in a pithy fashion: "Any damned fool can write a plan," he would say, but "it's the execution that gets you all screwed up."[47] Jack Welch, the former highly successful and legendary Chairman and CEO of General Electric, wrote that successful *execution* of a strategy requires a leader to ensure *accountability*. "Being able to execute means a person knows how to put decisions into action and push them forward to completion, through resistance, chaos, or unexpected obstacles. People who can execute know that [success] is about *results*."[48]

The person who immediately comes to mind in this context is Max Aitken, 1st Baron Beaverbrook, Churchill's first Minister of Aircraft Production in World War II.[49] When Churchill became Prime Minister in May 1940, Hitler was planning to use Germany's superior numbers of aircraft to control the skies over Britain for an invasion. The new Prime Minister knew that Britain would have to produce large numbers of aircraft if it was to win what became known as the Battle of Britain. Beaverbrook energized the system of aircraft production. He was ruthless, ran roughshod over everyone and refused to listen to arguments that supply "bottlenecks" were interfering with production by requiring that any manufacturer who made such a complaint submit to him a daily list of each purported bottleneck, which he then proceeded to attack with his personal intervention. His changes bore immediate results and Britain's production rate for fighter aircraft was soon two and a half times the rate of Germany.

When the 2022 Defense Strategy was released, many former senior defense officials from both political parties and Members of Congress were already very concerned that the Biden Administration, and even future Administrations, might not be able to execute the Strategy in time. Worried about the U.S. ability to deter Chinese aggression over the next five years when its armed forces will be at their strongest point, but before the U.S. can produce the new technologies and armaments that will be necessary for effective deterrence, even a former Obama-Biden Administration official conceded that: "A critical piece of the deterrence puzzle is still missing [from the new Defense Strategy]: a focused Department of Defense-wide effort to dramatically accelerate and scale the fielding of new capabilities needed to deter China over the next five years."[50] Therein lay another major failure of the Biden Administration, one that may cause irretrievable damage to our national security.

Thus it was that as the severity of the external threats to American security continued to grow, the overall complacency of the Government, the failure of recent Presidents to seriously address the dangers, the bitter partisan divide in Congress, and the apathy and uninformed, self-centered isolationists in the Left and Right wings of the two political parties, caused one informed student of geopolitics to attempt to explain what he called the "dizzying collapse in the quality of our leaders. Across the West," he wrote, "we are led by too many inferior people who shouldn't be left in charge of a Lego set, let alone the entire edifice of national government. Governing had become a heavily performative exercise played increasingly by a cast of professional political figures who never made a payroll, donned a uniform, or created anything other than a sharply worded press release. All this is exacerbated," he said, "by the unseriousness of a media and political culture in which the demand for constant gratification is met by "owning" your opponent, always on the lookout to exploit some alleged grievance."[51]

* * *

Joe Biden is not the first President to misjudge the common sense and will of the American people to do whatever is necessary for the safety of the country if their leaders will only be honest with them about the costs of not doing so. Jimmy Carter had certainly made such a misjudgment with his defense policies. It is important to remember that during Carter's campaign for reelection in 1980, his opponent, Ronald Reagan, had been quite blunt about how he would deal with the dangers then presented by the Soviet Union. In an address to the Veterans of Foreign Wars, he declared that he would change the policies of President Carter that had badly eroded our military strength, through a major peacetime buildup: "America has been sleepwalking for too long [and] we have to snap out of it," he said. "You are in the forefront of those who know that peace is not obtained or preserved by wishing and weakness," he told the audience of veterans. "If we are forced to fight, we must have the means and determination to prevail, or we will not have what it takes to secure the peace."

He continued with language and a tone that are directly relevant to the circumstances in which America finds itself today. "Firmness based on a strong defense capability is not provocative. But weakness can be provocative simply because it is tempting to a nation whose imperialist ambitions are virtually unlimited. ***The American people," he said, "must be given a better understanding of the challenge to our security and of the need for effort and, yes, sacrifice to turn the situation around. Our government must stop pretending that it has a choice between promoting the general welfare and providing for the common defense. Today, they are one and the same. ***Our best hope of persuading [potential enemies] to live in peace is to convince them they cannot win at war.[52]

After he was elected, Reagan made clear in the famous speech to the British Parliament, to which I referred in Chapter VII, why it was so important to rebuild the Armed Forces. "Our military strength," he said, "is a prerequisite to peace, but let it be clear we maintain this strength in the hope it will never be used, for the ultimate determinant in the struggle that's now going on in the world will not be bombs and rockets but a test of wills and ideas, a trial of spiritual resolve...." America responded to the President's call and after eleven more years of the test of wills, the Cold War ended and the Soviet Union ceased to exist.

Four decades after Reagan's speech to Britain's Parliament, a new study of Britain's appeasement policies in the 1930s was conducted for the purpose of determining the important lessons to be learned from such polices. Three simple conclusions were reached. First, that free countries must "try to understand the world as it is, not as it was or as we wish it to be." Second, that they must "maintain alliances and the structures of international discourse and cooperation" because as Churchill once observed, "There is only one thing worse than fighting with allies and that is fighting without them." Finally, and most importantly, they must accept "the grim necessity of maintaining those levers of force, that 'arsenal of democracy,' that may act as a deterrent, may be deployed in humanitarian causes and, in the last resort, ensure our liberty and safety."[53]

In the summer of 2022, there was some hope that a consensus might be slowly developing in Congress that the situation regarding the new, complex and very serious threats to the Nation was not quite yet hopeless, and that several immediate actions were imperative, including much larger and targeted Defense Budgets in the near term and a dramatic and immediate ramping up in the production of key weapons and munitions so that America has adequate stockpiles and active production lines when the shooting starts.[54] Many well informed senior U.S. officials believed that "America's defense-industrial base [wasn't] up to the job of supplying the U.S. military with weapons for a prolonged conventional conflict with a major power such as China."[55]

These steps would obviously require the Democrat leaders who were then in control of both Houses of Congress to "build liberal Democratic support for the kind of military buildup and alliance diplomacy that is necessary to make Taiwan [and implicitly, the U.S.] more secure and war less likely."[56] Very unfortunately, all of these issues were put on hold as Members of Congress returned home to engage in heavy politicking for the midterm elections in November.

> *Security against foreign danger is one of the primitive objects of civil society. It is an avowed and essential object of the American Union.*
>
> **James Madison**
> **The Federalist No. 41, 1788**

> *The country has to awaken every now and then to the fact that the people are responsible for the government they get. And when they elect a man to the presidency who doesn't take care of the job, they've got nobody to blame but themselves.*
>
> **Former President Harry S. Truman**

> *It is "obvious an unarguable" that no government interest is more compelling than the security of the Nation.*
>
> **United States Supreme Court**
> **Haig v. Agee, 1981**

> *This Ukraine crisis that we're in right now… is just the warmup. The big one is coming. ***And that is a very near-term problem.*
>
> **Admiral Charles A. Richard USN**
> **Commander, U.S. Strategic Command**
> **November 3, 2022**

XVII.

A REPUBLIC IF YOU CAN KEEP IT

Writing shortly after the death of Queen Elizabeth II on September 8, 2022, a Member of the British Parliament declared that "When the tectonic plates of history move, the great living organism that is the House of Commons feels the shift."[1] At the end of 2022 it remained to be seen how much the current and future occupants of the White House, both Houses of Congress, and the American people would feel the shift from the historic developments in geopolitics which took place during the previous twelve months, including the sharp decline in world order and the international rule of law, how much they understood the many new dangers to America's security that had developed, and whether they would do whatever was necessary to protect the Nation from those dangers.

The year had started peaceably enough. In January, the Biden Administration and Democrat leaders of both Houses of Congress were still celebrating their control of all the levers of political power in Washington and the passage of a huge $1.2 trillion infrastructure spending bill. Using the full range of their political powers, they were now preparing plans for even larger social spending bills. Staffers in the White House and political appointees in the Departments and Agencies of the Government were continuing to work with intensity to recommend to President Biden major changes in the policies of former President Trump that might be achieved solely by the issuance by Biden of a wide series of Executive Orders, since in a very closely divided Congress, those changes were unlikely to be included in any new legislation.

Very few people, if anyone in the Government, were interested in discussing and debating, much less taking action regarding the increasingly dangerous national security threats to the Nation. After all, national security had hardly been a major issue in the 2020 Presidential Election among registered Democrat voters. Barely 42% of them thought that anything relating to foreign policy generally was important. Polls had indicated that they were most interested in climate change, abortion and contraception policies, health care, the public health impact of Covid-19, issues involving race and ethnicity, and immigration, in that order. Since the Democrats gained power in January 2021 and now had control of the White House, the Senate and the House of Representatives, the main focus of their attention had been an effort to establish in law the Far-Left policies of people like Senator Bernie Sanders and Elizabeth Warren, now favored by an energized and increasing number of Democrat voters.

Moreover, most Americans were not even aware of the many early warning signs about the growing threats to America's security that have been discussed in previous chapters here. No recent President had possessed enough political courage to bring these developments to their attention in a meaningful way, much less to explain why it was necessary to take unpopular and unwelcome actions, both to prevent the threats from becoming more dangerous and to deter additional threats, all for the purpose of avoiding devastating wars. Recent Presidents had elected to pander directly to their political bases, and indirectly to the uninformed, by kicking the national security can down the road for some successor to deal with.

This had all happened many times before, and in other countries. After the end of World War II, to cite one example, Churchill had written about the lack of common sense, foresight, and essential prudence which had characterized the British public before the War and "how the malice of the wicked [had been] reinforced by the weakness of the virtuous."[2] He had observed that "The multitudes [had] remained plunged in ignorance of the simplest…facts, and their leaders, seeking their votes, did not dare to undeceive them." ***No one in great authority had the wit, ascendency, or detachment from public folly to declare these fundamental, brutal facts to the electorates…."[3] He reminded his readers that "the structure and habits of democratic states…lack those elements of persistence and conviction which can alone give security;" that "no policy is pursued for even ten or fifteen years at a time;" that counsels of prudence and restraint can "become the prime agents of mortal danger;" and that the public's desires for a quiet life and their tendency to live "from hand to mouth and from day to day, and from one election to another," may be found "to lead direct to the bull's-eye of disaster."[4] He had later written that "One day, President Roosevelt told me that he was asking publicly for suggestions about what the war should be called. I said at once, 'The unnecessary war,'" Churchill's intense desire to prevent future generations from making the same mistakes had caused him to explain the Theme of the last volume of his monumental history of the War with these words:

*How the Great Democracies Triumphed,
and so Were Able to Resume
the Follies Which Had so Nearly
Cost Them Their Life*

*   *   *

In the last days before the important 2022 congressional elections in the U.S., Ukraine's Army was about to retake the City of Kherson, a port city and the only Ukrainian regional capital that Russia had captured since the February 24 invasion. Only a few weeks earlier Putin had declared that Kherson would forever remain a part of Russia. On November 11, the Ukrainian Flag was hoisted in the center of the City, giving Vladimir Putin his most consequential political and military defeat in the war to date.

Meanwhile, Russia was continuing to escalate the war by launching brutal waves of cruise missiles and Iranian-produced drones at Ukraine's power-generation facilities, heating equipment, and other elements of its civilian electricity grids, destroying half of Ukraine's energy infrastructure and knocking out power and/or water supplies in nearly half a million homes, leaving six million people without power. All of the destruction was done in the apparent belief that the Ukrainian people would eventually lose their resilience, their ability to deal with the mass suffering, and their will to resist Russian control. Russia was also threatening to target U.S. commercial satellites if they were used to help Ukraine and using food as a political weapon by threatening to prevent Ukraine from exporting grain through the Black Sea to global markets.

On December 13, it was reported that after months of urgent requests from Ukraine for better air defense weapons to protect the country from Russian missiles, the Biden Administration had finally overcome their caution and agreed to provide Ukraine with a single Patriot missile battery. Administration officials had previously balked at sending that weapon out of fear that Russia would see such a move as an escalation of the war, but they finally recognized that it is only a defensive system. Although that issue was eventually resolved, for far too long the same kind of timidity by the Administration and Germany had prevented the West from responding to Ukrainian requests over several months for heavy tanks. The Administration still refused to give to Ukraine the long requested Army Tactical Missile System and F-16 Fighter Aircraft.[5]

There were still strong signs that Russia was preparing to launch a major offensive against Ukraine in the spring followed by a long war of attrition, which would clearly be to Ukraine's disadvantage because Russia has a much larger army and 3.5 times Ukraine's population. In addition, Russia had mobilized hundreds of thousands of new troops in September and had recently switched from a peacetime to a wartime economy, which would permit it to greatly increase its production of artillery, ammunition, and the other materials upon which its military power was based. Ukraine had no such capability. Its military industries had been effectively destroyed by Russia's missile attacks. Its reserves of old Soviet weapons were almost depleted. Time was not on Ukraine's side. Biden's wishful thinking and overly cautious decision-making were increasing the danger to the country daily.

It was imperative, therefore, and clearly necessary to protect vital U.S. security interests, that the West immediately give Ukraine the tools needed to impose a decisive defeat on Russia sooner, rather than later. There was, as one group of observers caustically declared, "no moral or strategic case for giving Ukraine just enough weapons to bleed for months with no chance of victory."[6] It was true that Putin might threaten some form of retaliation against the West for the escalation of its support for Ukraine, but a "long and ugly stalemate in Ukraine would put Russia in a position to menace its neighbors for years to come, which would be even more costly for the U.S. and Europe."[7]

The only alternative to helping Ukraine achieve an early victory would be far worse and would involve unacceptable consequences for the U.S. A Russian victory would inevitably result in a U.S. loss of trust and influence with allies. Xi Jinping would be convinced that America would never risk war with China in order to protect Taiwan. A Russian victory in Ukraine would also leave it in control of strategically important areas in Europe and much of Ukraine's large agriculture sector and industry. In order to prevent further Russian aggression in Europe, the U.S. would have to continue to focus great attention on that area and to send weapons and other important resources there that are badly needed to beef up the U.S. ability not only to deter China from further aggressions against Taiwan or U.S. interests elsewhere, but to win any war with China that cannot be avoided. The economic costs to the U.S. alone would be immeasurable.

The same month, Ukraine's Prime Minister Zelensky spoke to the G20 group of nations and indirectly proposed a negotiation process that would involve the West sending more sophisticated weapons to Ukraine; the protection of Ukraine's energy infrastructure; and a convening of a Global Peace Formula Summit at which other matters could be discussed. On December 13, Russia dismissed the proposal out of hand and its spokesman declared that Ukraine needed to accept the new territorial "realities."

There were no other prospects for negotiations to end the war. On the basis of information obtained from a former Russian intelligence officer and current and former U.S. and European officials, it was reported that Putin has an almost mystical belief that Russia is a 1,000 year old civilization "waging a holy struggle that will right historical wrongs and elevate him into a pantheon of conquering czarist leaders such as Peter the Great."[8] He also still believed that the people in the West would eventually tire and stop their support of Ukraine permitting him to achieve victory. Zelensky saw no reason to negotiate in view of Ukraine's recent gains on the battlefield, and in light of the savagery which the innocent people of Ukraine had suffered at the hands of Putin's brutal government and the sacrifices they had made, he could never agree to give up Ukrainian territory to purchase peace. There were other reasons not to negotiate at that time. Any cease fire during negotiations would give Russia an opportunity to regroup, strengthen supply lines, reinforce its defensive positions, and prepare men, equipment, and munitions for renewed ground attacks. For several reasons, a rushed, premature settlement might well be worse than no settlement at all. Still, Ukraine's continued success on the battlefield depended upon the capability and willingness of Western governments to continue their multibillion-dollar military assistance to Ukraine in a war in which the end could not yet be seen.

Very regrettably, at a Pentagon news conference on November 16, while giving lip service to the Biden Administration's policy that Ukraine would make all decisions relating to negotiations, if any, and not the U.S. or NATO, Army General Mark Milley, the Chairman of the Joint Chiefs of Staff, once again injected himself into political matters beyond his jurisdiction by suggesting a potential winter lull in the fighting might be a good time for Ukraine to consider negotiations. At the same time, however, former British Prime Minister Boris Johnson was asserting that "There is nothing to negotiate. ***[Y]ou can't negotiate," he said "with a murderous liar who will continue—whatever he may claim—to try to destroy your country. So, let's get real…there is only one possible set of circumstances in which a negotiation could take place—and that is when Mr. Putin has failed."[9]

* * *

Freshly emboldened by being given a third five-year term at the Chinese Communist Party's 20th National Party Congress, at which he warned attendees that "The world has entered a period of turbulence and transformation" and that China must be prepared for "dangerous storms," Xi Jinping was busy replacing senior members of the Chinese Government and Communist Party with loyal sycophants, most of them drawn from the military and security organizations, and officials with technical expertise in artificial intelligence, aerospace engineering, and other strategically important fields that would enable China to become a technology superpower. As a result, there now appeared to be no checks on Xi's power within the Chinese system. He was also engaging in a flurry of diplomatic activity by hosting meetings with senior representatives of several countries. This included Germany's Chancellor Olaf Scholz, who went to Beijing seeking new business deals with China despite political pressure back home in Germany for him to reduce Germany's economic dependence on China and to generally adopt a tougher stance with that country. Xi was also forging stronger economic ties with Russia and enabling Putin to sustain his war in Ukraine, by increasing Chinese imports of Russian oil and gas, increasing Chinese investment in Russia's railways and ports, and refusing to join Western sanctions against Russia.

On November 14, President Biden and Xi Jinping had their first-in-person meeting since Biden became President. There was every reason to believe that Xi saw the meeting as an opportunity to size up Biden's ability and toughness. He was presumably aware of the fact that a poll of registered American voters had found that more than half of the electorate believed that the soon to be 80 year old American President lacked "the mental capacity to effectively serve as President."[10] It was reported that consistent with his previous assertions that "the East is rising, and the West is declining," Xi told Biden that Taiwanese independence was as incompatible to peace and stability in the Taiwan Strait as "fire and water."[11] There were reports that Biden raised the issue of climate change, but observers did not believe that he raised the subject of China's continuing violation of international law in the seizure and militarization of islands in the South China Sea.

Unfortunately, at the same November 16 Pentagon news conference noted above, General Milley also left the impression that in an armed conflict with China over Taiwan, the U.S. could easily prevail. Noting again that China is the greatest geopolitical challenge to America and that it seeks to be militarily superior to the U.S. within the next five years, he boasted that "The U.S. military is, without question, ... the most lethal war fighting machine on earth, bar none," and that "We intend to stay Number One." That comment, while accurate to a limited degree, was, for the reasons I discussed in Chapter XIII, misleading in two ways. First, in the implied context of a war initiated by China against Taiwan. In such a conflict, China would likely quarantine Taiwan rather than engage in an amphibious invasion and the U.S. would be forced to attempt to break the quarantine. In that event, China would be able to rapidly reinforce its quarantine forces across the narrow Taiwan Strait, while the U.S. would have to support its forces in the conflict from bases thousands of miles away. Second, it didn't address the huge problems the badly under resourced U.S. Armed Forces would face if it became necessary for them to fight major armed conflicts against China and Russia, Iran, or North Korea at the same time.

On December 21, a Chinese J-11 jet fighter aircraft carrying air-to-air missiles intentionally flew within 20 feet of the nose of a U.S. Air Force aircraft which was flying in international airspace. Four days later, a total of 71 swarming Chinese jet fighters and other warplanes flew to a region surrounding Taiwan. On December 27, Taiwan announced that to improve its defensive capabilities, it was increasing the period of mandatory military service for male citizens from four months to a full year. U.S. officials continued to believe, however, that there was much more that the Taiwanese Government needed to do to improve and reform its defense forces and to instill a sense of urgency about defense matters among its public.

A development at the end of the first week of December involving China and Saudi Arabia should have created concern among the Biden Administration's national security officials. During an important, milestone visit to Riyadh by Xi Jinping, he sought to deepen the military and geopolitical aspects of the relationship between the two countries by signing dozens of new commercial contracts valued initially at more than $29 billion, including oil deals which would reduce the supremacy of the U.S. dollar, which is used in most worldwide energy contracts. Xi also signed a strategic partnership pact with Saudi King Salman by which Riyadh will be given top tier status in China's foreign relations. It was also reported that the two countries had discussed the possibility of building a naval base on the Red Sea, one of the world's most strategic waterways, and that Xi "is betting that [China's] hands off approach to... domestic [Saudi] politics would resonate in a region that bristles at what it considers U.S. moralizing on human rights."[12]

* * *

At that same moment in late 2022, Iran was attempting to deal with a growing protest movement that for weeks had called for the ouster of the Islamic Republic's clerical government,[13] but that did not prevent the Government from actively supporting Russia in its invasion of Ukraine. It was widely reported that Russia had launched more than 300 sophisticated Iranian drones against Ukraine in recent weeks, that Iran had deployed personnel to Crimea to train Russian military personnel in the use of the drones, and that the senior security chiefs of the two countries had met in Tehran to pledge deeper military cooperation in a relationship that was quickly expanding into a strong defense partnership and an "ideologically rooted anti-Western alliance.[14] More ominously, Iran announced that it had produced enough enriched uranium for at least one nuclear weapon, that it had also started producing near-weapons-grade enriched uranium at a second nuclear facility, and that it had a hypersonic missile capable of penetrating any air-defense system.

North Korea remained a fountain of belligerent rhetoric and, after threatening to take overwhelming measures in response to recent joint U.S. – South Korea military exercises, it continued its year-long burst of missile tests by launching a short-range ballistic missile off its east coast. As I previously noted, it had also tested an Intercontinental Ballistic Missile that had landed some 125 miles off the coast of Japan. North Korea asserted that its ICBM could reach the Continental U.S. The number of its test launches in 2022 was already greater than in any prior year by a wide margin. On November 22, Russia, and China, who had consistently opposed additional sanctions on North Korea, vetoed a United Nations Resolution condemning North Korea's latest ICBM test. It was reported that Kim Jong-un tested the missile for the purpose of "spooking U.S. allies like South Korea and Japan about the steadfastness of the U.S. defense commitment."[15] On December 26, North Korea added to its escalating tension with South Korea by flying five drones into South Korean air space, one of which reached the capital city of Seoul. It was also reported that the North Korean Government was continuing its use of hackers to commit cybercrimes such as hacking cryptocurrency exchanges, hacking banks, and using ransomware to extort cash from its victims to support its nuclear weapons programs.

* * *

Meanwhile, the body politic in America was rumbling loudly as the midterm elections approached. Election officials in various states were taking actions to prevent voter fraud, to prevent intimidation of voters by activists, and to prepare for expected lawsuits challenging the results of the elections in their state, whatever the results. Using the kind of histrionic, exaggerated, and often misleading kind of rhetoric which had come to characterize recent political campaigns, activists from both political parties were operating in emotional overdrive. In a televised speech on November 2, six days before the elections, President Biden campaigned against Donald Trump, who was not even on the ballot, and said nothing serious about foreign policy or any of the security threats to the Nation.

For reasons which were difficult to understand, isolationists and defense doves in both political parties were using the moment to argue against support for Ukraine. On the Left, the House [of Representatives] Progressive Caucus sent a letter to President Biden noting that for the time being, Putin "doesn't have a way out" of Russia's military setbacks in Ukraine, urging Biden to initiate direct negotiations with Putin to end that conflict, and implicitly suggesting that Biden help the besieged Russian dictator get out of the war which he started. When the Caucus letter was quickly and widely denounced, apparently by Democrats as well as Republicans, the Caucus Chair withdrew it. A former Democrat Member of Congress then criticized the Party's Left Wing for caving in to "the warmongers" in the Party.[16] On the Right, a group calling itself Citizens for Sanity[17] ran ads during baseball's World Series reportedly making the absurd claim that President Biden's domestic failures were the result of the financial and military support which the U.S. had been giving Ukraine.[18]

More disturbing was evidence that the U.S. support of Ukraine was becoming a partisan issue on a broader scale. On October 18, Republican House Minority Leader Kevin McCarthy made the comment that if Republicans gained a majority in the House of Representatives in the midterm elections, there would be no "blank check" for Ukraine. It was a silly and unnecessary comment since no one had even suggested a blank check. Much more concerning were the results of a new Wall Street Journal survey in which 30% of all respondents said that they believe the Biden Administration was doing too much to help Ukraine. Some 48% of the Republican respondents shared that view, up from only 6% in March. But, at the same time, 57% of all respondents said that they were in favor of sending additional aid to Ukraine.[19]

The new survey results strongly suggested that aside from what might be learned from Headline News reports since the Russian invasion of Ukraine in February, Americans largely remained very uninformed about the important relevance of the outcome of the war in Ukraine to America's own security; and that President Biden had failed to a degree not previously understood to educate the American public, to explain to Americans the nature and scope of the security threats to the Nation, especially the threats posed by Russia and China, the current state of the unpreparedness of America's Armed Forces to deter and if necessary to respond to those threats, why it was clearly in our own self-interest to prevent Putin and Xi Jinping from using force to achieve their territorial and other imperialistic ambitions, and that because no Americans or citizens of other NATO countries were fighting in Ukraine, the Ukrainian people were sacrificing and dying not only to save their own country, but also "to protect the West from…determined enemies."[20]

The situation called for Biden and the Members of Congress to somehow become immediately aware of the wisdom of Churchill which I described in the Preface of this book. He knew that words matter in a democracy. In the early 1930s, as Hitler was coming to power in Germany, he urged the British Government to "Tell the truth to the British people! They are a tough people, a robust people. They may be a bit offended at the moment, but if you have told them exactly what is going on, you have insured yourself against complaints, and reproaches which are very unpleasant when they come home on the morrow of some disillusion.[21] Speaking to the House of Commons on October 5, 1938, on the subject of the Chamberlain Government's Munich Agreement with Hitler, he asserted that "It is the most grievous consequence which we have yet experienced of what we have done and what we have left undone in the last five years—five years of futile good intention, five years of eager search for the line of least resistance, five years of uninterrupted retreat of British power, five years of neglect.…" He had then declared that the loyal, brave people of Britain "should know the truth. They should know that there has been gross neglect and deficiency in our defenses; they should know that we have sustained a defeat without a war, the consequences of which will travel far with us along our road."

A little more than three years later, three days after the attack on Pearl Harbor, the Japanese sank the British Battleship *Prince of Wales*, then the pride of the Royal Navy, along with the Battle Cruiser *Repulse*, off the coast of Malaya. More defeats at sea soon followed. After two months of siege, Singapore, the "Gibraltar of the East," surrendered to Japanese forces on February 15, 1942. The appalling defeats staggered Churchill, now the Prime Minister. His wartime leadership was called into question. The press urged him to cede direction of the war to someone else. The British public was embarrassed, unhappy, baffled.

On January 27, 1942, a Vote of Confidence debate opened in the House of Commons. Churchill refused to engage in the kind of happy talk and hyperbole which characterize most political speeches today. He believed that "There is no worse mistake in public leadership than to hold out false hopes soon to be swept away."[22] In his memoirs, he would later write that "The British people can face peril or misfortune with fortitude and buoyancy, but they bitterly resent being deceived or finding that those responsible for their affairs are themselves dwelling in a fool's paradise. I felt it vital…to discount future calamities by describing the immediate outlook in the darkest terms."[23] In his own remarks in the debate he provided a "realistic appraisal of Britain's predicament and, despite defeats, offered a path forward to victory."[24] Churchill's daughter, who observed the speech from the Visitors' Gallery, recorded that it was "Measured – exact – reasoned – dignified – & throughout an undertone of unalterable determination & sober hopefulness."[25] Americans deserve nothing less from their political leaders.

*   *   *

On November 3, 2022, only five days prior to what the media was calling the "High-Stakes Midterm Election" a thunderbolt development regarding America's defenses took place. It was all but lost in the noise of the last-minute electioneering. Admiral Charles A. Richard, the Four-Star Commander of the U.S. Strategic Command, addressed defense professionals at a conference. He may have ruffled some politically correct feathers at The Pentagon, but as a very senior military professional, he spoke about a hard truth as he saw it. "This Ukraine crisis that we're in right now…is just the warmup," he said. "The Big One is coming. And it isn't going to be very long before we're going to get tested in ways that we haven't been tested [for] a long time. As I assess our level of deterrence against China," he continued, "the ship is slowly sinking. It is sinking slowly, but it is sinking, as fundamentally they are putting capability in the field faster than we are. As those curves keep going, it isn't going to matter how good our [operating plan] is, or how good our commanders are, or how good our forces are—we're not going to have enough of them. And that is a very near-term problem." The phrase "near-term problem" immediately caught the attention of the relatively few who heard the Admiral's remarks, or who otherwise learned of them, because it exposed what one highly credible journal characterized as "a more urgent vulnerability than most of the political class cares to recognize."[26]

The Admiral noted that the U.S. retains an advantage in its submarine force ("maybe the only true asymmetric advantage we still have against our opponents"), but he asserted that "We have to do some rapid, fundamental change in the way we approach the defense of this Nation," because "unless we pick up the pace, in terms of getting our maintenance problems fixed, getting new construction going …if we can't figure that out, …we are not going to put ourselves in a good position to maintain strategic deterrence and national defense."[27] "We used to know how to move fast, and we have lost the art of that," he added. "We have got to get back into the business of not talking about how we are going to mitigate our assumed eventual failure, …and flip it to the way we used to ask questions., which is 'What's it going to take? Is it money? Is it people? Do you need authorities? What risk?' That's how we got to the Moon by 1969."[28] Less than 90 days later, Air Force General Michael Minihan, the Four-Star Commander of the Air Mobility Command, ordered his airmen to get their affairs in order and to increase the quality of their training in preparation for a possible war with China over Taiwan within two years.[29]

Only weeks after the Admiral's remarks, the results of a new study were released on the same subject. They were similarly disturbing. The study concluded that the U.S. is not prepared for a major war. "In a major regional conflict—such as a war with China in the Taiwan Strait—the U.S. use of munitions would likely exceed [its] current stockpiles," the report of the study said, and "it would likely run out of some munitions…in less than one week."[30] "Serious deficiencies [exist] in the U.S. defense industrial base," the report continued, "and serves as a stark reminder that a protracted conflict is likely to be an industrial war that requires a defense industry able to manufacture enough munitions, weapons systems, and material to replace depleted stockpiles."

Noting that the absence in the industrial base of an adequate surge capacity undermines the U.S. ability to deter war, the report said that "these problems are particularly concerning since China is heavily investing in munitions and acquiring high-end weapons systems and equipment five to six times faster than the United States...."[31] A failure to make critically important improvements in the industrial base the report concluded would fall into the category of what one defense analyst has called a "pink flamingo," which he defined as a "predictable event that is ignored due to cognitive biases of a senior leader or a group of leaders trapped by powerful institutional forces."[32]

To the continuing amazement of most senior military leaders and the relatively few other people who were fully aware of the dangerous weaknesses in the Armed Forces and the industrial base, those weaknesses had not been the subject of debate or even discussion in the midterm election campaigns. The truth about our military vulnerabilities might have offended part of the American public but if they had been told "exactly what is going on" by the President and Commander-in-Chief, it was very unlikely that the country would have been in the current precarious position. But, Biden had not had "the wit, ascendency, or detachment from public folly to declare these fundamental, brutal facts" to American voters. It could only be hoped that it was not too late for them to become aware of the facts and as the sovereign in the American Republic, to take the necessary actions to quickly change both the quality and the national security policies of their servants, i.e., those who occupy political leadership positions in the White House and Congress.

* * *

Washington's political analysts, pollsters, pundits, and eventually all of the Republicans currently serving in the Senate and House of Representatives, spent November 9, the day after the mid-term elections in shock, shaking their heads and asking each other "What is going on?" and "What does it all mean?" The election results were much different from those which had been predicted and expected. Despite the facts that historically, the political party that controls the White House loses several congressional seats in midterm elections, that almost 70% of Americans believed the country was going in the wrong direction, that President

Biden's approval rating was in the low 40s, that high inflation was a burning issue, and that a November 2 *Washington Post*/ABC News poll had found that voters believed Republicans were better than Democrats on the economy by 14 points, better on inflation by 12 points, and better on crime by 20 points, there had been no dramatic change in the political landscape. The "red wave" that had been over hyped and predicted by Republican leaders, particularly those in the House of Representatives, never materialized. It was the worst performance in a midterm election by an out of power political party in 20 years. Yes, several days later, after all ballots had been tallied, it was established fact that in the House races, the Republicans had won a majority of the national popular vote, and that they had picked up enough seats in the House of Representatives to give them a 222 to 213 majority and thus a thin control of that body, but when Democrats won a Senate runoff election on December 6, and despite the fact that one Democrat Senator announced on December 9 that she was leaving that Party to register as an Independent, Democrats retained a razor thin majority in that body, which gave them control and additional power to shape legislation.

One thing was clear from the results of the elections. Neither political party had been given a policy mandate and the new Congress would be as closely divided as the current one, which would end in January 2023. Exit polling of voters on Election Day found that when asked their opinion of the Democrat Party, 44% said Favorable and 53% said Unfavorable. When asked their opinion of the Republican Party, 44% said Favorable and 52% said Unfavorable.[33]

An explanation for the unexpected results and the "message" the voting public was sending to the politicians became widely accepted overnight: The public remained distrustful of the Government and very unhappy with the performance of both the Congress and President Biden, but that in many cases, when they considered the candidates offered by the out-of-power Republican Party for seats in the Senate and House, they were no more impressed with them than they were with the only alternative, i.e., sticking with the incumbent Democrats. Even though he was not on the ballot, it was widely believed by political analysts that the toxicity of former President Trump was also a factor. This was particularly the case with voters who identified as Independents. They voted for Democrats by wide margins in key states. An obvious exception to this factor was the election to the Senate of an apparent isolationist who had been endorsed by the former President and who is apparently a supporter of the way in which Trump handled foreign policy matters. The newly elected Senator soon attacked Trump's predecessors generally for "slavishly" following the "hawkish," but undefined, "foreign policy establishment." The Senator's own lack of any national security policy-making experience whatsoever, suggested that he would benefit from a good history course and association with those members of the presumed "establishment" who have had both.

Some of the Republican candidates were considered too extreme or were otherwise unappealing. Some lacked meaningful experience. Others were long on empty political rhetoric which described the major problems facing the country, but short on crafting and selling a message which proposed specific solutions and answers to the problems. According to one political professional, yet others were "knuckleheads with strange beliefs and closets full of problems."[34]

It was not necessary to read between the lines to conclude that voters were very unhappy with the Nation's political leadership and particularly with the extreme partisans in both political parties. Voters were desperate for change, but the change they wanted was to leaders who clearly placed the Nation's interests above their own political interests; leaders whose competence, character and experience had been strongly demonstrated in previous years; leaders who could develop policies to solve the problems, and get things done; leaders who, in the words of Jack Welch, to whom I referred in the previous chapter, could "put decisions into action and push them forward to completion, through resistance, chaos, or unexpected obstacles," i.e., who could produce results.

* * *

Immediately after the voting booths closed on Election Day and the closeness of the outcomes in the Senate and the House were recognized, intense speculation began on the consequences of the outcomes. The speculation was based on assumptions that the political gridlock would likely bring the legislative process to a near halt; that the shift in congressional power would effectively stop Biden from pursuing an ambitious legislative agenda and that he would therefore, use his executive powers as President and stretch them to their constitutional limit or even beyond; and that small, highly partisan factions within both political parties in the Senate and House would now have substantial leverage to influence proposed legislation. Republican leaders in the House were already describing some of their priorities, which included improvements in border security, reversing the Administration's plans to expand the Internal Revenue Service, and encouraging the states and cities to increase compensation for the police.

Very few members of Congress, however, were talking about substantial increases in the Defense Budget or the critical needs of the Armed Forces. Indeed, a number of the Republicans in the House were already talking about the actions they would take to cut Government spending, including attaching bills for spending cuts to proposed "must-pass" appropriations legislation, i.e., threatening a government shutdown if the spending cuts were not made, a dangerous tactic of very dubious value. Polls in recent years had found that voters strongly disapprove of shutdowns. There was no doubt that the Government's budgetary deficit and rapidly increasing debt was a major and increasingly dangerous problem and that it would be very difficult to resolve,[35] but budgetary chaos and political brinkmanship over the previous decade and a half and the continuing congressional requirement for the Armed Forces to do more with fewer resources had been the greatest impediment to U.S. military readiness. It would be disastrous if the new Republican-controlled House of Representatives continued that practice or permitted a few shortsighted isolationists to interfere with U.S. engagement in matters outside of our borders, even if they are necessary for our own security. As one informed observer noted, "The short version of navel gazing nationalism is that we have 'needs at home,' but what country doesn't?"[36]

Another national security problem exploded upon America's consciousness on November 15. A Federal Judge struck down a policy known as Title 42, which had initially been instituted in 2020 by the Trump Administration at the height of the Covid-19 pandemic for the purpose of expediting the processing of illegal immigrants so they could be more quickly deported. The policy had subsequently been continued by the Biden Administration as a means of slowing the huge numbers of illegal crossings by migrants across the southern border of the U.S. The effect of the court's ruling was a return by border authorities to the traditional and much slower processing of people who had crossed into the U.S. illegally.

The magnitude of the continuing border crisis was reflected in data provided by U.S. Customs and Border Protection. It was reported on October 5, 2022, that over the previous two years, nearly one million people had illegally crossed the border and disappeared into the U.S. and that "We don't know who these people are but, unlike asylum seekers, who turn themselves into border officials, they intentionally evade detention. They could be violent criminals, drug smugglers [Mexican transnational criminal organizations flood the U.S. with deadly Fentanyl and methamphetamine] or terrorists. And those are the ones we know of; many more could have crossed our porous southern border without being detected. Yet, the Biden Administration continued to insist, against all evidence, that 'the border is secure."[37] The reality was that thousands of illegal immigrants were entering the U.S. each day and that the millions of Americans who watched televised news programs each night could see the anarchy at our open southern border which was permitting more than 379 million doses of Fentanyl to enter the U.S. each year.[38] During the month of December 2022 alone, 251,487 people illegally crossed the border of the U.S. The flow of illicit narcotics across the border increased by 17.5 percent compared to November. This included a 52 percent increase in seizures of Fentanyl, and a 32 percent increase in seizures of cocaine.[39] And yet, in his entire political career, including his two years in the White House, President Biden had never made a single trip to the southern border to see for himself the dangerous chaos there. Congress was no less to blame. Politicians in both Houses of that institution had complained loudly about the illegal migration/border security problem for many years, but they had done little or nothing to resolve it because a workable solution would require partisans in the two political parties to compromise.

On December 27, the Supreme Court issued an order keeping Title 42 in place while it considered whether almost two-dozen states could intervene in long-standing litigation in federal courts on the question of the legality of the Title 42 border controls. Most observers had no confidence that Congress would be able to pass new immigration legislation or that the Biden Administration would develop a serious policy for the control of the southern border.

* * *

As America approached the week of Thanksgiving, many questions were on many minds, both at home and in foreign capitals. One group of questions related to President Biden. How would he govern during the final two years of his term? Now that the elections were over, would he remember the critical difference between political campaigns and the governance of a nation? Did he really understand that America's security is his most important constitutional responsibility and that for the protection of that security, he does not need a political mandate? The U.S. Supreme Court has made that principle very clear.[40] Was he willing to immediately commence a well-planned effort to better educate the American public on the serious threats to our security and what sacrifices must be made in order to quickly rebuild the Armed Forces for the purpose of deterring and, if necessary, winning potential armed conflicts against Russia and/or China, or other dangerous adversaries? As I have noted several times, it is a truism that no President can successfully pursue a policy involving our national security unless he has first educated the public about the risks of not pursuing the policy, instilled in the pubic a shared sense of direction, and informed them about what to expect and what is expected of them.

Would President Biden make the security threats and the need for immediate and substantial additional funding for the Armed Forces his highest priority and the only subject of a televised speech to the Nation? Was he willing to persuade those who argue that domestic problems require more attention than the Nation's security and those who oppose the rebuilding of the Armed Forces for any reason, that if we don't "provide for the common defense" as the Constitution demands of public officials, there will be no opportunity to "promote the general welfare?" Would he attempt to bring to their attention the words of John Stuart Mill, the famous British parliamentarian who was a fierce advocate for freedom from tyranny? In his Principles of Political Economy, he wrote that "War is an ugly thing, but not the ugliest of things. The decayed and degraded state of moral and patriotic feeling which thinks that nothing is worth war is much worse. ***A man who has nothing which he is willing to fight for, nothing which he cares about more than he does about his personal safety, is a miserable creature who has no chance of being free, unless made and kept so by the exertions of better men than himself."

More importantly, would Biden rigidly adhere to the same Left Wing political and policy agenda that he pursued during his first two years in the White House, or would he demonstrate the kind of leadership required of a President and Commander-in-Chief by reaching across the political divide in Congress to seriously seek pragmatic, workable compromises on these critically important defense issues? The President's initial reaction to the results of the elections was not encouraging. When he was asked on the day after the elections what he planned to do differently, he replied "Nothing."

The second group of questions related to the newly elected Congress which would take office on January 3, 2023. Given the thinness of the Republican majority in the House, which ideological factions would seek to wield power that is disproportional to their numbers? How well would the new Republican leaders of the House manage those factions? Since many Republicans in the House were self-described Budget Hawks, very concerned about the budget deficit and determined to cut even defense spending significantly as part of an effort to balance the Federal Budget, and many Democrats in the House opposed increased defense spending no matter what the facts were, would the kind of increases in the Defense Budget which the circumstances demanded take place? Would the Republican Budget Hawks remember and follow the principle articulated by President Reagan in his first term? He didn't have to defend his conservative credentials on fiscal matters to anyone, but, as noted in Chapter VII, he believed and had the *political will* to deal with the severe criticism of that belief–that the amount of money spent on defense should be dictated by national security needs and that it "could not be determined simply by looking at how much money the domestic budget had to spare."[41] Until he was halfway through his second term of office, he had to resist continued concern about the budget deficit and demands from Congress and from within his own Administration for more domestic spending. He consistently told his staff and the Cabinet that he too was concerned about the budget deficit, but that "If we have to put up with a deficit to protect our national security, that's what we're going to do."[42] And he did it, taking the Defense Budget from 4.5 percent of the Gross Domestic Product (GDP) in 1979 to 6 percent in 1986.

Would Republicans in the Senate and House work with Democrats and focus on producing the kind of results the public clearly wants, or would their frustration with the Biden Administration, the actions taken by Democrats in the House under Nancy Pelosi, and the results of the elections cause them to seek retribution against both the Democrat in the White House and those in Congress? Was political payback really inevitable?

The closing days of 2022 reminded us yet again of the many ways in which the world had become much more dangerous in the previous twelve months. The war and brutal suffering and devastation in Ukraine continued. Relying heavily on the Wagner Group, the private military contractor that had already been supplying mercenaries for Russia's war on Ukraine, tens of thousands of criminals released from its prisons (who faced execution if they deserted and amnesty if they survived six months in Ukraine), and some of its newly mobilized troops, Russia was massing men and arms for a new offensive as soon as January and no later than the spring.[43] Fears were also growing that Putin might force the neighboring country of Belarus to enter the war to support Russia. North Korea launched two more ballistic missiles adding to what had already been a historic year of its provocative tests of those weapons. China was continuing to solidify its already close partnership with Russia by engaging in live fire naval exercises in the Pacific involving detachments of ships from both countries.

On December 6, 2022, more than two months after the start of the Government's 2023 Fiscal Year, House and Senate negotiators finally agreed to a compromise bill for a new National Defense [policy] Authorization Act (NDAA). In the absence of cynical and irresponsible politicking, the bill could have been agreed to several months earlier.[44] Two days later, the bill was passed by the House of Representatives. On December 16, it was approved by the Senate. It authorized a total national security budget, including national security programs within the Department of Energy, of $857.9 billion, roughly a 10 percent increase over the $778 billion security budget which had been approved by Congress for FY 2022. Notably, and as I pointed out earlier in Chapter XVI, the authorized budget contained $45 billion more in military spending than President Biden had requested.

But these developments were not as good as they appeared. It should be remembered that during President Biden's first year in the White House, defense spending at 3.48 percent of the GDP was already below the historical average, and in his second year, it had declined further. The newly approved Defense Budget barely kept pace with inflation. Moreover, only about $160 billion of the total was for aircraft, missiles, ammunition, combat vehicles, Navy ships and other weapons and equipment.[45] A recent study had concluded that the Biden Administration's requested Defense Budget of only $773 billion contained "close to $109 billion in programs and activities that [did] not directly contribute to military capability" because "the Pentagon and its budget [had] become an 'easy button' to address problems that are not part of the defense core mission and function."[46]

The news would soon become worse. Only a few weeks after the close of 2022, Biden proposed to Congress another *reduction* in the Defense budget for FY 2024. Since defense spending in FY 2023 (ending

September 30, 2023) will turn out to be at or near an historic low of 3.0 to 3.3 percent of GDP, [47] he proposed only a 3.2% increase in spending. Although he claimed that his proposed Defense Budget was a record, the truth is that with inflation at 6%, if his proposal becomes law, the purchasing authority of the Defense Department will actually decline even further at a very dangerous time.

To put the projected Defense Budgets for 2023 and 2024 in perspective, it must be noted that in 1960, the last year of President Eisenhower's Administration, the U.S. spent 9% of its GDP on defense and that during the two Reagan Administrations, it spent just under 7%. The reduced Defense Budgets can be explained by the huge surge in nondiscretionary (entitlement) spending for domestic social programs that began with the Great Society programs of President Lyndon Johnson and which have skyrocketed since then. Members of Congress after Congress have refused to remember that social programs are nowhere mentioned in the U.S. Constitution, but that it mandates sufficient funding to provide "for the Common Defense."

By any reasonable standard, it is clear that none of the Defense Budgets proposed by the Nation's Commander-in-Chief, or even the increases approved by Congress, are close to being sufficient for the resolution of most of the readiness problems with which the Armed Forces are struggling to contend. Once again, the Nation's political leaders have failed to do everything possible to fulfill their highest duty to the American people.

On December 21, Ukrainian President Volodymyr Zelensky delivered an impassioned, dramatic address to a packed joint meeting of Congress wearing the same cargo pants and olive green sweatshirt which he had worn the previous day during a visit to his troops on the front lines of the war on his homeland. "Against all the gloom and doom scenarios," he said, "Ukraine didn't fall. Ukraine is alive and kicking." He reminded his listeners that the aid which was being provided to his country by the U.S. was "not charity," but rather "an investment in the global security and democracy that we handle in the most responsible way." It was rumored that during his very brief visit to Washington the Biden Administration had informed Zelensky of their view that Ukraine would never be able to drive Russia out of all of the Ukrainian territory it now occupied and that consequently peace negotiations should be commenced sooner, rather than later, but many military experts disagreed with both that conclusion and the recommendation. In any event, in remarks at the White House, Zelensky reiterated his previous declaration that Ukraine would not accept an outcome in the war that involved a loss of Ukrainian territory.

How would President Biden and the individual Members of Congress now respond collectively to the national security crises? A distinguished author of a book on the traits of good character has reminded us that to "respond" is to "answer," and that correspondingly, to be "responsible" is to be "answerable," to be *accountable*. But he has also correctly observed that "In Washington, D.C., common parlance makes ample use of the passive voice to avoid blame: "mistakes were made." But there is no rush to take responsibility.[48] Would our most senior public officials now accept responsibility for the self-centered mistakes, confusion, lack of preparation, unnecessary partisan bickering, and lack of good leadership on national security matters that had characterized the last several years? Did they really understand the message the voters had given them on November 8? When the new Congress convened, would it continue to be business as usual focused almost entirely on domestic matters?

*   *   *

As I noted in the Preface to this book, the several causes of the turbulence in the world order today are creating major problems for America's security. An ironic fact is that "the United States cannot insulate itself from world disorder for many reasons, and not least because, in some measure, it is necessarily a cause of it. American beliefs about political equality, rights (to include rights of women), religious freedom, and civil liberties, including the right to property, are a menace in many places, often without America's knowing or wishing it."[49] The obvious conclusion, which is also argued in the pages of this book, is that "The American stake in global order is enormous—and if it does not take the lead in maintaining it, its own prosperity and freedoms will suffer as well."[50]

Seven years ago, it was possible to believe that "American armed force, used wisely by American statecraft [could] not eliminate [the then existing challenges to our security]," but that "it [could] manage, contain, and reduce them."[51] In the intervening period, however, America's political leaders have not risen to the level of events. American statecraft has not used American military power wisely and has even permitted it to deteriorate. Because of previous neglect and the continuing neglect during that period, all in the face of the plainest warnings, we have now entered upon a period of danger greater than has befallen the U.S. since at least the end of the Cold War.

An experienced student of the historical developments in 2022 has reached the same conclusion. He has recently written that "the world is witnessing the revival of some of the worst aspects of traditional geopolitics: great-power competition, imperial ambitions, fights over resources. ***Meanwhile …China has embarked on a quest for regional and potentially global primacy, putting itself on a trajectory that will lead to …confrontation with the United States."[52] But, it is asserted, "that is not all – not by a long shot. These …risks are colliding with new challenges, …such as climate change, pandemics, and nuclear proliferation. ***U.S. leadership has underpinned what order there has been in the world for the past 75 years and remains no less central today. A United States riven internally, however, will become ever less willing and able to lead on the international stage" because America's "ability to deter rivals will diminish as its foes come to see the United States as too divided or reluctant to act."[53]

Many Americans remember from their school days the story of Abraham Lincoln's speech in 1858 in which he declared that "A house divided against itself cannot stand," but few recall President Eisenhower's speech in 1953 in which he declared that America had to remain militarily strong because "we cannot count upon any enemy striking us at a given, ascertainable moment," and that "All of us have learned— first from the onslaught of Nazi aggression, then from Communist aggression—that all free nations must stand together or they shall fall separately."[54] Fewer still are aware of the words of one of our Founding Fathers. Writing in *Federalist No. 41*[55] after the drafting of the Constitution had been completed, but still needed ratification from the states, James Madison, popularly known as the Father of the Constitution, declared that "Security against foreign danger is one of the primitive objects of civil society. It is an avowed and essential object of the American union. ***How could a readiness for war in time of peace be safely prohibited unless we could prohibit in like manner the preparations and establishments of every hostile nation? ***America united, …without a single soldier, exhibits a more forbidding posture to foreign ambition than America disunited, with a hundred thousand veterans ready for combat."

Americans have a constitutional right to expect that their elected officials in the White House and Congress will take all necessary measures to "faithfully execute" their office, to "preserve, protect and defend the Constitution of the United States," and to otherwise safeguard our freedoms and security. Very regrettably, many Americans have lost faith in Government officials. On January 30, 2023, the results of the annual Gallup Poll of the "most important U.S. problem" were released. The number one problem identified, even above inflation, was "the government/leadership." It must never be forgotten, however, that responsibility for the quality and performance of our elected officials rests with the American people. In notes that he made after he left the White House, former President Truman addressed this important principle in the context of presidential elections. "The country has to awaken every now and then to the fact," he wrote, "that the people are responsible for the government they get. And when they elect a man to the presidency who doesn't take care of the job, they've got nobody to blame but themselves."[56] The same comment is, of course, true with respect to congressional elections. The public's responsibility cannot be delegated or evaded.

Very regrettably, for many years, American voters who elect our national leaders have had relatively little information and weak attitudes on foreign and national security issues and on the Government's security policies. This is so for at least two reasons. First, except in times of immediate and easily seen danger, private interests and domestic issues have more direct consequences on people's lives and their material wellbeing. A much more disturbing reason is because of the public's ignorance about many political matters. Not long after the terrorist attacks of 9/11 2001, the results of a survey by the American Council of [University] Trustees and Alumni revealed that of the fifty-five top ranked universities in the Nation, not a single one required a course in American History.[57] Courses on U.S. military and political history are even more unusual. A 2016 study found that only about 34 percent of Americans could identify the three branches of the Federal Government.[58] One scholar has recently observed that these and related facts are "regrettable"—I would use the word 'tragic'—"not least because it impoverishes our debates on issues of war and peace."[59]

James Madison was under no illusion about the danger of voters who are uninformed or who have weak attitudes on important national issues. In a letter dated August 4, 1822, to a professor in Kentucky, Madison declared that "A popular Government, without …information is but a Prologue to Farce or Tragedy; or perhaps both. Knowledge will forever govern ignorance: And a people who mean to be their own

Governors, must arm themselves with the power which knowledge gives." It is of considerable urgency that Americans be helped to understand that it is up to us, as well as to elected officials, to take action to confront the dangers to our safety. Political leaders who are competent and fully informed on national security issues, and who make a continuous effort to educate the public on them, will not guarantee that future national security decisions will be the best ones possible. But, the absence of that competence and education will almost certainly guarantee that those decisions are no better than the failures of the last decade and a half.

* * *

It is reported that on September 18, 1787, the last day of the Constitutional Convention in Philadelphia, a lady asked Benjamin Franklin "Well Doctor, what have we got, a republic or a monarchy?" He is said to have replied "A republic, if you can keep it." Over the last 247 years, tens of thousands of American men and women have paid the highest possible price to preserve the Republic and its associated freedoms. It is now up to all of us to keep it. We are the Masters of our fate.

Si vis pacem, para bellum

> *We were living in a bubble in the 1990s, and as long we were inside that bubble, we as a Nation permitted ourselves every sort of indulgence, moral as well as material. For who could imagine that bad news would come, or what shape it would take, or what it might demand of us? The bubble burst on September 11, when the unimaginable became real and suddenly we found ourselves in an empty new and entirely unlovely world: vulnerable, warred upon, and at war.*
>
> Hon. William J. Bennett,
> Former Director of the White House Office
> of National Drug Control Policy, 2002

> *One reason the warnings [about the 9/11 2001 terrorist attacks] went unheeded was widespread national complacency in the 1990s about the rest of the world.... In the face of such public opinion, it was hard to mobilize enthusiasm for painful organizational change or dramatic increases in spending.*
>
> Hon. Joseph S. Nye,
> Former Assistant Secretary of Defense, 2001

POSTSCRIPT

In the months following the terrorist attacks of 9/11 2001, diplomats, national security analysts and certainly the American public searched desperately for answers. How did this happen to the world's only remaining superpower, and on its own soil? Why could we not prevent the attacks? Why were there no warning signs? The answer to the last question was simple. There had been warnings.

In 1996, a former Assistant Secretary of Defense and a former Director of the CIA had co-chaired a government study that warned of the lack of U.S. preparedness to deal with catastrophic terrorism and suggested several organizational changes. In 1999, the bipartisan Hart-Rudman Commission on National Security in the 21st Century warned that "Americans will likely die on American soil, possibly in large numbers" because the U.S. Government was not organized to meet the terrorist threat. A June 2000 report of the National Commission on Terrorism declared that the "number one priority" should be given to the loose affiliations of transnational terrorists who were seeking to inflict mass casualties on American soil. In February 2001, a much more specific warning was made public. In open testimony before the Senate Intelligence Committee, the Director of Central Intelligence declared that the most immediate and serious threat to the security of the United States was the global network of Osama bin Laden.

A few months after the 9/11 attacks, one of the co-chairs of the 1996 study wrote an article which described the difficulties that the co-chairmen had encountered when they attempted to educate senior Government officials on the seriousness of the terrorist threat. "When we gave briefings on our report to officials in several agencies," he said, "we received polite responses. But, ...one skeptic remarked: 'If it is so likely, why hasn't it happened?'"[1] A year after the completion of the 1996 study, the co-chairmen wrote in the *Lost Angeles Times* that "the very nature of U.S. society makes it difficult to prepare for [the terrorist] problem. We are unlikely to mount an adequate defense until we suffer an attack." One of the co-chairs would later write that "One reason the warnings ...went unheeded was widespread national complacency in the 1990s about the rest of the world," and that "In the face of such public opinion, it was hard to mobilize enthusiasm for painful organizational change or dramatic increases in spending."[2]

An official at the National Security Council put the matter this way, "there is a problem convincing people that there is a threat. There is disbelief and resistance. Most people don't understand."[3] A former Cabinet Member in two presidential administrations spoke to the issue with these words: "We were living in a bubble in the 1990s, and as long as we were inside that bubble, we as a Nation permitted ourselves every sort of indulgence, moral as well as material. For who could imagine that bad news would come, or what shape it would take, or what it might demand of us? ***The bubble burst on September 11, when the unimaginable became real and suddenly we found ourselves in an empty new and entirely unlovely world: vulnerable, warred upon, and at war. ***Our Government—where had it been all those years?"[4] He then expressed a national security concern that has been common among American leaders for more than half of a century: "I [am] afraid that, as a country, we had had it too good during the years of the bubble; having been softened up, we might not be able to sustain collective momentum in what we were now being called upon to do."[5]

Churchill addressed the dangers of continuing complacency in a speech in the House of Commons on May 2, 1935, four years before Britain became engaged in what developed into World War II. By that time, he had already spent a lifetime in politics and fighting in, leading Britain's response to, and writing about wars. "If only Great Britain, France and Italy had pledged themselves two or three years ago to work in association for maintaining peace and collective security," he had declared, "how different might have been our position. Indeed," he had continued, "it is possible that the dangers into which we are steadily advancing would never have arisen. But," he concluded, "the world and the Parliaments and public opinion would have none of that in those days. When the situation was manageable it was neglected, and now that it is thoroughly out of hand, we apply too late the remedies which then might have effected a cure."

In words which would soon become familiar to millions of people around the world who were fighting for their freedom, he had continued. "There is nothing new in the story. It is as old as the Sibylline Books. It falls into that long dismal catalogue of the fruitlessness of experience and the confirmed unteachability of a mankind. Want of foresight, unwillingness to act when action would be simple and effective, lack of clear thinking, confusion of counsel until the emergency comes, until self-preservation strikes its jarring gong—these are the features which constitute the endless repetition of history."

It has been more than 87 years since Churchill made that speech and Americans have still not learned the lessons in it. Despite our wonderful educational institutions and access to communications platforms and information technologies not even imaginable in 1935, we remain dangerously complacent about threats to our security. While much of that complacency can be laid at the feet of Congress and an increasingly partisan media, Theodore Roosevelt reminded us more than a century ago that "A council of war never fights and in a crisis the duty of a leader is to lead and not to take refuge behind the generally timid wisdom of a multitude of councilors."[6] While Congress has critically important constitutional responsibilities with respect to war and potential war, its 535 members cannot effectively educate. This is particularly true when the two houses of Congress are governed by different political parties, each operating with a razor-thin majority.

Only a President has the constitutional right and duty to serve as the Nation's Commander-in-Chief; only a President conducts diplomacy with other nations, and has the power to negotiate and sign treaties, which the Senate must then ratify; only a President receives extensive daily intelligence briefings and meets often with the most senior military leaders; only a President has a national platform and receives the kind of media and other attention which is required to effectively educate and persuade the American public. But he must have both the competence and the *will* to do so. Ideally, he should have significant national security experience, executive leadership experience in the Government, great political courage, and the ability to provide the clear direction, force and energy which are necessary to educate the public on the importance and complexities of the threats to our security; to make our response to those threats the highest national priority; and to "bust through bureaucratic log jams, hold federal departments and agencies accountable, and [to] integrate a Government wide …effort."[7]

Very regrettably, and as I have explained in this book, after Vladimir Putin's threatening speech at the Munich Security Conference in February 2007, to which I referred in Chapter IX, and during the administrations of three American Presidents, there were many additional warning signs of Putin's geopolitical intentions and of a potentially disastrous armed conflict in Europe. Starting in 2013, there were also many warning signs of Xi Jinping's hate of western values, including international law, of his increasingly aggressive conduct of China's foreign affairs, and of his ambition to make the Peoples Liberation Army the most powerful military force in the world. Actions taken by Iran and North Korea which were contrary to America's vital security interests were also reported in the news media on a regular basis. In addition to the many warning signs of Putin's and Xi's intentions, there was even more evidence of Russia's, China's, Iran's, and North Korea's rapidly increasing military strength.

Few people at senior levels of the American Government asked hard questions, such as "Why do the two largest land powers on the face of the earth, neither of which is in any danger of being attacked, much less invaded, need to build large navies and to develop the military capability to project power far beyond their own shores?" No President made any serious effort to explain to the American people why superior American military power is necessary to deter aggression by Russia and China which would be dangerous to vital American interests; why and how it is critically important to America's own security that the world order be based upon law and not upon Russian and Chinese nihilism and tyranny and Putin's and Xi's brutal personal ambitions for worldwide hegemony; and why in a world of Great-Power conflict, dictatorship and the spread of weapons of mass destruction, American leadership is essential. During at least a decade and a half of "passive incompetence," America's leaders "failed to anticipate, counter or deter China's massive military buildup"[8] and to take strong punitive actions in response to Russia's aggressions. They either sleepwalked through those developments, or intentionally avoided the subject because they did not want to fight for the resources that were required to maintain the kind of overwhelming U.S. military power that is necessary to deter these adversaries.

It is worth noting that prior to their elections, none of our last three Presidents had ever worn a military uniform, much less participated in the brutality of combat. Not one had ever carried the responsibilities of a Chief Executive of a Government Department or Agency, much less one that was involved in making national security policies. It is self-evident that service in uniform does not make one a military expert and that Chief Executive experience does not assure good judgment or otherwise make one a good President. But the two experiences at least focus one's attention on the critical importance of fully prepared Armed Forces and the many factors other than Party Politics which are relevant to decisions affecting America's security. They minimize the many risks of a new President having to learn everything on the job.

In April 1999, some 29 months prior to the 9/11 attacks, a military analyst described by the *Pittsburg Post-Gazette* as "arguably the best thinker …on international affairs" then in America, expressed his frustration with the failure of the Nation's political leaders to come to grips with the threats facing America at that time and to take action to address them. "Our problems," he said, "lie with a generation of leaders who deemed themselves of too much worth to serve in uniform, and who arrived at the pinnacle of power ignorant of what militaries can and cannot do. It is a generation accustomed to easy success, and it cannot understand why bloody-minded foreigners behave so badly.… [I]t is a generation sheltered from much of the world's reality. It knows how to win elections, but not how to lead. And leadership is crucial to the effective use of the military.… [T]he leader is the most important factor in deciding between victory or defeat.… This has not changed since The Battle of Jericho, or the fall of Troy."[9] The same thing may be said about many in the current generation of political leaders.

Unusually good presidential and congressional leadership and a bipartisan focus on policies and legislation which are badly needed are required promptly. To the surprise and dismay of many American voters who had made it clear in the recent 2022 congressional elections that they do not support extremists in either of the political parties, and that they want their political leaders to compromise as necessary on bitter partisan issues in order to get things done, the first days of the new 118th Congress, which convened on January 3, 2023, only demonstrated the characteristics of dysfunction in the new House of Representatives. In 15 rounds of voting over five days, a Right-Wing group of only 20 of the 222 Republicans who had been elected, prevented the House from even completing its first order of business—the election of a new Speaker. It was the first time in one hundred years that a new Speaker had not been elected on the first round of voting and the number of rounds of voting that were required were the most since before the Civil War.

Ignoring the obvious fact that elections have consequences and that they constituted only 10 percent of the Republicans who had just been elected to the House, and only 5 percent of the entire House, the fringe group claimed that they were only interested in changing the House rules which govern the legislative process, a landable goal, but they seemed to thrive in what a U.S. Senator characterized as "the chaos of the current moment."[10] Their apparent preference for deadlock prevented the House from even swearing in its new members. Their demand for a rule change that would permit a single Republican member to significantly reduce the authority of any Speaker to get things accomplished by calling for a motion to "vacate the chair"—essentially a vote to oust whoever was serving Speaker, threatened to plunge the House into continuing chaos.[11] The small group offered no plausible candidate for Speaker as an alternative to Representative Kevin McCarthy, who had served as Minority Leader for several years and who was supported by all of the other Republicans, nor did they offer any policy proposals that were significantly different from those of McCarthy.

More than a few observers concluded that the fringe holdouts preferred "combative sound bites to actual governing."[12] Some of the dissidents were reportedly seeking personal advancement, i.e., "positions of power that they hadn't earned through seniority or influence with colleagues,"[13] e.g., seats on important committees or the chair of particular subcommittees—or at least, broader name recognition and notoriety. Even friendly critics believed that some of the group's members were in it for the showboating.

Among the concessions that McCarthy made to the fringe group was a pledge that the top-line budget figure for discretionary spending in FY 2024 will not exceed what it was in FY 2022. Some Republicans were expected in the future to demand severe budget cuts on both defense programs and entitlement programs before they will agree to raise the ceiling on the national debt.[14] Instead of substantially increasing the Defense Budget to address the many military readiness problems I have previously described, the effect of these developments was to increase the danger that the small group of Republicans might join a fringe group on the Left Wing of the Democrat Party, which seeks a reduction of the armed Forces for other reasons, to prevent a closely Congress from increasing the Defense Budget at all.

In the context of the Nation's many national security problems, it is important to remember that even if the new Congress that convened on January 3 had immediately passed and President Biden had immediately signed a military appropriations bill that dramatically increased the Defense Budget for the rebuilding of the Armed Forces, that objective could not have been accomplished for several years. Even in normal times the defense industry cannot turn on a dime to the production of weapons systems, munitions, and other tools of war. It is true that after the attack on Pearl Harbor the U.S. produced weapons at a rate that "defied all past experience;" that between the summer of 1940 and the summer of 1945, "American shipyards produced 141 aircraft carriers, eight battleships, 807 cruisers, destroyers, and destroyer escorts, and 203 submarines;"[15] and that during the same period American automobile manufacturers and other industries "converted their assembly lines to produce 88,410 tanks and self-propelled guns, 257,000 artillery pieces, 2.4 million trucks, 2.6 million machine guns and 41 billion rounds of ammunition."[16] But, the U.S. no longer has that kind of manufacturing capacity. Over the last several years, defense industry companies have pursued business strategies of consolidation. As a result, we now have many fewer arms manufacturers. We no longer have either the number of shipyards or the number of skilled workers that would be required to build the number of ships that would be essential if the U.S. was forced to fight in more than one major regional conflict or even a single conflict that was prolonged. This problem has been exacerbated in recent years by shortages of parts and labor and other supply-chain disruptions. It takes years to build new ships and combat aircraft and to train officers and non-commissioned officers. By their nature, democracies are notoriously slow compared to authoritarian regimes.

* * *

Almost four years after he left the White House, former President Ronald Reagan accepted an invitation from the Oxford Union Society at Oxford University to deliver one of his last public addresses. When he arrived on December 4, 1992, he was subjected to a few boos from somewhat aggressive and cocky students, but he was given a standing ovation after the speech.

Reflecting upon the toppling of the "massive, creaking machine of oppression known as communism" and the end of the Cold War, to which he was the major contributor, he expressed concern about the isolationism and complacency which appeared to be growing. "Ironically," he said, the end of communist tyranny has robbed much of the West of its uplifting, common purpose.... With the Soviet empire defeated, will we fall into petty, self-absorbed economic rivalries? Will we squander the moral capital of half a century? Will we turn inward, lulled by a dangerous complacency and the short-sighted view that the end of one Evil Empire means the permanent banishment of evil in all its forms?"

"It is a fashionable assertion in these troubled times," he continued, "that nations must focus on economic, not military strength. Over the long run, it is true, no nation can remain military strong while economically exhausted. But I would remind you that defeats on the battlefield occur in the short run. More precisely, economic power is not a replacement for military power."

"Evil still stalks the planet," he said and "the work of freedom is never done."

*   *   *

Whatever national security problems may be encountered in the months and years ahead, it is essential that we anticipate them and start addressing them now. The Nation has no leader like Churchill, so we must rely on an informed and aroused public to wake up a sleeping Congress and the indifferent and often incompetent occupants of the White House to the stark national security realities and push them into action. Theodore Roosevelt emphasized the importance of the average American citizen in such circumstances. In a lecture at the University of Paris on April 23, 1910, he declared that the success or failure of the American Nation "will be conditioned upon the way in which the average man, the average woman, does his or her duty, first in the ordinary, everyday affairs of life, and next in those great occasional crises which call for the heroic virtues." We cannot exercise heroic virtues by just sitting at home as spectators. As the highly honored American historian David McCullough observed, 'Citizenship isn't just voting."[17] It is, as Benjamin Franklin said, up to all of us to protect and to keep our Republic. Much is at stake and as I said in the Preface to this book, time is short.

ACKNOWLEDGMENTS

I wish to record my gratitude to Mrs. Michelle Perdue for her invaluable help in preparing and revising the text of this and several other of my books with her customary enthusiasm. I am also indebted to Mrs. Nancy Newland of Rare Bird Design for many helpful, professional suggestions, and very creative energy on the structure and design of the book. It was a real pleasure for me to be able to work with two ladies who are themselves, real craftsmen.

NOTES

Preface

1. William Macaskill, "Surviving the Era of Catastrophic Risk," *Foreign Affairs: The Age of Uncertainty*, September/October 2022, p.10.
2. Richard Haass, "The Dangerous Decade," *Foreign Affairs: The Age of Uncertainty*, *op.cit.*, p.25.
3. Jamie Dimon, "The West Needs America's Leadership," *The Wall Street Journal*, January 4, 2023.
4. Richard Haass, *op.cit.*
5. William J. Bennett, *Why We Fight* (New York: Doubleday, 2002), p.2.
6. *Ibid.*
7. The Heritage Foundation, "Executive Summary of the 2023 Index of U.S. Military Strength," October 18, 2022.
8. Editorial Board, "'The Big One Is Coming,'" *The Wall Street Journal*, November 5-6, 2022, p.A16.
9. *Ibid.*
10. In his seminal book *Strategy*, B. H. Liddell Hart, the respected British soldier, military historian and military theorist, distinguished between "the sphere of *policy*, or the higher conduct of war, which must necessarily be the responsibility of the government and not of the military leaders it employs as its agents in the executive control of operations," and *strategy*, and applying military means to fulfill the ends of policy," B. H. Liddell Hart, *Strategy*, 2d rev. ed. (New York: Meridan, 1991), pp.319-21. War policy and strategy are, of course, intimately connected.
11. Robert Kagen, "A Free World If You Can Keep It," *Foreign Affairs*, January/February 2023.

Chapter I: The Beginning of a Tradition and the Necessary Departures From It

1. In what became known as the Citizens Genet Affair, the French Ambassador to the U.S., the audacious Edmond-Charles Genêt, traveled throughout the country building support for France at a time when Washington's opposition to any such foreign entanglement was well known.
2. James Thomas Flexner, *Washington: The Indispensable Man* (New York: Sterling Publishing Co., Inc., 2012), p.360.
3. Ron Chernow, *Washington: A Life* (New York: The Penguin Press, 2010), p.756.
4. *Ibid.*; John Rhodehamel, ed., *George Washington, Writings* (New York, 1997), p.973.
5. *Ibid.*
6. Robert D. Kaplan, *Earning the Rockies: How Geography Shapes America's Role in the World* (New York: Random House, 2017), p.141.
7. These were the words of Winston Churchill in a BBC Broadcast from London on July 14, 1940, some 64 days after he became Prime Minister and only 4 days after the beginning of an effort by Hitler's Air Force to obtain control of the air as the first stage of a planned invasion of Britain. The German effort became known as The Battle of Britain.
8. Henry Kissinger, *World Order* (New York: Penguin Press, 2014), p.1.
9. Thomas Jefferson, Letter to Dr. Joseph Priestly, June 19, 1802.

10. For several reasons, Britain's Royal Navy was often short of recruits to man its worldwide fleet of ships. It had long engaged in the practice of using "press gangs" of its sailors to go ashore to forcibly "recruit" additional sailors. While it was true that some of the impressed sailors were deserters from British ships, many were not. In June 1807, during Jefferson's presidency, a 50-gun British warship hailed a smaller American frigate off the coast of Virginia and a British officer insisted upon inspecting the American ship to look for British deserters. When the American ship refused, the British ship fired three broadsides into the American vessel, killing three American sailors and wounding 18 more. The American public was outraged, but Jefferson decided not to start a war over the incident because the small American Navy was not capable of defending itself against the much more powerful Royal Navy. Public resentment remained, however, and it added to the belief of the young American Government that Britain did not take American independence or the Government seriously.
11. Margaret Leech, *In the Days of McKinley* (New York: Harper & Brothers, 1959), pp.66-67.
12. *Ibid.*, p.146.
13. *Ibid.*
14. In March, 1898, an official U.S. Naval Court of Inquiry ruled that the ship was sunk by a mine. No blame was placed directly on Spain, but a majority of the American public and many members of Congress expressed little doubt that Spain was responsible. In 1976, a team of investigators concluded that the explosion of the *Maine* was likely caused by a fire that ignited the ammunition stored in its magazines.
15. Eugene Secuuda, Terrence P. Moran, *Selling War to America* (Westport, CT: Praeger Security International, 2007), p.20.

Chapter II: The Big Stick Policy and a New Broad View of American Interests

1. Sidney Milkis, "Theodore Roosevelt: Foreign Affairs," Miller Center, University of Virginia.
2. David McCullough, *The Path Between the Seas: The Creation of the Panama Canal,1870-1914* (New York: Simon and Schuster, 1977), p.382.
3. William N. Tilchin, "Power and Principle: The Statecraft of Theodore Roosevelt," in Cathal J. Nolan, Ed., *Ethics and Statecraft: The Moral Dimension of International Affairs, Second Edition* (Westport, CT: Praeger, 2004), pp.103-104.
4. During the fourteen-month long deployment, the ships traveled 43,000 nautical miles and made 20 port calls on six continents. Kenneth Wimmel, *Theodore Roosevelt and the Great White Fleet* (Washington: Brassey's, Inc., 1998), p.xvii.
5. Theodore Roosevelt, Speech to the Progressive National Committee, June 22, 1916.
6. Saladin Ambar, "Woodrow Wilson: Foreign Affairs, Miller Center, University of Virginia.
7. The Allies referred to wartime military alliance of Germany, Austria-Hungary, Bulgaria, and The Ottoman Empire as the "Central Powers."
8. See, e.g., Barbara W. Tuchman, *The Guns of August* (New York: Ballantine Books, 1962).
9. Theodore Roosevelt, Letter to W. W. Sewall in Island Falls, Maine, April 7, 1917.
10. Theodore Roosevelt, "Shall We Prepare?", Video by Paramount Pictures 1916, Library of Congress Online Catalog (No. 1,238,592).
11. Theodore Roosevelt, Speech at Cooper Union, New York City, November 3, 1916,
12. See Theodore Roosevelt, Letter to John J. Richardson, March 21, 1917.

Chapter III: The Fury of An Aroused Democracy

1. James MacGregor Burns, *Roosevelt: The Lion and the Fox* (New York: Harcourt, Brace and Company, 1956), pp.247-249.
2. The Locarno Treaties were a series of seven post-World War I agreements which were negotiated at Locarno, Switzerland in October 1925, whereby Great Britain, France, Germany, Italy, and Belgium mutually guaranteed peace in western Europe. The existing frontiers of Germany–Belgium and Germany-France were made inviolable. Germany, Belgium and France agreed that they would never attack each other except in "legitimate defense" or in consequence of a League of Nations obligation.
3. The Rhineland is the name used for a loosely defined region which includes land on the banks of the River Rhine in Central Europe.
4. James MacGregor Burns, *op.cit.*, p.260.
5. *Ibid.*, p.262.
6. *Ibid.*, p.390.
7. Warren F. Kimball, Ed., *Churchill & Roosevelt: The Complete Correspondence (I. Alliance Emerging)* (Princeton: Princeton University Press, 1984), p.38.
8. Charles A. & Mary R. Beard, *The Beards' New Basic History of the United States* (Garden City, N.Y.: Doubleday & Company, Inc., 1960), p.434.
9. United States Department of State Office of the Historian, "Lend-Lease and Military Aid to the Allies in the Early Years of World War II."
10. James MacGregor Burns, *op.cit.*, p.458.
11. David Bergamini, *Japan's Imperial Conspiracy* (New York: William Morrow and Company, Inc., 1971), pp.798-816.
12. Winston S. Churchill, *The Second World War: The Grand Alliance* (Boston: Houghton Mifflin Company, 1950), pp.606,607.
13. Eliot A. Cohen, "The Might-Have-Beens of Pearl Harbor," in Robert Cowley, Ed., *No End Save Victory: Perspectives on World War II* (New York: G.P. Putnam's Sons, 2001), p.126.
14. *Ibid.*, p.129.
15. Dan Kurzman, "Sabotaging Hitler's Bomb," in Robert Cowley, *op.cit.*, p.378.
16. *Ibid.*
17. Stephen E. Ambrose, "Beware the Fury of An Aroused Democracy," *The Wall Street Journal*, October 1, 2001.

Chapter IV: Isolationism and the Start of The Cold War
1. James Chace, "The Day the Cold War Started," in Robert Cowley, Ed., *The Cold War: A Military History* (New York: Random House, 2005), p.3.
2. *Ibid.*
3. David McCullough, *Truman* (New York: Simon & Schuster, 1992), p.608.
4. *Ibid.*
5. Seventy-seven British and American airmen lost their lives in the operation, but some 238,616 flights had transported over two million tons of supplies into the blockaded city.
6. John Lewis Gaddis, *The Cold War: A New History* (New York: The Penguin Press, 2005), p.42.
7. Arthur M. Schlesinger, Jr., *The Cycles of American History* (Boston: Houghton Mifflin Company, 1986), p.28.
8. Harry S. Truman, *Years of Trial and Hope, 1946-1952* (Garden City, N.Y.: Doubleday & Company, Inc., 1956), pp.332-333.

9. David Halberstam, *The Coldest Winter: America and the Korean War* (New York: Hyperion, 2007), p.138.
10. Robert Cowley, Ed., *The Cold War: A Military History* (New York: Random House, 2005), p.70.
11. *Ibid.*, pp.138-143.

Chapter V: Stand Together or Fall Separately
1. Michael T. Hayes, "The Republican Road Not Taken," *The Independent Review*, v. VIII, n.4, Spring 2004, pp.514-516.
2. *Ibid.*, p.510.
3. Lee Edwards, "The Political Thought of Robert A. Taft," *The Heritage Foundation*, October 39, 2020.
4. Dwight D. Eisenhower, *Mandate for Change, 1953-1956*, (Garden City: Double-Day & Company, Inc., 1963), pp.8-9.
5. Dwight D. Eisenhower, Address at the Annual Convention of the National Junior Chamber of Commerce, Minneapolis, Minnesota, June 10, 1953.
6. Eisenhower served as Connor's Executive Officer in the 20th Infantry Brigade in the Panama Canal Zone from 1922 to 1924. The deep-thinking Connor assigned several classics of strategy, military campaign histories, and treaties on war for Eisenhower to read and discuss. He impressed upon Eisenhower three primary principles: Never fight unless you have to; Never fight for long; and Never fight alone.
7. William I. Hitchcock, *The Age of Eisenhower: America and the World in the 1950s* (New York: Simon & Schuster, 2018), pp.103-104.
8. Theodore C. Sorensen, *Kennedy* (New York: Harper & Row Publishers, 1965), p.245.
9. Richard Reeves, *President Kennedy: Profile of Power* (New York: Simon & Schuster, 1993), p.261.
10. Bernard Brodie, *War & Politics* (New York: The Macmillan Company, 1973), p.127.
11. Robert A. Caro, *The Years of Lyndon Johnson: The Passage of Power* (New York: Alfred A. Knopf, 2012), pp.402-403.
12. 1H. R. McMaster, *Dereliction of Duty: Lyndon Johnson, Robert McNamara, the Joint Chiefs of Staff, and the Lies that Led to Vietnam* (New York: Harper-Collins, 1997), pp.62,326.
13. 1Hugh Sidey, *A Very Personal Presidency: Lyndon Johnson in the White House* (New York: Atheneum, 1968), pp.236-237.
14. David Halberstam, The Best and the Brightest (New York: Random House, 1969), p.593.
15. See Arthur M. Schlesinger, Jr., *op.cit.*, pp.27-29.
16. James Webb, "History Proves Vietnam Victors Wrong," *The Wall Street Journal*, April 28, 2000.
17. The comment was made by Dr. John Sloan Dickey, the then President of Dartmouth College at the College's 1965 Convocation.
18. James Webb, *op.cit.*
19. The Tet Offensive involved coordinated attacks by some 85,000 troops against five major South Vietnamese cities, dozens of military installations, and many towns and villages.
20. U.S. and South Vietnamese forces almost completely eliminated the Viet Cong forces and regained all of the territory that had been lost initially. Moreover, the South Vietnamese people did not rise up to support the Offensive as the North had expected.
21. Tim Page, John Pimlott, Consultant Editors, *NAM: The Vietnam Experience 1965-1975* (New York: Mallard Press, 1988), pp.376-379.
22. Doris Kearns Goodwin, *Leadership in Turbulent Times* (New York: Simon & Schuster, 2018), pp.341-342.

Chapter VI: Pragmatism, Political Will and Human Rights
1. Roland Evans, Jr., Robert D. Novak, *Nixon in the White House* (New York: Random House, 1971), p.79.
2. Ken Hughes, "Richard Nixon: Foreign Affairs," *Miller Center*, University of Virginia.
3. Roland Evans, Jr., Robert D. Novak, *op.cit.*, p.100.
4. Remarks by Dr. Henry Kissinger at Richard Nixon's Funeral, April 27, 1994.
5. Stephen M. Duncan, *First Duty: Presidents, the Nation's Security and Self-Centered Politics* (Mount Vernon, VA: Highland & Claymore Press, 2019), p.118.
6. Dave Richard Palmer, *Summons of the Trumpet: U.S.-Vietnam in Perspective* (Novato, CA: Presidio Press, 1978), p.259.
7. Robert T. Kelley, "Introduction," in William Bowman, Roger Little, G. Thomas Sicilia, eds., *The All-Volunteer Force after a Decade* (Washington, D.C.: Brassey's, 1986), p.21.
8. Richard Nixon, *U.S. Foreign Policy for the 1970s: A New Strategy for Peace*, Report to the Congress, February 1970 (Washington, D.C.: Government Printing Office, 1970), p.129.
9. Secretary of Defense James R. Schlesinger, Memorandum, "Readiness of the Selected Reserve," August 23, 1973, pp.1-2.
10. See Stephen M. Duncan, *Citizen Warriors: America's National Guard and Reserve Forces & the Politics of National Security* (Novato, CA: Presidio Press, 1997), pp.93-130.
11. Gerald R. Ford, *A Time to Heal* (New York: Harper & Row Publishers, The Readers Digest Association, Inc., 1979), p.61.
12. In May 1904, Ion Perdicaris, an elderly, wealthy American, was dining with his family at his home in the hills above Tangier. He was suddenly kidnapped by a number of armed Moors who were led by a powerful Berber chieftain named Mulai Ahmed er Raisuli, Lord of the Rif and last of the Barbary pirates. Raisuli made ransom demands of the Sultan of Morocco, with whom he was engaged in a struggle for power. When the Sultan did not move quickly enough, and consistent with his Big Stick Policy, Roosevelt directed Secretary of State John Hay to send a telegram to the U.S. Counsel-General of Morocco, which read "This Government wants Perdicaris alive or Raisuli dead." He also ordered part of the Great White Fleet to Tangier. Upon his release, Perdicaris wrote to the Counsel-General. "Few indeed," he said "are the Americans who can have appreciated as keenly as I did then what the presence of our Flag in foreign waters meant at such a moment and in such circumstances." Ironically, Roosevelt learned in the middle of the crisis that Perdicaris was a Greek citizen who had relinquished his American citizenship years earlier. But, the President was undeterred since he knew that Raisuli believed he had kidnapped an American, and thus a larger principle was at stake. See Barbara W. Tuchman, "Predicaris Alive or Raisuli Dead," *American Heritage*, Vol. 10, Issue 5, August 1959.
13. Henry Kissinger, *Years of Renewal* (New York: Simon & Schuster, 1999), p.551.
14. Gerald Ford, *op.cit.*, p.275.
15. Henry Kissinger, *Years of Renewal*, p.558.
16. See, e.g., Julian E. Zelizer, *Jimmy Carter* (New York: Henry Holt and Company, 2010), p.147.
17. U.S. Department of State, Office of the Historian, "Carter's Foreign Policy," https://history.state.gov.
18. See Harold Brown, *Thinking About National Security: defense and foreign policy in a dangerous world* (Boulder, CO: Westview Press, 1983), p.267.
19. Don Oberdorfer, "Carter's Decision on Korea Traced Back to January 1975,"

Washington Post, June 12, 1977.
20. Jimmy Carter, *Keeping Faith: Memoirs of a President* (Toronto: Bantam Books, 1982), p.155.
21. James Kitfield, *Prodigal Soldiers* (New York: Simon and Schuster, 1995), pp.198-200.
22. See David R. Segal, Nathan L. Hibler, "Manpower and Personnel Policy in the Reagan Years," in William P. Snyder, James Brown, eds., *Defense Policy in the Reagan Administration* (Washington, D.C.: National Defense University Press, 1988), p.205.
23. Scott Kaufman, *Plans Unraveled: The Foreign Policy of the Carter Administration* (DeKalb: Northern Illinois University, 2008), p.183.
24. Cross-decking is a naval term which generally refers to the informal or ad hoc sharing of resources between naval vessels. One or more experienced individuals with required specialties may be cross-decked to another ship to help the second vessel come to a full state of readiness. Spare parts may also be cross-decked between ships which operate comparable equipment.
25. James Kitfield, *op.cit.*
26. Julian E. Zelizer, *op.cit.*, pp.96-97.
27. Zbigniew Brzezinski, *Power and Principle: Memoirs of the National Security Adviser, 1977-1981* (New York: Farrar, Straus, Giroux, 1983), p.493.
28. James Fallows, "The Passionless Presidency: The trouble with Jimmy Carter's Administration," *The Atlantic*, May, 1979.

Chapter VII: The End of the Cold War and a New Hot War in Iraq

1. Caspar W. Weinberger, *In The Arena: A Memoir of the 20th Century* (Washington, D.C.: Regnery Publishing, Inc., 2001), p.278.
2. William Inboden, *The Peacemaker: Ronald Reagan, The Cold War, and the World on the Brink* (New York: Dutton, 2022), p.1.
3. Telegram 1978, June 1, 1982, from Thatcher Manuscripts, THCR 1/10/33, Churchill Archives Centre, Churchill College, University of Cambridge.
4. William Inboden, *op.cit.*, p.155.
5. Matthew Continetti, "'The Peacemaker' Review: Ronald Reagan's Cold War," *The Wall Street Journal*, November 25, 2022.
6. Robert Kagen, "When America Blinked: How we unlearned the art of war," *New Republic*, December 3, 2001, p.35.
7. Vincent Dais, "The Reagan Defense Program: Decision Making, Decision Makers and Some of the Results," Stephen J. Cimbola, ed., *The Reagan Defense Program: An Interim Assessment*, Wilmington Scholarly Resources, Inc., 1986, p.49.
8. Dinesh D'Souza, *Ronald Reagan: How an Ordinary Man Became an Extraordinary Leader* (New York: The Free Press, 1997), p.98.
9. Tom Bowman, "Reagan guided huge buildup in arms race," *The Baltimore Sun*, June 8, 2004.
10. Michael Beschloss, *Presidential Courage* (New York: Simon & Schuster, 2007), p.280.
11. Robert Love, "Rethinking Reagan," *AARP*, October/November 2015, p.65.
12. Robert Kagan, *op.cit.*.
13. William Inboden, *op.cit.* p.479.
14. *Ibid.*, p.478.
15. *Ibid.*
16. *Ibid.*, p.479.
17. Robert D. Kaplan, *Earning the Rockies: How Geography Shapes America's Role in the World* (New York: Random House, 2017), p.141.

18. Michael Gerson, "Demolishing America's mission in the world," *Washington Post* July 20, 2018, p.A17.
19. Paul Lettow, *Ronald Reagan and His Quest to Abolish Nuclear Weapons* (New York: Random House, Inc., 2005), p.xi.
20. Martin Anderson, Annelise Anderson, *Reagan's Secret War: The Untold Story of His Fight to Save the World from Nuclear Disaster* (New York: Crown Publishers, 2009), pp.60, 63, 143, 156, 161.
21. *Ibid.*, p.x.
22. The Treaty resulted in the destruction of 859 U.S. nuclear missiles and 1,836 Soviet nuclear missiles in Europe which had ranges between 300 and 3,400 miles.
23. Henry Kissinger, *Diplomacy* (New York: Simon & Schuster, 1994), p.764.
24. Cited by Richard Ned Lebow and Janice Gross Stein, "Reagan and the Russians," *Atlantic Monthly*, February 1994, p.35; Dinesha D'Souza, *Ronald Reagan* (New York: The Free Press, 1997), p.196.
25. Margaret Thatcher, *The Downing Street Years* (New York: HarperCollins, 1993), p.813.
26. Reagan's final approval rating in the Gallup poll was 63 percent. His final approval rating in the *New York Times* – CBS Poll was 68 percent.
27. At that time, the People's Republic of China had not been formally recognized by the U.S., which maintained diplomatic relations only with the Republic of China on Taiwan.
28. Lou Cannon, *President Reagan: The Role of a Lifetime* (New York: Simon & Schuster,1991), pp.305-306.
29. *Ibid.*
30. Stephen M. Duncan, *First Duty: Presidents, the Nation's Security and Self-Centered Politics* (Mount Vernon, VA: Highland & Claymore Press, 2019), p.178.
31. David E. Hoffman, "He kept his cool as the world caught fire," *Washington Post*, December 2, 2018, pp.A1, A14.
32. John H. Sununu, *The Quiet Man: The Indispensable Presidency of George H. W. Bush* (New York: HarperCollins Publishers, 2015), p.91.
33. George Bush, Brent Scowcroft, *A World Transformed* (New York: Alfred A. Knopf, Inc.,1998), pp.xiii, xiv.
34. See Stephen M. Duncan, *First Duty*, p.178.
35. The Warsaw Pact was a Communist political and collective defense (military) treaty which was signed on May 14, 1955, between the Soviet Union and seven Soviet satellite states in Central and Eastern Europe during the Cold War. Those states included East Germany, Poland, Bulgaria, Hungary, Romania, Albania, and Czechoslovakia. The Pact was established in response to the integration of West Germany into NATO.
36. Christopher Maynard, *Out of the Shadow: George H. W. Bush and the End of the Cold War* (College Station: Texas A&M University Press, 2008), pp.42-43.
37. Michael R. Beschloss, Strobe Talbott, *At the Highest Levels: The Inside Story of the End of the Cold War* (Boston: Little, Brown and Company, 1993), p.135.
38. Jon Meacham, *Destiny and Power: The American Odyssey of George Herbert Walker Bush* (New York: Random House, 2015), p.382.
39. *Ibid.*, p.495.
40. Jeffrey A. Engel, *When the World Seemed New: George H. W. Bush and The End of The Cold War* (Boston: Houghton Mifflin Harcourt, 2017), p.484.
41. Alex Yacoubian, "U.S.-Iran Showdown in the Gulf – Déjà vu?" *The United States Institute of Peace (The Iran Primer)*, July 29, 2019.

42. William Inboden, *op.cit.*, pp.450-451.
43. Jon Meacham, *op.cit.*, p.428; The Defense Intelligence Agency estimated that the Iraqi Army included 540,000 troops, more than 4,200 tanks, 2,800 armored personnel carriers, and approximately 3,100 artillery pieces.
44. Rick Alkinson, *Crusade: The Untold Story of the Persian Gulf War* (Boston: Houghton Mifflin Company, 1993), p.54.
45. "The Vietnam Syndrome," *The Economist*, April 15, 2004.
46. William J. Taylor, Jr., James Blackwell, "The Ground War in the Gulf," *Survival*, Vol. 33, No. 3 (May/June 1991), p.245.
47. Rick Atkinson, "U.S. Victory is Absolute," *Washington Post*, March 1, 1991, p.1.

Chapter VIII: The Dangerous Road to Ineffective Deterrence
1. Frederick W. Kagan, "Strategy and Force Structure in an Interwar Period," *Joint Forces Quarterly* (Spring/Summer, 2001), p.94.
2. Adam Kuper, "'Why We Fight' Review: Give Peace a (Bigger) Chance," *The Wall Street Journal*, May 6, 2022; See also, Christopher Blattman, *Why We Fight: The Roots of War and the Paths to Peace* (New York: Viking, 2022).
3. *Ibid*.
4. See Stephen M. Duncan, *A War of a Different Kind: Military Force and America's Search for Homeland Security* (Annapolis, MD: Naval Institute Press, 2004); p.xiv.
5. *Ibid*.
6. David Halberstam, *War in a Time of Peace: Bush, Clinton, and the Generals* (New York: Scribner, 2001), p.193.
7. See, Dick Morris, Eileen Morris, *Because He Could* (New York: Regan Books, 2004), pp.123-124.
8. Richard K. Betts, "Are Civil-Military Relations Still a Problem?" in *American Civil-Military Relations: The Soldier and the State in a New Era*, ed. Suzanne C. Nielson and Don M. Snyder (Baltimore: Johns Hopkins University Press, 2009), p.14.
9. See Stephen M. Duncan, *Only the Most Able: Moving Beyond Politics in the Selection of National Security Leaders* (Lanham, MD: Rowman & Littlefield Publishers, Inc., 2013), pp.60-62.
10. The operation became the subject of the 2001 film *Black Hawk Down*, which was based on the 1999 book of the same name by Mark Bowden.
11. Charles Krauthammer, "How to Deal With Countries Gone Mad," *Time*, September 21, 1987.
12. George E. Bogden, "How Bill Clinton Sealed Ukraine's Fate," *The Wall Street Journal*, March 25, 2022.
13. David Halberstam, *War in a Time of Peace*, p.283.
14. Nigel Hamilton, *Bill Clinton: Mastering the Presidency* (New York: Public Affairs, 2007), p.86.
15. Anthony Lake, *6 Nightmares: Real Threats in a Dangerous World and How America Can Meet Them* (New York: Little, Brown and Company, 2000, Emphasis Added); Nigel Hamilton, *op.cit.*, p.196.
16. Strobe Talbott, "Democracy and the National Interest," *Foreign Affairs*, November/December 1996, pp.48-49.
17. Ralph Peters, "The Decadence of Deterrence," *Strategika* (Hoover Institution), February 15, 2022.
18. *Ibid*.
19. Newsweek Staff, "The Peace Dividend," *Newsweek*, January 25, 1998.
20. Department of the Army, *U.S. Army Field Manual* 100-5, p.13-0.

21. William Matthews, "Reserves Get Larger Role in Battle on Domestic Ills, *Army-Times*, July 25, 1994, p.22.
22. Deborah R. Lee, Remarks to the National Guard Association of the United States, Boston, Massachusetts September 2, 1994.
23. Hannah Hartig, Carroll Doherty, "Two Decades Later, the Enduring Legacy of 9/11," *Pew Research Center*, September 9, 2021.
24. *Ibid.*
25. Andrew Kohut, "American International Engagement on the Rocks," *Pew Research Center*, July 11, 2013.
26. See Stephen M. Duncan, *First Duty, op.cit.*
27. Churchill served as Home Secretary (1910-1911), First Lord of the Admiralty (1911-1915) and (1939-1940), Minister of Munitions (1917-1919), Secretary of State for War and Air (1919-1921), Prime Minister and Minister of Defence (1940-1945) and (1951-1955).
28. Andrew Roberts, *Churchill: Walking with Destiny* (New York: Viking, 2018), P. 279; Hastings L. Ismay, *The Memoirs of General Lord Ismay* (New York: Viking, 1960), p.166.
29. Paul D. Miller, "Ending the 'Endless War' Trope," *Atlantic Council*, March 26, 2020.
30. Peter D. Feaver, Jim Golby, "The Myth of 'War Weary' Americans, *The Wall Street Journal*, December 1, 2020.
31. Latest Reagan National Defense Survey Shows Declining Confidence in U.S. Military But Broad Support for American Leadership in the World," Ronald Reagan Presidential Foundation and Institute, March 10, 2021.
32. Lucian Stalno-Daniels, "America Doesn't Control Forever Wars," *foreignpolicy.com*, January 15, 2022.
33. Daniel Henniger, "Progressive to Uyghurs: Drop Dead," *The Wall Street Journal*, January 19, 2022.
34. *Ibid.*

Chapter IX: Russia: The Early Warning Signs
1. Winston S. Churchill, *The Gathering Storm* (Boston: Houghton Mifflin Company, 1948), p.393.
2. The KGB was the primary security agency for the Soviet Union from March 13, 1954 to December 3, 1991. It was a military service in the same fashion as the Soviet Army. Its functions included foreign intelligence, secret police, and internal security and it was used to combat dissident, religious, and "anti-Soviet" activities.
3. Yaroslav Trofimov, "How Far Do Putin's Imperial Ambitions Go?", *The Wall Street Journal*, June 24, 2022.
4. Daniel Fried, Kurt Volker, "The Speech In Which Putin Told Us Who He Was," *www.politico.com/news/magazine*, February 18, 2022.
5. Michael R. Gordon, Bojan Pancevski, Noemie Bisserbe, Marcus Walker, "Putin Targeted Ukraine for Years. Why Didn't the West Stop Him?", *The Wall Street Journal*, April 2-3, 2022, p.C1.
6. Lynne Harnett, "The long history of Russian imperialism shaping Putin's war," *Washington Post*, March 2, 2022.
7. *Ibid.*
8. *Ibid.*
9. Daniel Treisman, "Searching for the roots of Russia's aggression," *Washington Post*, September 25, 2015.
10. Shaun Walker, "How the Soviet Union's Fall Pushed Putin to Try and Recapture

Russia's Global Importance," *www.history.com/news*, February 28, 2022.
11. Hitler used this term in a speech to the Germany Reichstag on September 1, 1939, the day that Germany invaded Poland.
12. Michael S. Goodman, Daniel Frey, David Giol, "Alexi Navalny poisoning: what theatrical assassination attempts reveal about Vladimir Putin's grip on power in Russia," *theconversation.com*, September 9, 2020.
13. Peggy Noonan, "Putin Really May Break The Nuclear Taboo in Ukraine," *The Wall Street Journal*, April 28, 2022.
14. Michael S. Goodman, Daniel Frey, David Giol, *op.cit.*
15. *Ibid.*
16. Michael R. Gordon, Bajan Pancevski, Noemie Bisserbe, Marcus Walker, *op.cit.*
17. Andrew A. Michta, "China, Russia and the West's Crisis of Disbelief," *The Wall Street Journal*, August 7, 2022.
18. Alec Blivas, "Sino-Russian Military Exercises Signal A Growing Alliance, U.S. Naval Institute *Proceedings*, June 2021.
19. *Ibid.*
20. *Ibid.*
21. Jon Meacham, *op.cit.*, p.596; Philip Seib, "President George H. W. Bush and Diplomacy"in *Security, Culture, Diplomacy, www.pacificcouncil.org.*
22. Daniel Fried, Kurt Volker, *op.cit.*
23. George E. Bogden, "How Bill Clinton Sealed Ukraine's Fate," *The Wall Street Journal*, March 25, 2022.
24. Michael R. Gordon, Bojan Pancevski, Noemie Bisserbe, Marcus Walker, *op.cit.*
25. Yaroslav Trofimov, "How Far Do Putin's Imperial Ambitions Go?", *op.cit.*
26. "Why NATO Is at the Center of the Russia-Ukraine Conflict," *The Wall Street Journal*, February 18, 2022.
27. *Lessons from Russia's Operation in Crimea and Eastern Ukraine* (Santa Monica, CA: Rand Corporation, 2017), p.14.
28. Yaraslav Trofimov, "Ukraine Is the West's War Now," *The Wall Street Journal*, February 25-26, 2023, p. C1.
29. Charles Krauthammer, "Russia Rising," *Washington Post*, March 28, 2014.
30. Yaroslave Trofimov, "Ukraine Is the Wast's War Now, *op.cit.*
31. Charles Krauthammer, "Russia Rising," *op.cit.*, p.227
32. Kipp Hanley, "Advocating for Change in Europe;" "A former NATO commander speaks out on recount events," *Military Officer Magazine*, June 22, 2022, pp.20-21.
33. *Lessons from Russia's Operation in Crimea and Eastern Ukraine, op. cit.* p.xii.

Chapter X: Russia: The Failure of Deterrence, A Hot War in Ukraine and Cold War II

1. Russian Battalion Tactical Groups number approximately 700-800 troops each. They are built around mechanized infantry or tank battalions and are reinforced with artillery, air defenses, electronic warfare and other specialized units. Michael R. Gordon, Thomas Grove, Yaroslav Trofinov, Bojan Pancevski, "Russia Accelerates Troup Buildup Along Ukraine Border," *Wall Street Journal*, February 14, 2022.
2. David Rennick, "The Weakness of the Despot," *The New Yorker*, March 11, 2022.
3. The Editorial Board, "With Russia's Invasion of Ukraine, a New Cold War Arrives," *The Wall Street Journal*, February 22, 2022; The Editorial Board, "The 80s Got Their Foreign Policy Back," *The Wall Street Journal*, February 23, 2022, p.A16.
4. Michael R. Gordon, Bojan Pancevski, Naomie Bisserby, Marcus Walker, "Vladimir Putin's 20-Year March to War in Ukraine – And How the West Mishandled It," *The Wall Street Journal*, April 1, 2022.

5. Stephen M. Walt, "Liberal Illusions Caused the Ukraine Crisis," *Foreign Policy* (foreignpolicy.com), January 19, 2022.
6. *Ibid.*
7. Michael R. Gordon, Bojan Pancevski, Naomie Bisserby, Marcus Walker, *op.cit.*
8. Nicholas Mulder, "Don't Expect Sanctions to Win the Ukraine War," *The Wall Street Journal*, April 21, 2022.
9. Dan Balz, "Bush Promises an 'American Internationalism'", *www.washingtonpost.com*, November 19, 1979.
10. Tom Rosentiel, "Bush's Concern Over Isolationism Reflects More Than Just Rhetoric," *Pew Research Center*, February 3, 2006.
11. See Stephen M. Duncan, *First Duty*, pp.233-240.
12. Bob Woodward, *Obama's Wars* (New York: Simon & Schuster, 2010), p.336.
13. See Stephen M. Duncan, *First Duty*, pp.240-245.
14. Dan DeLuce, "Hagel: The White House Tried to Destroy Me," *Foreign Policy*, December 18, 2015.
15. Leon Panetta, Jim Newton, *Worthy Fights* (New York: Penguin Press, 2014), pp.450-451. Ian Schwartz, "Panetta: When Presidents Don't Stand By Red Lines It Sends A Message of Weakness To World," *RealClear Politics*, April 14, 2017.
16. Pamela Engel, "Former U.S. Defense Secretary: Obama hurt U.S. credibility when he backed down from his red line on Syria," *Business Insider*, January 26, 2016.
17. Greg Jaffe, "The Problem with Obama's account of the Syrian red-line incident," *The Washington Post*, October 4, 2016.
18. Bret Stephens, "The Price of Obama's Mendacity," *The Wall Street Journal*, April 11, 2017, p.A15
19. The Editorial Board, "Why Obama Didn't Arm Ukraine," *The Wall Street Journal*, March 8, 2022, p.A20.
20. Stephen M. Duncan, *First Duty*, pp.263-267, 278.
21. *Ibid.*, pp.270-274, 278-279; John Walcott, "'Willful Ignorance': Inside President Trump's Intelligence Briefings," *Time (www.msn.com)*, February 3, 2019.
22. See Philip Rucker, Paul Sonne, "Trump, first lady visit U.S. troops at air base in Iraq," *Washington Post*, December 27, 2018, pp.A1,A2; Josh Rogin, "Trump's new foreign policy whisperer," *Washington Post*, December 28, 2018, p.A19.
23. Winston S. Churchill, *The Hinge of Fate* (Boston: Houghton Mifflin Company, 1950), p.405.
24. Mark T. Esper, *A Sacred Oath* (New York: William Morrow, 2022), p.356.
25. *Ibid.*, p.8.
26. Mark T. Esper, *Ibid.*, p.364.
27. *Ibid.*, p.339.
28. *Ibid.*, p.338.
29. Bryan Metzger, "Former National Security Adviser John Bolton says 'Putin was waiting' for Trump to withdraw the United States from NATO in his second term," *Business Insider* (bmetzger@insider.com), March 4, 2022.
30. Charles Krauthammer, "To Die for Estonia?" *Washington Post*, June 2, 2017.
31. After Trump announced his candidacy in the 2024 Presidential Election for another term in the White House, and despite the huge stakes for the U.S. in the outcome of the war in Ukraine, he made it clear that he would limit or even end the U.S. support of Ukraine. Declaring that "this thing has got to stop, and it's got to stop now," he posted a video in which he pledged to "clean house of all the warmongers and America's last globalists." See Kimberly Stassel, "Ron DeSantis's Security Test," *The Wall Street Journal*, Febarury 24, 2023, p. A15.

32. Karl Rove, "Zelensky Defines Courage in Our Time," *The Wall Street Journal*, March 17, 2022, p.A19.
33. Dan DeLuce, "Biden under fire from Congress for waiving sanctions on Russian gas pipeline company," www.nbcnews.com, May 19, 2021.
34. Michael R. Gordon, *Degrade and Destroy* (New York: Farrar, Straus and Giroux, 2022) p.394.
35. *Ibid.*, p.397.
36. Tony Abbot, "Putin Gambles That the West is Weak," *The Wall Street Journal*, February 28, 2002, p.A21.
37. Gerard Baker, "Biden at the Improv: Ukraine and the Dangers of Foreign Policy by Open Mic," *The Wall Street Journal*, March 28, 2022.
38. Robin Wright, "Russia and China Unveil A Pact Against America And the West," *The New Yorker*, February 20, 2022.
39. *Ibid.*
40. Sidharth Kaushal, Sam Cranny-Evans, "Russia's Aggressive New Nuclear Strategy," *The Wall Street Journal*, July 23-24, 2022, p.C3.
41. A poll taken immediately after Biden announced the U.S. sanctions indicated that 56 percent of the American public were of the opinion that this response to the Invasion was not strong enough.
42. *Swift* is a Belgian-based cooperative which is owned and operated under European law by its member banks for the purpose of providing secure financial messaging services to banks for quick cross-border payments and the smooth flow of international trade.
43. Walter Russell Mead, "A Rogue Russia Tries to Reset the World Order," *The Wall Street Journal*, February 24, 2022.
44. The Editorial Board, "Putin's New World Disorder," *The Wall Street Journal*, February 24, 2022.
45. Steven Erlanger, "With the Ukraine Invasion, NATO is Suddenly Vulnerable," *New York Times*, February 24, 2022.
46. Stephen M. Duncan, *op.cit.*, p.270.
47. Germany imports 55 percent of its gas and 45 percent of its oil from Russia, thereby making it strategically dependent on Putin.
48. Daniel Henninger, "Progressive to Uyghurs: Drop Dead," *The Wall Street Journal*, January 19, 2022.
49. Daniel Henniger, "Ukraine Changes Everything," *The Wall Street Journal*, March 3, 2022, p.A19.
50. Joseph Gideon, "Trump calls Putin 'genius' and 'very savvy' for Ukraine invasion," *Politico*, February 23, 2022.
51. Timothy Bella, "Tucker Carlson, downplaying Russia-Ukraine conflict, urges Americans to ask, 'Why do I hate Putin?'" *Washington Post* (www.washingtonpost.com), February 23, 2022.
52. Tim Hains, *RealClear Politics* (www.realclearpolitics.com) February 27, 2022.
53. Andrew Roberts, "Churchill, Zelensky and the American Right," *The Wall Street Journal*, April 2-3, 2022, p.A13.
54. Jeffrey Scott Shapiro, "The Right's Russia Temptation," *The Wall Street Journal*, April 10, 2022.
55. Karl Rove, "Republicans Stand Up for Ukraine," *The Wall Street Journal*, March 9, 2022.

Chapter XI: The Will and Moral Courage of Free Men and Women

1. Andrew Roberts, "Leadership for the West," *International Churchill Society*, June 30, 2022.

2. Robert Burns, "Russia's failure to take down Kyiv was a defeat for the ages," *AP News*, April 7, 2022.
3. Yaroslav Trofimov, "Ukraine Is the West's War Now," *op. cit.*
4. Ibid.
5. Aaron Blake, Michael Birubam, "Trump says he threatened not to defend NATO against Russia," *Washington Post*, April 22, 2022.
6. The Editorial Board, "A GOP Faction Votes Against Ukraine," *The Wall Street Journal*, May 17, 2022.
7. Sune Engel Rasinussen, "How Putin Drove Finland Into NATO'S Arms," *The Wall Street Journal*, May 13, 2022.
8. Finland reportedly had an artillery arsenal of 1,500 weapons, the largest in Western Europe, an Active Army of 280,000 troops and, 600,000 additional Reservists, making the country's armed forces among Europe's largest on a per capita basis. Finland also retains its *Sisu*, the Finnish fighting spirit which characterized its courageous fight against the much stronger forces of the Soviet Union in World War II (referred to in Finland as the Winter War or the First Soviet-Finnish War).
9. Yaroslav Trofimov, "Ukraine Will Fight Until All Russian Forces Are Expelled, Military Intelligence Chief Says," *The Wall Street Journal*, May 20, 2022.
10. Charlotte Plantiv, Dmitry Zaks, Patrick Fort, "Zelensky: Only diplomacy can end conflict with – Russia," *The Times of Israel*, May 21, 2022.
11. Andrew A. Michta, "China, Russia and the West's Crisis of Disbelief," *op.cit.*
12. Ralph Gert Schöllhammer, "Why Europe Hedges Its Support for Ukraine," *The Wall Street Journal*, May 23, 2022, p.A17.
13. Walter Russell Mead, "Managing a World Order in Crisis," *The Wall Street Journal*, May 3, 2022.
14. *Ibid*.
15. Bojan Pancevski, "Cracks Show in Western Front Against Russia's War in Ukraine," *The Wall Street Journal*, May 31, 2022.
16. The Editorial Board, "Biden's Ukraine Ambivalence," *The Wall Street Journal*, May 30, 2022.
17. Yaroslav Trofimov, "How Far Do Putin's Imperial Ambitions Go?", *op.cit.*; Ishaan Tharoor, "Putin makes his imperial pretensions clear," *Washington Post*, June 13, 2022.
18. *Ibid*.
19. *Ibid*.
20. *Ibid*.
21. Daniel Henniger, "Progressive to Uyghurs: Drop Dead," *op.cit.*
22. *Ibid*.
23. The Wagner Group is a Russian state-backed mercenary group, i.e., a private military contractor, which is reportedly tightly integrated with Russia's Defence Ministry and its intelligence arm, the CRU. It has been accused of war crimes by several countries.
24. The High Mobility Artillery Rocket System, or *HIMARS*, fires multiple GPS-guided precision rockets, each of which can hit a different geo-located target. Each rocket can be fitted with either a 200-pound explosive warhead for armored targets or fragment charges for hitting personnel. Each *HIMARS* carries one six-rocket pod "that can effectively land thepunch of more than 100,000 pounds of traditional artillery shells." Because of its mobility and a speed as high as 53 mph, a *HIMARS* system can fire its rockets and quickly move to a new location in order to avoid an enemy's counterfire. Stephen Kalin, Daniel Michaels, "The Himars Revolution In Warfare," *The Wall Street Journal*, October 8-9, 2022.

25. Yaroslav Trofimov, "Captured Arms Fuel Kyiv Offensive," *The Wall Street Journal*, October 6, 2022, p.A6.
26. Stephen Fidler, Kim Mackrael, "Europe Is Tested Anew, This Time by Energy, Inflation and Putin," *The Wall Street Journal*, July 22, 2022.
27. Alan Gullison, "Protests Persist Over Russia Draft," *The Wall Street Journal*, September 26, 2022, p.A6.
28. Drew Hinshaw, Kate Vtorygina, "Russians Crowd Borders as Many Evade Draft," *The Wall Street Journal*, September 30, 2022, p.A7.
29. Alan Gullison, "Escalation of War Raises Risks to Putin, *The Wall Street Journal*, September 30, 2022, p.A7.
30. Yaroslav Trofimov, Matthew Luximoore, "Ukraine's Zelensky Says a Cease-Fire With Russia, Without Reclaiming Lost Lands, Will Only Prolong War," *The Wall Street Journal*, July 22, 2022.
31. William A. Galston, "How Russia's Invasion Changed the World," *The Wall Street Journal*, September 21, 2022, p.A15.
32. The Editorial Board, "Ukraine Takes the Offensive," *The Wall Street Journal*, September 12, 2022, p.A16.
33. Winston Churchill, "Fifty Years Hence" (originally published in *Strand*, London, December 1931), in *Thoughts and Adventures* (New York: W.W. Norton, 1991), p.201.
34. Peggy Noonan, "The Uvalde Police Scandal," *The Wall Street Journal*, June 4-5, 2022, p.A15.

Chapter XII: China: The Early and Recent Warning Signs

1. Jim Garamone, "U.S. Intel Officials Detail Threats From China, Russia, *DOD News*, March 8, 2022.
2. Christopher Wray, "The Threat Posed by the Chinese Government and the Chinese Communist Party to the Economic and National Security of the United States," Remarks delivered to The Hudson Institute, July 7, 2020.
3. "Report on Military and Security Developments Involving the People's Republic of China," U.S. Department of Defense, November 3, 2021, p.1.
4. The term "Peoples Liberation Army" is used to apply to all of China's individual military services.
5. "Report on Military and Security Developments Involving the Peoples Republic of China, pp.III, V.
6. Peter Martin, Understanding Chinese "Wolf Warrior Diplomacy," an interview with The National Bureau of Asian Research, October 21, 2021.
7. Jeffrey Wasserstrom, "Why Are There No Biographies of Xi Jinping?", *The Atlantic*, January 30, 2021.
8. The Cultural Revolution was a sociopolitical upheaval in China from 1966 until Mao Zedong's death in 1976. The declared objective of the Revolution, which was launched by Mao, was to preserve Chinese Communism by purging remnants of traditional and capitalistic elements from Chinese society and to re-focus the population on Mao Zedong thought. In fact, much of Mao's purpose was to regain total political power and to ensure his own place in history.
9. "Xi Jinping: Early life, "*Encyclopedia Britannica* (www.britannica.com), November 22, 2021.
10. The Princelings are the descendants of influential senior officials of the CCP, especially those prominent leaders who had power in the first generation after the founding of the CCP. Since Princelings have opportunities and influence which are not available to the

common people in China, somewhat like crown princes in hereditary monarchies, their fortunes and political power are often the result of cronyism and nepotism.
11. See Cindy Yu, "What shaped today's CCP leaders?/Chinese Whispers," *Spectator* TV, May 31, 2022.
12. "Xi Jinping: Early life," *Encyclopedia Britannica*
13. The Editorial Board, "Opinion: Truth emerges about Chinese repression of Uyghurs – no thanks to the U.N.," *Washington Post*, May 29, 2022; "Leaked papers link top Chinese leaders to Uyghur crackdown," *BBC*, November 30, 2021.
14. "Leaked papers link Chinese leaders to Uyghur crackdown," *BBC*.
15. "China's Xi responsible for Uyghur 'genocide,' unofficial tribunal says," *Reuters*, December 10, 2021. In June 2022, new American legislation, the Uyghur Forced Labor Prevention Act, went into effect. It presumes that all items produced in China's Xinjiang region, or by entities linked to the government there, are made with forced labor and blocks American companies from importing such products. Liza Lin, Yoko Kubota, "U.S. Import Ban Targets Xinjiang Region, *The Wall Street Journal*, June 22, 2022, p.A8.
16. Jeffrey Wasserstrom, *op.cit.*
17. Kevin Rudd "The World According to Xi Jinping," *Foreign Affairs, Vol. 101, Number 6*, November/December, 2022, pp.10,21.
18. Francis Pike, "How long will Xi Jinping rule China? *The Spectator*, June 12, 2022.
19. Zbigniew Brezezinski, *The Grand Chessboard* (New York: BasicBooks, 1997), p.161.
20. Alastair Gale, "China's Military Catches Up," *The Wall Street Journal*, October 21, 2022, p.A11.
21. Niharika Mandhana, "How Beijing Boxed America Out of the South China Sea," *The Wall Street Journal*, March 11, 2023.
22. The Editorial Board, "Meanwhile, Watch China in the Pacific," *The Wall Street Journal*, March 24, 2022.
23. Niharika Mandhana, op. cit.
24. "Remarks by Vice President Pence on the Trump Administration's Policy Toward China," The Hudson Institute, Washington, D.C., October 4, 2018; See also Dexter Filkins, "A Dangerous Game: China has coveted its island neighbor for decades. Is Xi Jinping ready to seize it?", *The New Yorker*, November 21, 2022, p.32.
25. Advantage at Sea: Prevailing with Integrated All-Domain Naval Power, December 2020.
26. Josh Rogin, "This Asia strategy goes on the road," *Washington Post*, November 9, 2018, p.A25.
27. William Schneider, Jr., "China Sees Its Nuclear Arsenal as More Than a Deterrent," *The Wall Street Journal*, September 7, 2021.
28. *Ibid.*
29. Gordon Lubold, Nancy A. Youssef, "Advanced Maneuver in China Hypersonic Missile Test Shows New Military Capability," *The Wall Street Journal*, November 21, 2021.
30. David Martin, "Top military official discloses new details about China's hypersonic test," *CBS NEWS*, November 16, 2021.
31. Gordon Lubold, Warren P. Strobel, "China Nears Launch of Advanced Aircraft Carrier Satellite Images Show," *The Wall Street Journal*, June 2, 2022.
32. Chun Han Wong, "China Launches Third Aircraft Carrier, Advancing Naval Ambitions," *The Wall Street Journal*, June 17, 2022.
33. James T. Areddy, "China Has Built Mock-Ups of U.S. Aircraft Carrier, Warships In the Desert," *The Wall Street Journal*, November 8, 2021.
34. Alastair Gale, "China Recruited Western Pilots With Knowledge of Stealth Fighters And Aircraft Carriers," *The Wall Street Journal*, December 14, 2022.

35. *Ibid.*
36. Elaine Luria, "Does the Pentagon Take China seriously?" *The Wall Street Journal*, July 5, 2021.
37. Jake Sullivan, Hal Brands, "China Has Two Paths to Global Domination," *Foreign Policy*, May 22, 2020.
38. The Editorial Board, "The Chinese Navy's Great Leap Forward," *The Wall Street Journal*, June 7, 2022.
39. *Ibid.*
40. Michael M. Phillips, "China Seeks First Military Base on Africa's Atlantic Coast, U.S. Intelligence Finds," *The Wall Street Journal*, December 5, 2021.
41. Michael Cunningham, "Chinese Spies Violate U.S. Sovereignty and Americans Rights," *The Wall Street Journal*, May 6, 2022.
42. Dustin Volz, "U.K. Spy Chief Warns Of China Tech Threat," *The Wall Street Journal*, October 12, 2022, p.A9.
43. Liza Liu, "Chip Rules Entangle Executives from U.S.," *The Wall Street Journal*, October 17, 2022, p.A1.
44. Anders Fogh Rasmussen, "Europe's Complacency Heightens the China Challenge," *The Wall Street Journal*, October 10, 2021.
45. Robin Wright, *op.cit.*
46. See The Editorial Board, "President Biden's Saudi Arabia Flip Flop," *The Wall Street Journal*, June 14, 2022.
47. John Bolton, "Biden Has a Summit With Xi, but No Strategy for China," *The Wall Street Journal*, November 17, 2021.
48. Andrew A. Michta, "Russia and China's Dangerous Decline," *The Wall Street Journal*, December 14, 2021.
49. "China's Partnership With Russia Seen as Serious Problem for the U.S.," *Pew Research Center*, April 28, 2022.
50. Lingling Wei, Sha Hua, "China's Xi Reaffirms Support for Moscow in Call With Putin," *The Wall Street Journal*, June 15, 2022.
51. Graham Allison, *Destined For War: Can America and China Escape Thucydides's Trap?*, (New York: HarperCollins Publishers, 2018).

Chapter XIII: China: Taiwan and Other Acts of Aggression

1. An Air Defense Identification Zone (ADIZ) is the airspace of a country and an additional wider area over land and water in which a country tries to identify, locate and control any aircraft in the interest of national security.
2. Aaron Mehta, "Chinese flights near Taiwan look like 'rehearsal' US officials warn," *Reagan National Defense Forum 2021*, December 6, 2021.
3. Walter Russell Mead, "Xi Jinping's Two-Track Foreign Policy," *The Wall Street Journal*, October 11, 2021. The *Global Times* is a daily tabloid newspaper under the auspices of the Chinese Communist Party's flagship newspaper. It reports news from a nationalistic perspective and it is part of a broader set of Chinese state media outlets that constitute the Chinese Government's foreign propaganda apparatus.
4. Eric Cheung, "Taiwan won't be forced to bow to China, President Tsai says during National Day celebration" *CNN*, October 11, 2021.
5. Yuka Hayashi, "U.S. Launches Initiatives to Boost Economic Ties With Taiwan," *The Wall Street Journal*, June 1, 2022.
6. The Editorial Board, "Biden's Real Taiwan Mistake," *The Wall Street Journal*, May 23, 2022.
7. Paul D. Shinkman, "China 'Clearly' Developing Ability to Invade Taiwan, Top

General Says," *U.S. News*, November 3, 2021.
8. Richard Bush, "Taiwan's Democratic Politics and Its Relations with China," The Brookings Institution, November 10, 2021.
9. *Ibid.*
10. *Ibid.*
11. *Ibid.*
12. See "Freedom in the World 2022," *Freedom House* (freedomhouse.org), March 30, 2022.
13. Erin Hale, "Taiwan Ranks Among Top 10 Democracies in Annual Index," *Voice Of America News (voanews.com)*, February 11, 2022.
14. Abe Shinzō, "U.S. Strategic Ambiguity Over Taiwan Must End, *Project Syndicate*, April 12, 2022.
15. In August 2021, after his pathetic and abrupt withdrawal of all U.S. forces from Afghanistan, Biden had compared the U.S. commitment to defend Taiwan to Article 5 of the NATO Treaty. "We made a sacred commitment to Article Five," he said, "that if in fact anyone were to invade or take action against our NATO allies, we would respond. Same with Japan, same with South Korea, same with Taiwan."
16. See David Brunnstrom and Trevor Hummicutt, "Biden says U.S. forces would defend Taiwan in the event of a Chinese invasion," *Reuters*, September 19, 2022; Amy B. Wang, "Biden says U.S. troops would defend Taiwan in event of attack by China," *Washington Post*, September 19, 2022.
17. The conference, the Shangri-La Dialogue, was organized by the London-based Think Tank International Institute for Strategic Studies.
18. Chaff is a radar countermeasure in which aircraft spread a cloud of small pieces of aluminum, which either appears as a cluster of primary targets on radar screens or swamps the screen with multiple returns to confuse and distract the radar operator.
19. See, e.g., Thomas J. Shattuck, "Believe Biden When He Says America Will Defend Taiwan," *Foreign Policy Research Institute*, May 25, 2022.
20. Considerable concern exists about the training, combat readiness, and morale of Taiwan's armed forces and its defense budget. According to one report, Taiwan spent $13 billion on defense in 2020, while Israel, with less than half of Taiwan's population, spent $22 billion. Joyce Wang, Alastair Gale, "Does Taiwan's Military Stand a Chance Against China? Few Think So," *The Wall Street Journal*, October 26, 2021; See also Dexter Filkins, "A Dangerous Game: China has coveted its island neighbor for decades. Is Xi Jinping ready to seize it?", *The New Yorker*, November 21, 2022.
21. Captain Sam J. Taugredi USN (Ret.), "Bigger Fleets Win," U.S. Naval Institute *Proceedings*, January 2023.
22. *Ibid.*, See also Ronald O'Rourke, *China Naval Modernization: Implications for U.S. Navy Capabilities—Background and Issues for Congress*, Updated March 8, 2022, Congressional Research Service, RL 33153
23. *Ibid.*
24. Richard J. Samuels, "After Abe, Japan Tries to Balance Ties to the U.S. and China," *The Wall Street Journal*, July 30-31, 2022.
25. Ralph Peters, "Thucydides in Beijing," *Strategika* (Hoover Institution), Issue 77, June 6, 2022.
26. Aaron Blake, "Americans aren't that tired of war, it seems," *Washington Post*, October 12, 2021; Thomas J. Shattuck, *op.cit.*
27. James P. Delgado, *Across the Top of the World* (Vancouver, BC: Douglas & McIntyre, Ltd., 1999), p.197.
28. The Northwest Passage is an oceanic shortcut from the Atlantic to the Pacific across the top of North America. It is located 500 miles north of the Arctic Circle

and less than 1,200 miles from the North Pole.
29. Canada, which officially required the archipelago along with Britain's remaining possessions in North America in 1880, claims sovereignty over the Passage. The Canadian Government has declared that because all of the routes of the Passage run between islands that are Canadian territory, "All of the waters within the Canadian Arctic Archipelago are Canadian historic internal waters over which Canada exercises full sovereignty." That view appears to be supported by Article 8 of the United Nations Convention on the Law of the Sea 1982.
30. See Advantage at Sea: Prevailing with Integrated All-Domain Naval Power, December 2020.
31. *Ibid.*, p.3.
32. *Ibid.*, pp.1,6.
33. Paul Vieira, "Canada Plans Billions in Military Spending to Counter Russia Threat in Arctic," *The Wall Street Journal*, June 20, 2022.
34. NATO 2022 Strategic Concept, June 29, 2022, pp.4-5.
35. The Editorial Board, "Pelosi and Biden, Taiwan and China," *The Wall Street Journal*, July 23, 2022.
36. The Editorial Board, "Who Would Win a War Over Taiwan?" *The Wall Street Journal*, January 20, 2023, p.A14.
37. "PLA DRILLS AROUND Taiwan continue to 'rehearse reunification operation' amid Pelosi's visit, 'exercises blockading island to become routine,'" *Global Times*, August 3, 2022.
38. Hal Brands, Michael Beckley, "The Coming War Over Taiwan," *The Wall Street Journal*, August 4, 2022.
39. Seth Cropsey, "Will the U.S. Really Defend Taiwan?" *The Wall Street Journal*, January 27, 2023, p.A15.
40. *Ibid.*
41. *Ibid.*
42. *Ibid.*
43. Walter Russell Mead, "A Costly Passivity Toward China, *The Washington Post*, August 9, 2022.
44. See Andrew A. Michta, "China, Russia and the West's Crisis of Disbelief," *op.cit.*
45. Hal Brands, Michael Beckley, "The Coming War Over Taiwan," *op.cit.*
46. *Ibid.*
47. Editorial Board, "The B-21 Bomber Is Needed Now," *The Wall Street Journal*, December 6, 2022, p.A20.
48. Dexter Filkins, *op.cit.*, pp.43,45.
49. Tunku Varadarajan, "The Ascent To Hyperpower," *The Wall Street Journal*, June 29, 2022, p.A15.

Chapter XIV: Iran: Nuclear Armed Terrorist?
1. Melvyn P. Laffler, *For the Soul of Mankind: The United States, the Soviet Union and the Cold War* (New York: Hill and Wang, 2007), p.301.
2. "Iran Hostage Crisis ends," *This Day in History, January 20, 1981*.
3. Zbigniew Brzeginski, *Power and Principle: Memoirs of the National Security Adviser, 1977-1981* (New York: Farrar, Straus, Giroux, 1983), p.493.
4. J. L. Holloway III, "[Iran Hostage] Mission Rescue Report," Special Operations Review Group (1980), pp.9-10.
5. Michael Kohler, "Two Nations, a Treaty and the World Court – An Analysis of United States-Iranian Relations under the Treaty of Amity before the International Court of Justice,"*Wisconsin International Law Journal*, 18 (Winter 2000), p.287.

6. Sarah Pruitt, "How the Iran Hostage Crisis Became a 14-Month Nightmare for President Carter and the Nation," *History*, October 16, 2019.
7. In Islamic Law, "fatwa," an Arabic word, means "a decision from a mufti, where a "mufti"is a Muslim legal authority. In English usage, the word has become equated with a death sentence. Ben Zimmer, "A Legal Edict Now Known as A Death Sentence," *The Wall Street Journal*, August 18, 2022.
8. Reuel Marc Gerecht, "How the Salman Rushdie Fatwa Changed the World," *The Wall Street Journal*, August 25, 2022.
9. Stephen J. Hadley, "The George W. Bush Administration," *United States Institute of Peace*, October 5, 2010.
10. Charles Krauthammer, "The Iran Charade on Capitol Hill," *Washington Post* (www.washingtonpost.com), September 10, 2015.
11. Gary Samore, Ed., "The Iran Nuclear Deal: A Definitive guide," *Harvard Kennedy School* (Belfer Center), August 3, 2015.
12. Eric Brewer, "Iran on the Nuclear Brink," *Foreign Affairs*, June 17, 2022.
13. Joe Biden, "Why I'm going to Saudi Arabia, *Washington Post*, July 9, 2022.
14. Dion Nissenbaum, Dov Lieber, Aresu Eqbali, "Israel Expands Operations Against Iranian Nuclear, Military Assetts," *The Wall Street Journal*, June 20, 2022; Jonathan Spyer, "Israel's Shadow War With Iran Goes Nonnuclear," *The Wall Street Journal*, June 15, 2022.
15. Walter Russell Mead, "The Iran Nuclear Deal's Convulsive Death," *The Wall Street Journal*, July 25, 2022.
16. "Will Use Force As "Last Resort" to Prevent Iranian Nuclear Weapons: Biden," *Reuters*, July 14, 2022.
17. Walter Russell Mead, "The Iran Nuclear Deal's Convulsive Death," *op.cit.*
18. *Ibid.*
19. Eric Brewer, "Iran on the Nuclear Brink."
20. Robert S. Litwak, "Iran's Nuclear Challenge and the Military Option: Nonproliferation Precedents and the Case for Containment, *Wilson Center*, January 19, 2022.
21. *Ibid.*
22. Dustin Volz, Vivian Salama, "John Bolton Was Target of Assassination Plot by Iranian National," *The Wall Street Journal*, August 10, 2022.
23. The Associated Press, "A judge denies bail for the man accused of trying to kill Salman Rushdie," August 18, 2022.
24. William A. Galston, "Biden's focus Turns to Foreign Policy," *The Wall Street Journal*, August 9, 2022.
25. William P. Strobel, "War Game Finds U.S., Taipei Countering Invasion," *The Wall Street Journal*, August 10, 2022, p.A10.
26. The Editorial Board, "The Military Needs More Ammo," *The Wall Street Journal*, September 30, 2022, p.A16, Emphasis Added.
27. *Ibid.*
28. William A. Galston, "Biden's Focus Turns to Foreign Policy," *op.cit.*
29. Eliot A. Cohen, *The big Stick: The Limits of Soft Power & the Necessity of Military Force* (New York: Basic Books, 2016), p.226.
30. The Editorial Board, "Iran Tells the Truth About Inspections and the Nuclear Deal," *The Wall Street Journal*, August 29, 2022.
31. William A. Galston, "Biden's Focus Turn's to Foreign Policy," *op.cit*. Many current news articles were discussing the tighter ties that Iran and Russia were forging in order to circumvent Western sanctions. Russia was particularly interested in Drone (Unmanned Aerial Vehicles) technologies designed by Iran and in an Iranian

satellite that could be used by Tehran to monitor Ukrainian troop movements.
32. Winston S. Churchill, *The World Crisis 1911-1918*, Volume I (London: Odhams Press Limited, 1938), p.33.

Chapter XV: North Korea: International Outlaw
1. Harry S. Truman, *Memoirs: Years of Trial and Hope 1946-1952, Volume Two* (Garden City, NJ: Doubleday & Company, Inc., 1956), p.533.
2. David McCullough, *Truman* (New York: Simon & Schuster, 1992), p.779.
3. David Halberstam, *The Coldest Winter: America and the Korean War* (New York: Hyperion, 2007), pp.2-3.
4. David Halberstam, "Command Performance," *Smithsonian*, November 2007, p.58.
5. David McCullough, *op.cit.*, pp.782-783.
6. David Halberstam, *The Coldest Winter*, *op.cit.*, p.624.
7. Text an Address by Dwight D. Eisenhower, Republican Nominee for President, Delivered at Detroit, Michigan, October 24, 1952.
8. Evan Thomas, *Ike's Bluff: President Eisenhower's Secret Battle to Save the World* (New York: Little, Brown and Company, 2012), pp.70-71.
9. William I. Hitchcock, *The Age of Eisenhower: America and the World in the 1950s* (New York: Simon & Schuster, 2018), pp.103-104.
10. Dwight D. Eisenhower, *Mandate for Change, 1953-1956* (Garden City: DoubleDay & Company, Inc., 1963), p.181.
11. David Halberstam, *The Coldest Winter*, *op.cit.*, p.642.
12. *Ibid.*, p.639.
13. *Ibid.*, pp.639-640.
14. Arlow Oliver, "Kim Jong-il keeps $4bn 'emergency fund' in European banks," *The Sunday Telegraph*, March 14, 2010.
15. According to a report by the Institute for National Security Strategy, a South Korean think tank, Kim has ordered the execution of more than 340 individuals since he took power. See George Petras, "North Korea executions under Kim Jong Un," *USA Today*, February 27, 2017; K. J. Kwon, Ben Westcott, "Kim Jong Un has executed over 300 people since coming to power," *CNN*, December 29, 2016.
16. Jake Tapper, Wolf Blitzer, Jeremy Diamond, "Top Source: Trump believes North Korea is greatest threat," *CNN*, February 28, 2017.
17. Libby Johnson, "The End of Strategic Patience," *The Strategy Bridge*, September 29, 2017.
18. Eleanor Albert, "North Korea's Military Capabilities," *Council on Foreign Relations*, September 5, 2017.
19. *Ibid.*
20. Jacqueline Klimas, "Trump's North Korea Strategy: A lot like Obama's, "*Politico* (www.politico.com), August 8, 2017.
21. Stephen M. Duncan, *First Duty*, *op.cit.*, p.267.
22. Trump sowed considerable confusion when he parroted North Korean propaganda by calling U.S.-South Korea joint military exercises "Very provocative." Secretary of Defense Jim Mattis found it necessary to call his counterparts in South Korea and Japan to assure them of America's "ironclad defense commitments" and "determination to maintain the readiness of its forces in the region." See Editorial, "A Troops for Nukes Trade?", *The Wall Street Journal*, June 18, 2018, p.A16.
23. See Bruce Klinger, "North Korean Cyberattacks: A Dangerous and Evolving Threat," *The Heritage Foundation*, September 2, 2021; Benjamin R. Young, "North Korea Knows How Important Its Cyberattacks Are," *Foreign Policy*, February 9, 2022.
24. The pandemic triggered the Kim regime to close all borders and to otherwise seal

the country off from all of the outside world. That action cut off vital trade with neighboring China. The regime even rejected vaccines offered through the Covak Initiative, a program financed primarily by Western governments to assist lower-income countries obtain the medication.
25. See Chapter XII.
26. On December 9, 2022, off the coast of Southern California, the U.S. Air Force successfully conducted its first test launch of a fully operational prototype of an air-launched Hypersonic Missile. The successful test followed three consecutive test failures in 2021.
27. "U.S. think tank identifies North Korea base likely intended for ICBMs," *Reuters*, February 7, 2022.
28. Timothy W. Martin, Chieko Tsuneoka, "North Korea Test-Fires Intercontinental Ballistic Missile, *The Wall Street Journal*, March 24, 2022.
29. Min Joo Kim, "North Korea codifies right to launch preemptive nuclear strikes," *Washington Post*, September 9, 2022.

Chapter XVI: Inexcusable and Unacceptable Failures of Leadership
1. This phrase is taken from the speech made by Winston Churchill in the House of Commons on November 11, 1936 during a debate on the British Government's lack of preparation for a war initiated by Germany.
2. Stephen M. Duncan, *First Duty: Presidents, the Nation's Security and Self-Centered Politics {Prologue}, op.cit.* p.xiv.
3. *Ibid.*
4. The Strategic Petroleum Reserve (SPR) is a national energy safety net which was created in response to the 1973 oil embargo which was imposed by the Organization of Petroleum Exporting Countries (OPEC) because of the U.S. support of Israel during the Fourth Arab-Israeli War. A President can authorize an emergency drawdown from the SPR in response to a "severe energy supply interruption." The SPR can hold up to 74 million barrels of oil.
5. Daniel Henninger, "The Biggest Midterm Issue: Chaos," *The Wall Street Journal*, October 19, 2022, P.A15.
6. Jason Lange, Biden approval holds near lower level of his presidency," *Reuters*, October 11, 2022.
7. Redfield and Wilson Strategies, Joe Biden Administration Approval Ratings and Hypothetical Voting Intention," October 14, 2022.
8. The Heritage Foundation, "Executive Summary of the 2023 Index of U.S. Military Strength," October 18, 2022.
9. *Ibid.*
10. The Heritage Foundation, News Release, "Heritage Foundation Releases 2023 Index of U.S. Military Strength, Gives U.S. Military First-Ever 'Weak' Overall Rating, October 18, 2022.
11. Walter Russell Mead, "The High Cost of Low Military Spending," *The Wall Street Journal*, November 1, 2022, p.A13. George F. Will, "Opinion: Biden's China policy is admirable but underfunded," *Washington Post*, October 1, 2021.
12. The Editorial Board, "Congress Rejects Biden's Defense Budget," *The Wall Street Journal*, July 10, 2022.
13. *Ibid.*
14. See, e.g., Jimmy Bym, "What if They Gave a War and Everybody was Woke?", *The Wall Street Journal*, July 30-31, 2022; There is no widely agreed-upon definition of the term *woke*. Originally, it implied alertness to racial discrimination. More recently,

it has come to mean a left wing, radically progressive, or moralizing and intolerant (politically correct) ideology on such matters as race, gender, LGBTQ, and religion.
15. See Ronald Reagan Institute, "Reagan National Defense Survey," November 2022; Editorial Board, "Americans Are Losing Trust in the Military, *Wall Street Journal*, December 1, 2022, p.A18.
16. "Executive Order 13583 – Establishing a Coordinated Government-wide Initiative to Promote Diversity and Inclusion in the Federal Workforce, The White House, August 18, 2011.
17. An April 26, 2022, poll by the Pew Research Center found that 79% of White adults, 68% of Hispanic adults, 63% of Asian American adults, 59% of Black adults, 87% of Republicans, and 62% of Democrats, believe that neither race nor ethnicity should be factored into admissions decisions. Vianney Gomez, "U.S. public continues to view, grades, test scores as top factors in college admissions," *Pew Research Center*, April 26, 2022; Scott Jaschik, "Poll Finds Public Doesn't Favor Affirmative Action, *Inside Higher Ed*, May 2, 2022.
18. On October 31, 2022, the U.S. Supreme Court heard oral argument on the issue of whether race can be considered in the admissions practices of Harvard University a private institution, and the University of North Carolina, a public institution. In a closely-divided case in 2007, Chief Justice Roberts signaled the possible future end of most affirmative action matters when he wrote in a concurring opinion that: "The way to stop discrimination on the basis of race is to stop discriminating on the basis of race." See *Parents Involved in Community Schools v. Seattle School District No. 1*, 551 U.S. 701 (2007).
19. In Fiscal Year 2022, the Army missed its recruiting goal by approximately 20,000 new soldiers or 25 percent. The other military services were having similar problems. Meghann Myers, "Is the military too 'woke' to recruit?" *Military Times*, October 13, 2022; The Editorial Board, "The Pentagon's Recruiting Woes," *The Wall Street Journal*, October 15-16, 2022, p.A14.
20. *Ibid.*
21. Lieutenant General Thomas Spoehr, USA (Ret.), "The Rise of Wokeness in the Military," *Imprimis*, June/July 2022.
22. *Ibid.*
23. Meghann Myers, *op.cit.*
24. Haley Britzky, "Army Secretary to Leaders: stay out of online 'culture wars,'" Task & Purpose, October 10, 2022.
25. Henry Kissinger, *Leadership: Six Studies in World Strategy* (New York: Penguin Press, 2022), pp.395-416.
26. Robert M. Gates, *Duty: Memoirs of a Secretary at War* (New York: Alfred A. Kopf, 2014), p.288.
27. Alex Thompson, "'The President Was Not Encouraging': What Obama Really Thought About Biden," *POLITICO (Magazine)*, August 14, 2020.
28. *Ibid.*
29. *Ibid.*
30. In September 1987, after indisputable evidence emerged that Biden had made false statements and "lifted phrases and mannerisms from a British Labour Party politician while making closing remarks at a debate," he was forced to end his first presidential campaign. Examples soon surfaced of Biden using material from other politicians without attribution. He had already been accused of hyperbole and imprecision. In 1987, a week in which he was presiding over the Senate Judiciary Committee's Confirmation Hearing on the nomination by President Reagan of Judge Robert Bork to the U.S.

Supreme Court, it was confirmed that while he was in law school, Biden had used five pages of a Law Review article in a 15-page paper "without quotation or citation." At about the same time, reporters found a video of Biden speaking to a voter in New Hampshire in which he claimed that he had attended law school on a full academic scholarship and graduated in the top half of his class, adding, "I was the outstanding student in the Political Science Department at the end of my year." In fact, he had attended law school on a partial-need based scholarship, and his academic career was certainly not impressive. He "repeated the Third Grade, earned all C's and D's in his first three semesters at the University of Delaware except for A's in PE, a B in 'Great English Writers,' and an F in ROTC, and graduated 76th in his Syracuse Law School Class of 85 students." Always sensitive about suggestions that he was dumb or a lightweight, he tended to dismiss his falsehoods with a minimum of explanation: "I exaggerate when I'm angry." Neena Satija, "Echoes of Biden's 1987 plagiarism scandal continue to reverberate." *Washington Post*, June 5, 2019; Alex Thompson, *op.cit.*

31. Editorial Board, "Biden's New Border Record," *The Wall Street Journal*, October 24, 2022, p.A16.
32. Courts in which criminal and civil matters are litigated are part of the Judicial Branch of the U.S. Government pursuant to Article III of the Constitution. Immigration Judges are Administrative Judges who are appointed by the U.S. Department of Justice.
33. Alicia A. Caldwell, "Migration Wave Fuels Record Arrests at the Border," *The Wall Street Journal*, October 24, 2022, p.A3.
34. Mark Morgan, "The Disaster at Our Southern Border," *Imprimis*, August 2021.
35. Charlotte Cuthbertson, "Former Border Commissioner: 'We have Lost Control of the Southwest Border'," *The Epoch Times*, January 12, 2022, p.A5.
36. United States Senate Committee on Foreign Relations Minority Report, "Biden's Border Crisis: Examining Policies That Encourage Illegal Migration," June 22, 2022.
37. Mark Morgan, "The Disaster at Our Southern Border," *op.cit.*
38. Mark Morgan, *op.cit.*
39. The Council on Foreign Relations, "U.S. – Saudi Arabia Relations," December 7, 2018; Stephen Kalin, Summer Said, Dion Nissenbaum, "Animosity Strains U.S. - Saudi Ties," *The Wall Street Journal*, October 25, 2022, p.A1.
40. See, e.g., Karen Elliott House, "The U.S. – Saudi Rift Over Oil Prices Is Déjà Vu All Over Again," *The Wall Street Journal*, October 20, 2022, p.A7.
41. *Ibid.* The author of this article is also the author of *On Saudi Arabia: Its People, Past, Religion, Fault Lines – and Future*.
42. *Ibid.*
43. Karen Elliott House, "Both Sides Lose in the U.S.-Saudi Feud," *The Wall Street Journal*, November 2, 2022, p.A17.
44. Richard Haass, "The Dangerous Decade," *Foreign Affairs*, September/October 2022, p.37.
45. Stephen M. Duncan, *Only The Most Able: Moving Beyond Politics in the Selection of National Security Leaders* (Lanham, MD: Rowman & Littlefield Publishers, Inc., 2013), pp.121-144.
46. Eliot A. Cohen, "Churchill and His Generals in *No End Save Victory*, ed. Robert Cowley (New York: G.P. Putnam's Sons, 2001), p.283.
47. Army Lieutenant General James F. Hollingsworth was recognized by General George Patton as one of the two best armor battalion commanders in World War II. He later served as the commander of all combined forces in South Korea.
48. Jack Welch, Suzy Welch, *Winning* (New York: HarperCollins, 2005), p.87. Emphasis added.

49. Lord Beaverbrook was a highly successful Canadian-British newspaper publisher who was elected to the House of Commons in 1910 and subsequently served in several senior positions in the British Government for more than three decades. Churchill often disagreed with Beaverbrook, but he respected him. He would later explain his appointment of the man this way: "I needed his vital and vibrant energy."
50. Michael R. Gordon, Brett Forrest, "Defense Strategy Casts China as Greatest Threat," *The Wall Street Journal*, October 28, 2022, p.A4.
51. Gerard Baker, "Free Expression," *The Wall Street Journal*, October 25, 2022, p.A15. Gerard Baker is a British writer who was educated in Oxford. He has broad international experience and previously served as the Editor-in-Chief of the *Wall Street Journal*.
52. Ronald Reagan, Address to the Veterans of Foreign Wars Convention in Chicago, August 18, 1980.
53. See Tim Bouverie, "Churchill Appeasement, and the Lessons of History," *Finest Hour*, First Quarter 2023, p.37.
54. *Ibid*. By August 2022, the number of high-explosive 155mm rounds in U.S. military storage, ammunition which is fired by howitzers, was already "uncomfortably low" and dormant supply chains and production lines were not at the required capacity. See Gordon Lubold, Nancy Youssef, Ben Kesling, "Ukraine War Is Depleting U.S. Ammunition Stockpiles, Sparking Pentagon Concern," *The Wall Street Journal*, August 29, 2022. Critical components for Stinger and Javelin missiles were not being produced in sufficient quantity to meet demand.
55. Elbridge A. Colby, Alexander B. Gray, "America's Industrial Base Isn't Ready for War With China," *The Wall Street Journal*, August 18, 2022.
56. 56. *Ibid*.

Chapter XVII: A Republic If You Can Keep It

1. Robert Courts, "Elizabeth the Great: Inside the House of Commons," *Finest Hour*, Special Issue 2022, No. 199, p.24.
2. Winston S. Churchill, *The Second World War: The Gathering Storm* (Boston: Houghton Mifflin Company, 1948), p.17.
3. *Ibid.*, p.7.
4. *Ibid.*, pp.17-18.
5. For several years German governments have failed to meet the NATO standard of defense spending and have based their security on policies promoting trade. For weeks, German Chancellor Olaf Scholz refused to send any of Germany's Leopard 2 Tanks to Ukraine and to approve request from other NATO countries to donate German-made Tanks to Ukraine until the U.S. first sent its MIAI Abrams to the besieged country. Scholz's admitted purpose was to give Germany greater protection from a possible angry Russian reaction.
6. Editorial Board, "A Crucial Moment for Ukraine," A Crucial Moment for Ukraine," *The Wall Street Journal*, January 19, 2023.
7. *Ibid*.
8. Evan Gershkovich, Thomas Grove, Drew Hinshaw, Joe Parkinson, "Putin Leans on Hard-Line Advisers," *The Wall Street Journal*, December 24-25, 2022, pp.A1, A10.
9. Boris Johnson, "Victory is the Only Option for Ukraine," *The Wall Street Journal*, November 15, 2022, p.A17.
10. The poll of more than 94,000 registered voters was sponsored by the Associated Press, *The Wall Street Journal*, and Fox News. See Tarini Parti, Natalie Andrews, Lindsay Wise, "Political Gridlock Is Poised to Return," *The Wall Street Journal*,

November 17, 2022, p.A4.
11. Andrew Restuccia, Keith Zhai, Ken Thomas, "Biden, Xi Strive to Stabilize Relations," *The Wall Street Journal*, November 15, 2022, p.A1.
12. Stephen Kalin, "Xi and Arab Leaders Bolster Links," *The Wall Street Journal*, December 10-11, 2022, p.A9.
13. On December 7, 2022, Badri Hosseini Khamenei, the sister of Iranian Supreme Leader Ali Khamenei, posted a letter on Twitter calling her brother a despotic caliph and declaring "I hope to see the victory of the people and the overthrow of this tyranny ruling Iran soon."
14. Sune Engel Rasmussen, "Moscow, Iran Vow Stroger Ties," *The Wall Street Journal*, November 10, 2022, p.A9; Ken Thomas, "Russia, Iran Deepen Military Ties, U.S Says," *The Wall Street Journal*, December 10-11, 2022, p.A7.
15. Editorial Board, "North Korea's U.N. Protectors," *The Wall Street Journal*, November 26-27, 2022, p.A12.
16. Daniel Henninger, "Putin's Nonnuclear War in Ukraine," *The Wall Street Journal*, November 3, 2022, p.A13.
17. Citizens for Sanity is purportedly a nonprofit PAC led by former advisers to President Trump.
18. Daniel Henninger, "Putin's Nonnuclear War in Ukraine," *op.cit.*
19. Vivian Salama, "Republicans Increasingly Opposed To Aid for Ukraine, New Poll Finds," *The Wall Street Journal*, November 4, 2022, p.A4.
20. Daniel Henninger, "Putin's Nonnuclear War in Ukraine," *op.cit.*
21. Richard M. Langworth, "English-Speaking Peoples: We Must Be United, We Must Be Undaunted, and We Must Be Inflexible," *Finest Hour*, No. 122, Spring 2004, p.30.
22. Winston S. Churchill, *The Hinge of Fate* (Cambridge: Houghton Mifflin Company, 1950), p.61.
23. *Ibid.*
24. John H. Maurer, "Churchill and the Hinge of Fate: Confronting the Onslaught of Japan" *Finest Hour*, No. 200, Fourth Quarter 2022, p.12.
25. Emma Soames, ed. *Mary Churchill's War: The Wartime Diaries of Churchill's Youngest Daughter* (London: Two Roads, 2021), p.150.
26. Editorial Board, "'The Big One Is Coming,'" *The Wall Street Journal*, November 5-6, 2022, p.A16.
27. C. Todd Lopez, "Stratcom Commander Says U.S. Should Look to 1950s to Regain Competitive Edge," *DOD News*, November 3, 2022.
28. *Ibid.*
29. Editorial Board, "Telling the Truth About War Over Taiwan," *The Wall Street Journal*, January 30, 2023, p.A16.
30. Seth Jones, "Empty Bins in a Wartime Environment: The Challenge to the U.S. Defense Industrial Base," *Center for Strategic & International Studies*, January 23, 2023.
31. *Ibid.* The problems with the industrial base include several elements, the study concluded. First, the fact that for two decades the Armed Forces were engaged in troop-intensive insurgency conflicts, but the year in Ukraine is a conventional conflict that involves greater use of heavy weapons. A war in the Taiwan Strait would require the use of different weapons systems. Second, "onerous business processes and regulations," involving years of poor "acquisition policy, culture and behavior have prioritized efficiency and cost control over speed and capacity." Another element involves workforce and supply chain constraints.
32. *Ibid.*
33. Source: Media exit poll, November 8, 2022.

34. Karl Rove, "With No Red Wave, Trump Is Out at Sea," *The Wall Street Journal*, November 10, 2022.
35. A former Speaker of the House of Representatives described the problem in this fashion: "[V]arious factors–demographics, health, inflation, declining labor-force growth and declining productivity–have built in an unsustainable rise in the national debt. The Federal Government is making promises to citizens that it can't keep." Paul Ryan, "A Plan to Save America's Finances," *The Wall Street Journal*, November 17, 2022, p.A17.
36. Daniel Henniger, "Putin Heists a Nation's Identity," *The Wall Street Journal*, December 8, 2022, p.A19.
37. Marc A. Thiessen, "To Stop Inflation, We Need to Secure the Border," *Washington Post*, October 5, 2022.
38. Daniel Henniger, "Biden's Title 42 Catastrophe," *The Wall Street Journal*, December 22, 2022, p.A15.
39. U.S. Customs and Border Protection, "December 2022 Monthly Operational Update," January 20, 2023.
40. In the opinion for the Court in the 1981 case of Haig v. Agee, 453U.S.280, 307, Chief Justice Warren Burger declared that "It is 'obvious and unarguable' that no governmental interest is more compelling than the security of the Nation."
41. Dines D'Souza, *Ronald Reagan: How an Ordinary Man Became an Extraordinary Leader* (New York: The Free Press, 1997), p.98.
42. Edwin Meese, III, *With Reagan: The Inside Story* (Washington, D.C.: Regnery Gateway, 1992), pp.54-55
43. Yaroslav Trofimov, "Looming Battle to Test Kyiv, Moscow," *The Wall Street Journal*, December 19, 2022, p.A1.
44. Democrat Senate Leader Chuck Schumer held up approval of the bill in an aggressive effort to attach to it a provision which was favorable to Democrat political donors, but which could not receive approval standing alone, namely, language that would have made bank financing easier for marijuana companies in Schumer's home state of New York.
45. Katz Steck Ferek, Natalie Andrews, "Congress Clears Defense Bill And Stopgap Spending Fix," *The Wall Street Journal*, December 16, 2022, p.A1.
46. Elaine McCusker, "Defense Budget Transparency and the Cost of Military Capability," *American Enterprise Institute*, November 9, 2022.
47. Robert Kagan, "Challenging The U.S. Is A Historic Mistake," *The Wall Street Journal*, February 4-5, 2023, p.C1; Editorial Board, "About That 'Record' Defense Budget," *The Wall Street Journal*, March 10, 2023, p.A14.
48. William J. Bennett, *The Book of Virtues*, (New York: Simon & Schuster, 1993), p.185.
49. Eliot A. Cohen, *The Big Stick, op.cit.*, p.25.
50. *Ibid.*, p.28.
51. *Ibid.*
52. Richard Haass, "The Dangerous Decade: A Foreign Policy for a World in Crisis," *Foreign Affairs*, September/October 2022, p.26.
53. *Ibid.*
54. See Chapter V.
55. *Federalist No. 41* was, of course, one of *The Federalist Papers*, several essays which were published in 1788 by Alexander Hamilton, Madison and John Jay, who were co-authors under the pseudonym "Publius." The essays were written in support of the draft Constitution.
56. Jon Meacham, *The Soul of America: The Battle for Our Better Angels* (New York:

Random House, 2018), p.265.
57. See William J. Bennett, *Why We Fight, op.cit.,* p.145.
58. Jared Meyer, "The Ignorant Voter," *Forbes,* June 27, 2016. 59. Michael O'Hanlon, "The Lessons of Military History," *The Wall Street Journal,* January 28-29, 2023, p.C4.
59. Michael O'Hanlon, "The Lessons of Military History," *The Wall Street Journal,* JNUey 28-29, 2023, pl C4.

Postscript

1. Joseph S. Nye, Jr., "Government's Challenge: Getting Serious About Terrorism," in James G. Hoge, Jr., Gideon Rose, Eds., *How Did it Happen?* (New York: Public Affairs, 2001), pp.199-200.
2. *Ibid.*
3. *Ibid.,* pp.200-201.
4. William J. Bennett, *Why We Fight, op.cit.,* pp. 166-168.
5. *Ibid.*
6. Theodore Roosevelt, *An Autobiography* (New York: MacMillan Company, 1914), p.563.
7. Stephen M. Duncan, *A War of a Different Kind: Military Force and America's Search for Homeland Security* (Annapolis, MD: Naval Institute Press, 2004), p.46.
8. Walter Russell Mead, "America Is Stronger Than Biden," *The Wall Street Journal,* December 20, 2022, p.A15.
9. Ralph Peters, *Beyond Terror* (Mechanicsburg, PA: Stackpole Books, 2002), pp.331-332; Ralph Peters, "The Future of War," *Macleans,* April 26, 1999.
10. Ben Sasse, "America's True Divide: Pluralists vs. Zealots," *The Wall Street Journal,* January 3, 2023.
11. Kimberley Strassel, "GOP Rebels Need to Take the Win," *The Wall Street Journal,* January 6, 2023, p.A13.
12. Editorial Board, "The GOP's Chaos Caucus Returns," *The Wall Street Journal,* January 4, 2023, p.A14.
13. Editorial Board, "The Price for Speaker McCarthy," *The Wall Street Journal,* January 7-8, 2023, p.A12.
14. Azi Paybarah, "Republicans defend messy speaker fight as House readies for business," *Washington Post,* January 8, 2023. The national Debt Ceiling, or Debt Limit, is the total amount of money that the U.S. Government is authorized to borrow to meet its existing legal obligations, including Social Security and Medicare benefits, military salaries, interest on the national debt, tax refunds, and other payments. In order to maintain the Government's creditworthiness, it is necessary for Congress to periodically raise the Debt Ceiling to allow the Treasury Department to issue more debt to pay for existing obligations.
15. Robert Kagan, "Challenging The U.S. Is A Historic Mistake," *The Wall Street Journal,* February 4-5, 2023, p.C1.
16. *Ibid.*
17. David McCullough, *The American Spirit: Who We Are and What We Stand For* (New York: Simon & Schuster, 2017), p.119.

Made in the USA
Middletown, DE
03 April 2023

27619694R00166